best ever

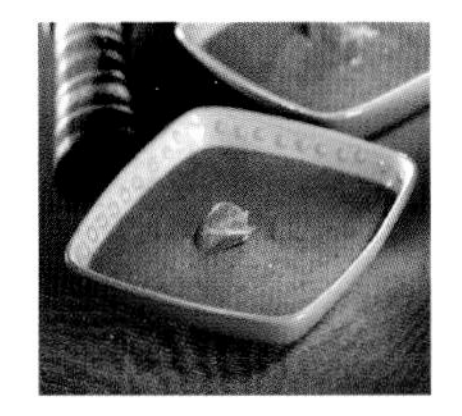

indian

p

This is a Parragon Book
This edition published in 2004

Parragon
Queen Street House
4 Queen Street
Bath BA1 1HE
United Kingdom

Created and produced by
The Bridgewater Book Company Ltd,
Lewes, East Sussex

Photographer Ian Parsons
Home Economists Brian Wilson & Richard Green

ISBN: 1–40542–041–3

Printed in China

NOTE

This book uses metric and imperial measurements. Follow the same units of measurement throughout; do not mix metric and imperial. All spoon measurements are level: teaspoons are assumed to be 5 ml and tablespoons are assumed to be 15 ml. Unless otherwise stated, milk is assumed to be full fat, eggs and individual fruits and vegetables such as mangoes or potatoes are medium, and pepper is freshly ground black pepper.

The times given for each recipe are an approximate guide only because the preparation times may differ according to the techniques used by different people and the cooking times may vary as a result of the type of oven used. Ovens should be preheated to the specified temperature. If using a fan-assisted oven, check the manufacturer's instructions for adjusting the time and temperature. The preparation times include chilling and marinating times, where appropriate.

The nutritional information provided for each recipe is per serving or per portion. Optional ingredients, variations or serving suggestions have not been included in the calculations.

Recipes using raw or very lightly cooked eggs should be avoided by infants, the elderly, pregnant women, convalescents and anyone suffering from an illness.

contents

introduction

Indian cuisine is among the most diverse and versatile in the world, employing a wide range of cooking techniques and a vast array of ingredients and flavours. This is hardly surprising given the sheer size of the country and its long and eventful history. The story of Indian food is, indeed, one of geography and history, but it is also profoundly influenced by religion, and these three elements are closely interwoven with one another.

Each region of India has its own specialities and characteristic dishes. For example, Mumbai, formerly Bombay, is famous for its pork curries, while Bengali cuisine features fish and Madras is well known for its superb vegetarian food. Nevertheless, in broad culinary terms the country can be divided into the north and south. The dishes of the north bear witness to a succession of invasions throughout the centuries, whereas foreign influences are less pronounced in the south. The Moghuls left a heritage of finely prepared, creamy and rich-tasting dishes, while India is indebted to the Persians for pulaos and many other rice dishes, and to the Portuguese for the introduction of vinegar, the defining ingredient of vindaloo curries. Portuguese and Spanish explorers were also responsible for introducing the chilli to Asia from its native South America, although nowadays it is difficult to imagine Indian food without this almost ubiquitous spice. India is now one of the world's largest producers of chillies. Only the British, it seems, had little effect on the country's cooking. However, so enamoured were they of Indian seasonings and chutneys that they did much to spread the word of this distinctive and delicious cuisine.

The cooking style of the north evolved in the palaces and mansions of princes and nobles, whereas that of the south has more humble origins. An abundance of fruit and vegetables grows in the south and, together with lentils and rice, feature in the staple dishes of the region. The north is a wheat-growing area and a wide variety of different breads are produced. The main religion in southern India is Hinduism and so the majority of the population is vegetarian. There are, of course, many Hindus in the north too, but observance of a vegetarian diet is often less strict. Meat, mainly lamb and chicken, does feature in lots of traditional dishes, although no Hindu would ever eat beef, as the cow is regarded as a sacred animal. In coastal areas, even in the south, many Hindus eat fish, not classifying it as meat. Muslim communities, on the other hand, eat all kinds of meat, apart from pork or other products derived from pigs, which are thought to be unclean. Other groups who practise other religions are scattered throughout the country, whether Christians in the former Portuguese colony of Goa, Middle Eastern Jews or Parsees in the west, all of whom have their own dietary regulations and traditional foods.

There is also an east-west culinary divide, although the difference is less pronounced than that between north and south. Both regions have plentiful supplies of fish and seafood, but lamb and chicken also feature in the west, perhaps as a result of greater foreign influences. Probably the defining characteristic of eastern Indian cuisine is the widespread use of mustard oil.

cooking techniques and equipment

One of the great things about Indian cooking of all kinds is that it rarely requires much last-minute attention. It also needs little, if anything, in the way of special equipment. Most Western kitchens will already include virtually

everything you need to prepare the recipes in this book. The proper blending of spices is an essential part of Indian cooking, regardless of the region from which the dish originates. Indian cooks grind fresh spices for each dish, using a stone rolling pin and flat stone called a sil and batta, or a heavy stone or cast-iron pestle and mortar called a hamal-dista. These are available from specialist shops, but you can also achieve an authentic flavour with an ordinary pestle and mortar or spice grinder kept specifically for the purpose.

A heavy-based frying pan is essential and, if you are keen on Balti dishes, you might want to invest in a karahi or Balti pan. Resembling a wok, this has a round base and two handles. Karahis are made in a variety of sizes, including small ones suitable for individual portions that are accompanied by wooden stands for serving at the table. Cast iron is the traditional material, but nowadays these pans are manufactured in a variety of metals. Like woks, they need to be able to withstand high cooking temperatures and must be seasoned before they are used for the first time. A tava or tawa is a kind of griddle used by Indian cooks for roasting spices and cooking chapatis and other flat breads. However, neither a karahi nor a tava is essential if you have a good-quality frying pan.

Other specialist equipment, which is also available from many specialist Asian shops, includes a coconut grater, called a narial kas, which consists of rotating curved blades, and a fine wood or metal sieve called a chalni. While it is fun to use authentic tools, an ordinary grater and sieve will serve the purpose.

The one piece of specialist equipment for which there is no Western equivalent is the tandoor, a clay or brick oven, which is popular in parts of northern India. Food cooked in a tandoor has a distinctive, smoky flavour and a crisp texture. Tandoori chicken is probably one of the best-known and most-loved dishes cooked in this way, although bread, fish, prawns and kebabs are also popular. Several tandoori recipes that have been adapted for cooking in a Western-style oven are included in this book.

the importance of spices

Happily, the time is past when the majority of Westerners thought Indian food and curry were synonymous and that it always consisted of the same thing with just a change in the main ingredient from, say, chicken to prawns. In fact, the word curry is derived from the Tamil word for sauce and applies to only some kinds of dishes.

However, whether ingredients are being prepared in a curry, a korma – braised in yogurt – or a mollee – stewed in coconut milk – the right balance of spices is crucial. The masala or blend of spices is carefully combined to ensure that each spice retains its integral flavour, but does not predominate over the others in the mixture. On rare occasions, one spice, often cumin, is chosen to stand out, but usually Indian cooks take great care to create a pleasing combination.

The recipes in this book include dishes from as many regions as possible with a consequent wide range of flavours and masalas. However, you should feel free to change the combinations of spices and their proportions to suit your taste – a wholly authentic approach to Indian cooking. Most of the spices are readily available from supermarkets, but you may need to visit an Asian food shop for some of the less familiar ones. For the best flavour, buy whole spices and grind as you need them. Whether whole or ground, it is best to buy spices in small quantities, as they lose their flavour and aroma in storage. Therefore, resist the temptation to buy every spice in sight. However, a good basic stock might include cardamoms, cumin, cinnamon, coriander, cloves, turmeric and chilli powder, as well as black peppercorns. Store them in airtight containers in a cool, dark place. A colourful spice rack on the kitchen wall looks lovely, but the light, heat and humidity make it the worst possible place and spices will degenerate very quickly.

the indian meal

Unlike Western meals, in India all the savoury dishes are placed on the table at the same time. There is no separate starter or soup course, even on formal occasions. The dishes may all be vegetarian or may consist of a mixture of meat, poultry, fish and vegetable dishes and will often include rice. What is important is to get the balance right and provide a complementary selection of textures and flavours, and also a mixture of milder and more hotly spiced dishes. A typical meal will consist of a meat or fish dish and three or four vegetable dishes, frequently including lentils. Bread is also a common accompaniment, and there will often be a mass of little dishes containing selections of raw vegetables and a variety of sauces, chutneys and raitas.

Indian meals are traditionally served on a thali, a round tray containing a number of small bowls. Each diner is served separately and it is considered extremely bad manners to eat from someone else's thali or to offer something from your own. These trays are made of metal – stainless steel, brass or silver – and are available from specialist Asian shops. In southern India, banana leaves often take the role of plates and bowls. This is an attractive way to present food and makes clearing up afterwards extremely easy. In many areas, it is customary to eat with your right hand, scooping up the food with your fingers. (The left hand is never used for eating or serving food.) However, Westerners may prefer to use knives and forks. Neither wine nor beer is served with meals, but tea may be drunk afterwards. Muslims are forbidden to drink alcohol at any time. It is worth noting that drinking water is also not recommended if you are consuming hotly spiced food.

Fresh fruit is a popular dessert, but Indians tend to have a sweet tooth and produce a range of delicious sweetmeats, cakes and ice cream. Many of these are based on nuts, such as pistachio nuts and cashew nuts, and may be delicately flavoured with rose petals or orange flower water. Naturally, rice and semolina milk desserts are also common, but these bear little resemblance to their Western counterparts.

special ingredients

Many ingredients, from chicken to potatoes, are common to both Indian and Western cooks. These days, a vast range of tropical fruits and vegetables are available from major supermarkets and many exotic ingredients have become familiar. However, there are some ingredients typically used in Indian cooking that may not have become quite so well known.

asafoetida: This is a distinctive and pungent spice, which is also known as devil's dung. Its foul smell disappears on cooking and it adds a pleasant flavour to fish, meat and vegetables. It is also added to pulses and dals as it is reputed to have anti-flatulence properties. It is a hard resin from a type of fennel and is best bought ground. Store in an airtight container.

ata flour: Also known as chapati flour, this is a wholemeal flour widely used for making breads. It is available from Asian food shops and many supermarkets. Well-sifted wholemeal flour can be used instead.

banana leaves: These are used for wrapping ingredients, particularly fish, before steaming. They are available from Asian food shops and should be soaked briefly in hot water to make them pliable.

basmati rice: This fragrant rice from the foothills of the Himalayas is known as the prince of rices because of its fine flavour and aroma. Not all rice labelled basmati is of the same quality and there are plans in India for greater control over which varieties may be officially included in this group to protect its quality. At the moment, because of unscrupulous trading, more so-called basmati rice is exported than actually grows in the whole of the country. It should be rinsed in several changes of water and, ideally, soaked for 10 minutes before using.

besan: Also known as gram flour, this is made from chickpeas. It is used to flavour and thicken curries and for making pakoras and bhajias.

black-eyed beans: Available dried or canned, these cream-coloured, kidney-shaped beans have a black spot or eye. They have a mild flavour and are widely used in Indian cooking.

cardamom pods: Used in both sweet and savoury dishes, cardamoms are one of India's favourite spices and are native to the country. The pods may be used whole or the seeds can be extracted and used alone. Whole pods are usually removed and discarded before a dish is served. Green cardamoms are the most common, but there are also black and cream varieties. The black pods are used only in savoury dishes. Cardamom is the world's second most expensive spice.

cayenne pepper: This is a type of chilli powder made from a particularly hot variety of chilli. It includes both the ground seeds as well as the dried flesh.

chana dal: A split yellow lentil with a slightly sweet taste, chana dal are used in a variety of vegetable dishes and as a binding agent.

chickpeas: A round, nutty flavoured pulse, this is widely used in many vegetarian dishes. It is available dried and canned. It is also ground to make flour (besan or gram).

chillies: Available both dried and fresh, these hot peppers are essential to Indian cooking. The level of heat varies, depending on the variety, so it is sensible to err on the side of caution. Removing the seeds before cooking tones down the heat of the dish. As a general rule, dark green chillies tend to be hotter than light green ones, which in turn, tend be hotter than red chillies. Small, pointed chillies are usually hotter than larger, more rounded varieties. However, this is not invariably the case. Always wash your hands thoroughly after handling fresh chillies and avoid touching sensitive areas, such as the eyes or lips. If you have very sensitive skin, protect your hands with rubber gloves.

chilli powder: Made from dried, ground chillies, this is a hot spice to be used with caution. Some brands are hotter than others and some also include other spices.

cinnamon: Available in sticks or ground, this is a warm, aromatic spice. It is quite difficult to grind yourself.

cloves: Available whole or ground, this warm spice is used in both savoury and sweet dishes. In India, it is usually used whole.

coconut: Widely used in southern Indian cuisine, coconut is available fresh, desiccated (that is, dried and shredded), and as milk in cans and cartons. Coconut milk is not the same as the liquid found in the shells, but a mixture of pulped flesh and water. Coconut is used in both savoury and sweet dishes.

coriander: Also known as dhania, the fresh herb is very fragrant and frequently used in many dishes and as a garnish. It is usually added towards the end of cooking to preserve its fresh aroma. It does not dry successfully.

coriander seeds: Available whole or ground, this slightly sweet and extremely aromatic spice is widely used in Indian cooking.

cumin: Also known as zeera, and available whole or ground, this fragrant, mildly hot spice is used to flavour many savoury dishes and curries. It is often fried or toasted first to release its aroma. The seed is ridged and greenish, beige in colour, although it is often known as white cumin. Black cumin is not, in fact, cumin at all but a different spice, which is also known as nigella or kalonji.

curry paste: Curry spices may be combined with oil and heated to make a convenient paste, which can be stored for up to a month. Shop-bought, ready-made curry pastes vary in quality, and you can easily make your own (see page 12).

curry leaves: These look rather like bay leaves and are used in much the same way, particularly in southern Indian cuisine. When crushed they give off an aroma similar to a mixture of curry spices. They are available dried and, sometimes, fresh from Asian food shops. The fresh leaves freeze well.

curry powder: Indian cooks mix their own combination of curry spices and never use a ready-made powder. They may, however, make a batch of the spice mixture and store it for a short while for later use.

fennel seeds: This sweet spice tastes a little like aniseed and is used in some curries. Roasted fennel seeds are chewed to freshen the breath after meals.

fenugreek: The fresh herb is used in a number of vegetable dishes and in some meat dishes. Always discard the stalks, which taste unpleasantly bitter, and use only the small leaves.

fenugreek seeds: This pungent seed gives curry spice mixes their characteristic, strong aroma. They have a bitter flavour.

five-spice powder: This is a mixture of spices that can be bought ready-made, or you can make it yourself (see Panch Phoran on page 12). If you buy five-spice powder, make sure that you obtain the Indian mixture, not the Chinese one, which contains different spices.

garam masala: Originally from northern Indian, this is the most widely used spice mixture in Indian cooking and is available ready-made, or you can make it yourself (see page 12). There is no fixed recipe – masala simply means blended spices – and it varies from region to region and from cook to cook. It typically contains roasted whole spices such as cloves, cardamoms, cumin, peppercorns and cinnamon, that are ground. It is often added to dishes towards the end of cooking.

garlic: Indispensable in curries and many other Indian dishes. Garlic may be used fresh or in the convenient form of Garlic Paste (see page 12). Garlic powder is also used in some spice mixtures.

ghee: Clarified butter or ghee used to be the standard cooking fat throughout India. Nowadays, vegetable ghee, often corn oil, is more popular because it contains less saturated fat.

ginger: This aromatic fresh root is as indispensable as garlic in curries and other dishes. It should be peeled before chopping or pulping. Ground ginger is no substitute, but Ginger Paste (see page 12) is convenient.

kalonji: Also known as nigella, these tiny black seeds have a slight peppery flavour and are used mainly in vegetable dishes. They are also erroneously called black cumin, but come from a completely different plant, and are sometimes confused with onion seeds, which they resemble in appearance.

mace: This is the lacy dried covering of the ripe nutmeg seed and has a similar, slightly bitter taste. It is sometimes available intact with nutmeg, but is more usually sold in fragments called blades, or ground.

mango: This tropical fruit is sweet and juicy when ripe and is used in many Indian desserts. Unripe mangoes are also used in some curries and to make chutney.

mango powder: Used to flavour vegetable dishes, this sour powder is made from unripe mangoes.

masoor dal: These split red lentils are widely available and are used in many dishes. They are actually orange in colour and become much paler when they are cooked.

mint: This is a widely used herb often paired with lamb. Indian mint has a stronger flavour and more pungent aroma than Western varieties.

moong dal: This split yellow lentil is quite similar to chana dal, but smaller.

mustard oil: A speciality of Bengali cuisine, this has a completely unique flavour and aroma. Mustard oil should be bought from a specialist Asian food shop – never use the pharmaceutical variety for cooking.

mustard seeds: Black mustard seeds, also known as brown mustard seeds, have a strong flavour and are used in curries, particularly with vegetables and pulses, and in pickles. They are often fried in oil first to release their full flavour and aroma. The larger, yellow variety, known as white mustard seeds, are much less pungent.

onion seeds: These small black seeds are used in many pickles and curries, especially with vegetables.

panch phoran: This is an Indian mix of five spices – cumin seeds, onion seeds, mustard seeds, fenugreek seeds and aniseed. Five-spice powder is available from Asian food shops, or you can mix the whole seeds (see page 12) and grind as required.

paneer: This smooth, white cheese with a delicate flavour is used throughout India by both vegetarians and meat eaters – it is often combined with meat. It is available in vacuum packs from Asian food shops and can be made easily at home (see pages 12–13). Ricotta cheese may be used instead.

pomegranate seeds: These are added to vegetable dishes to give them a tangy, acidic flavour. You can use fresh pomegranate seeds directly from the fruit, or dried seeds, called anardana, which are available from Asian food shops.

poppy seeds: White poppy seeds are quite different from the tiny black ones popular in the West. They are often ground and used as a thickener.

raw sugar: Also known as crude sugar or jaggery, this is the sugar that remains after cane sugar juice has been boiled and the molasses separated. It is available from Asian food shops. Alternatively, you can substitute muscovado or dark brown sugar.

saffron: This fragrant spice is made from the dried stigmas of the saffron crocus and is very expensive. It is used in both sweet and savoury dishes and has a delicious aroma and flavour, as well as a lovely yellow colour. It is available in threads and as a powder.

tamarind: Sour tasting and strongly flavoured, this is the sticky, dried, dark brown pod of the tamarind plant. It has to be soaked in hot water, then sieved before use. Tamarind paste is more convenient to use and is available in jars from Asian food shops. You can use lemon juice as a substitute.

toor dal: This split lentil is similar to chana dal.

toovar dal: This orange split pea is available plain or in an oily variety. It has a distinctive flavour.

turmeric: This bright yellow spice is mainly used to provide colour and should be added with discretion because it has a bitter flavour. It is usually sold ground, but you can sometimes buy the fresh root. Wear rubber gloves when handling fresh turmeric as it will stain your hands yellow.

urid dal: This lentil is available with its hull, which is black, and may be called black gram, or hulled, when it is creamy white. It takes quite a long time to cook.

basic recipes

panch phoran

preparation time: 5 minutes
cooking time: 0 minutes

1 tsp cumin seeds
1 tsp onion seeds
1 tsp mustard seeds
1 tsp fenugreek seeds
1 tsp aniseed

1 Mix all the seeds together in a small bowl and store in an airtight jar.

garlic paste

preparation time: 5 minutes
cooking time: 0 minutes

115 g/4 oz garlic cloves, halved
125 ml/4 fl oz water

1 Place the garlic cloves and water in a food processor or blender and process to make a paste. Transfer to a glass jar with a lid and store in the refrigerator for up to 1 month.

ginger paste

preparation time: 5 minutes
cooking time: 0 minutes

115 g/4 oz fresh root ginger, roughly chopped
125 ml/4 fl oz water

1 Place the ginger and water in a food processor or blender and process to make a paste. Transfer to a glass jar with a lid and store in the refrigerator for up to 1 month.

curry paste

preparation time: 10 minutes, plus 20 minutes cooling
cooking time: 10 minutes

4 tbsp coriander seeds
2 tbsp cumin seeds
1 tbsp fenugreek seeds
1 tbsp fennel seeds
2 curry leaves
2 dried red chillies
2 tsp ground turmeric
2 tsp chilli powder
5 tbsp white wine vinegar
2 tbsp water
125 ml/4 fl oz vegetable oil, plus extra for sealing

1 Grind the coriander seeds, cumin seeds, fenugreek seeds, fennel seeds, curry leaves and dried red chillies in a spice grinder. Alternatively, use a mortar and pestle. Transfer to a bowl and stir in the turmeric, chilli powder, vinegar and water to make a smooth paste.

2 Heat the vegetable oil in a large, heavy-based frying pan, add the paste and cook over a low heat, stirring constantly, for 10 minutes, or until all the water has been absorbed and the oil rises to the surface.

3 Leave to cool, then spoon into a glass jar with a lid. To preserve the curry paste, heat a little more vegetable oil in a clean saucepan and pour it over the surface. Store in the refrigerator for up to 1 month.

garam masala

preparation time: 10 minutes, plus 10 minutes cooling
cooking time: 10 minutes

1 cinnamon stick
8 dried red chillies
5 tbsp coriander seeds
2 tbsp cumin seeds
2 tsp cardamom seeds
2 tsp black peppercorns
1 tsp fennel seeds
1 tsp black mustard seeds
1 tsp whole cloves

1 Dry-fry the cinnamon and chillies in a heavy-based frying pan over a low heat, stirring constantly, for 2 minutes. Add the remaining spices and dry-fry, stirring and shaking the frying pan constantly, for 8 minutes, or until they give off their aroma.

2 Remove the frying pan from the heat and leave to cool. Transfer the contents to a spice grinder and process until ground. Alternatively, use a mortar and pestle. Store in an airtight container in the refrigerator for up to 3 months.

paneer

preparation time: 10 minutes, plus 3 hours standing
cooking time: 5–10 minutes

1 litre/1¾ pints milk
2 tbsp lemon juice

1 Bring the milk to the boil in a heavy-based saucepan over a low heat, then reduce the heat and simmer gently for a few minutes. Add the lemon juice, stirring constantly until the milk begins to curdle.

2 Drain the mixture through a muslin-lined sieve, then rinse the contents of the sieve under cold running water. Gather up the corners of the muslin, tie them together and squeeze gently to extract any moisture.

3 Hang the muslin-wrapped cheese for 1 hour to drain, then press under a heavy weight for 1½–2 hours. Transfer to an airtight container and store for up to 1 week.

stocks If you like your food spicy, choose the Indian variations:

indian vegetable stock

makes: 3 litres/5¼ pints
preparation time: 10 minutes, plus 3 hours standing
cooking time: 1 hour 40 minutes

3 tbsp ghee or vegetable oil
1 tsp Garlic Paste (see page 12)
1 tsp Ginger Paste (see page 12)
2 tsp coriander seeds
1 tsp cumin seeds
5 cloves
10 black peppercorns
5-cm/2-inch cinnamon stick
6 cardamom pods
1 onion, cut into 8 wedges
1 carrot, chopped
3 litres/5¼ pints water

1 Heat the ghee in a large, heavy-based saucepan. Add the Garlic Paste, Ginger Paste, coriander seeds and cumin seeds. Cook over a low heat, stirring constantly, for 1 minute. Add the cloves, peppercorns, cinnamon stick, cardamoms, onion and carrot. Cook, stirring frequently, for 8 minutes.

2 Add the water and bring to the boil. Cover and simmer for 1½ hours.

3 Remove from the heat and sieve the stock into a bowl. Leave to cool, then chill in the refrigerator. When chilled, carefully remove and discard any fat on the surface. Use immediately.

basic vegetable stock

makes: 3 litres/5¼ pints
preparation time: 10 minutes
cooking time: 40 minutes

2 tbsp sunflower oil
115 g/4 oz onions, finely chopped
115 g/4 oz leeks, finely chopped
115 g/4 oz carrots, finely chopped
4 celery sticks, finely chopped
85 g/3 oz fennel, finely chopped
85 g/3 oz tomatoes, finely chopped
2.25 litres/4 pints water
1 bouquet garni

1 Heat the oil in a large saucepan. Add the onions and leeks and cook over a low heat, stirring occasionally, for 5 minutes, or until softened.

2 Add the remaining vegetables, cover and cook over a low heat, stirring occasionally, for 10 minutes. Add the water and bouquet garni, bring to the boil and simmer for 20 minutes.

3 Remove from the heat and sieve the stock into a bowl. Leave to cool, then chill. Remove and discard any fat on the surface. Use immediately or freeze in portions for up to 3 months.

indian meat stock

makes: 1.7 litres/3 pints
preparation time: 15 minutes, plus 1 hour cooling/chilling
cooking time: 2 hours 45 minutes

1 kg/2 lb 4 oz chicken, duck or lamb
1-cm/½-inch piece fresh root ginger, thinly sliced
5-cm/2-inch cinnamon stick
1 fresh green chilli, chopped
pinch of ground mace
pared rind of 1 lemon

1 Place all the ingredients in a large, heavy-based saucepan and pour in enough water to cover generously. Bring to the boil, then reduce the heat, cover and leave to simmer for 40 minutes.

2 Using a slotted spoon, remove the chicken, duck or lamb and cut the meat off the bone. Reserve it for use later. Return all the bones to the saucepan and return to the boil, then leave to simmer for a further 2 hours.

3 Remove the saucepan from the heat and sieve the stock into a bowl. Leave to cool, then chill in the refrigerator. When chilled, carefully remove and discard the layer of fat that has set on the surface. Use immediately.

basic meat stock

makes: 2.5 litres/4½ pints
preparation time: 15 minutes, plus 1 hour cooling/chilling
cooking time: 3 hours 30 minutes

1.3 kg/3 lb chicken or duck wings and necks, or lamb on the bone
2 onions, cut into wedges
4 litres/7 pints water
2 carrots, roughly chopped
2 celery sticks, roughly chopped
10 fresh parsley sprigs
4 fresh thyme sprigs
2 bay leaves
10 black peppercorns

1 Place the chicken, duck or lamb and the onions in a large, heavy-based saucepan and cook over a low heat, stirring frequently, until lightly browned.

2 Add the water and stir thoroughly to scrape off any sediment on the base of the saucepan. Bring to the boil and skim off the scum that rises to the surface. Add the carrots, celery, parsley, thyme, bay leaves and peppercorns, partially cover and leave to simmer gently for 3 hours.

3 Remove the saucepan from the heat and sieve the stock into a bowl. Leave to cool, then chill in the refrigerator. When chilled, carefully remove and discard the layer of fat that has set on the surface. Use immediately or freeze in portions for up to 6 months.

snacks & starters

As a general rule, meals in India don't begin with a separate first course, but Indians are inveterate snackers, so there is a wealth of delicious nibbles that can be served as appetizers and canapés. You can, of course, also enjoy them in the traditional way as early evening nibbles with the inevitable cup of tea, and many of them make great after-school snacks.

This chapter includes some familiar favourites, such as Samosas (see page 26) – with both a vegetable and a meat filling – and Onion Bhajias (see page 36), as well some more unusual tempting treats, such as Spicy Pancakes (see page 18) and Stuffed Meatballs (see page 21). Choose from an array of vegetable, meat or seafood delicacies to wake up the taste buds and stimulate the appetite, whether you are planning to serve an authentic Indian meal or simply want an interesting, more unusual starter for a Western-style supper.

There are also some delicious soups, ranging from quite fiercely spiced to milder and more subtle in flavour. All of them would make a delicious and substantial lunchtime snack, perhaps served with some Indian bread, or as an imaginative start to a dinner party menu.

pakoras

serves 4 | **prep: 15 mins** | **cook: 15–20 mins**

Pakoras are eaten all over India. This savoury snack is made in many different ways and with a variety of fillings. Sometimes pakoras are served with yogurt or other dipping sauces.

INGREDIENTS

- 6 tbsp gram flour
- ½ tsp salt
- 1 tsp chilli powder
- 1 tsp baking powder
- 1½ tsp white cumin seeds
- 1 tsp pomegranate seeds
- 300 ml/10 fl oz water
- 2–3 tbsp fresh coriander leaves, finely chopped
- vegetables of your choice, such as cauliflower cut into small florets, onions cut into rings, sliced potatoes, sliced aubergines, or fresh spinach leaves
- vegetable oil, for deep-frying
- fresh coriander sprig, to garnish

NUTRITIONAL INFORMATION	
Calories	331
Protein	9g
Carbohydrate	27g
Sugars	5g
Fat	22g
Saturates	3g

variation

You can serve these pakoras with a cooling Raita (see page 228) or Mango Chutney (see page 230).

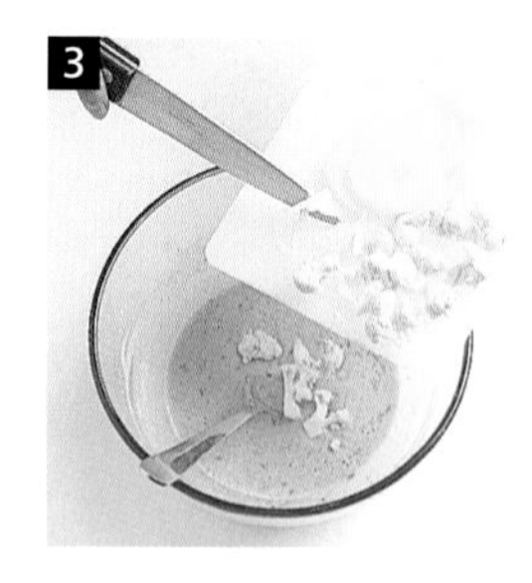

1. Sift the gram flour into a large bowl. Add the salt, chilli powder, baking powder, cumin seeds and pomegranate seeds and blend together well.

2. Pour in the water and beat well to form a smooth batter. Add the coriander and mix well.

3. Add the prepared vegetables of your choice to the batter, then remove with the tip of a sharp knife or a fork, carefully shaking off any excess batter.

4. Heat the vegetable oil in a large, heavy-based saucepan to 180–190°C/350–375°F, or until a cube of bread browns in 30 seconds. Using a slotted spoon, lower the battered vegetables into the hot oil, a few at a time, and deep-fry, turning once. Remove with the slotted spoon and drain thoroughly on kitchen paper. Repeat this process until all of the batter has been used up.

5. Place the pakoras on a large serving plate and garnish with a fresh coriander sprig. Serve immediately.

cook's tip

When deep-frying, it is important to use oil at the correct temperature. If it is too hot, the outside of the food will burn before the inside is cooked. Draining on kitchen paper absorbs excess oil.

spicy pancakes

serves 6 **prep: 25 mins, plus 12 hrs soaking/standing** **cook: 1 hr 20 mins**

Packed with flavour, these southern Indian snacks make a delicious light lunch, especially if served with Mango Chutney (see page 230). However, you will need to allow plenty of time to make them.

INGREDIENTS

- 140 g/5 oz basmati rice, soaked for 2–3 hours in cold water and drained
- 140 g/5 oz urid dal, soaked for 2–3 hours in cold water and drained
- 2 fresh green chillies, deseeded and finely chopped
- 1 tsp dark brown sugar
- salt
- 300 ml/10 fl oz water
- 1.25 kg/2 lb 12 oz potatoes
- 3 tbsp grated fresh coconut
- 2.5-cm/1-inch piece fresh root ginger, finely chopped
- 4 tbsp ghee or vegetable oil, plus extra for frying
- 2 tsp black mustard seeds
- 2 tsp cumin seeds
- 1 tsp ground turmeric
- 3 tbsp chopped fresh coriander
- fresh coriander sprigs, to garnish
- chutney, to serve

NUTRITIONAL INFORMATION	
Calories	330
Protein	13g
Carbohydrate	66g
Sugars	3g
Fat	3g
Saturates	2g

variation

If you can't find fresh coconut, you can substitute 2 tablespoons of unsweetened coconut cream.

1

4

4

cook's tip

When buying a fresh coconut, choose one that feels heavy for its size, and make sure that it contains a good amount of coconut milk.

1. Place the rice and dal in a food processor and process until ground. Tip into a bowl. Stir in half the chillies, the sugar and a pinch of salt. Gradually add the water and mix to a smooth batter. Cover and leave to stand in a warm place overnight.

2. Cook the potatoes in lightly salted boiling water for 20–25 minutes, or until tender. Drain and mash. Mix the remaining chillies, coconut and ginger to a paste.

3. Heat the ghee in a large, heavy-based frying pan, add the mustard and cumin seeds and stir until they give off their aroma. Stir in the coconut and ginger paste and cook for 1 minute, then add the mashed potatoes, turmeric and coriander and cook, stirring, for 5 minutes. Remove from the heat.

4. Heat a little ghee in a 20-cm/8-inch frying pan. Stir the batter. Pour one-sixth into the frying pan, tilting the pan to spread it over the base. Cook for 1–2 minutes, or until the underside is golden. Flip over and cook the other side for 2 minutes. Transfer to a plate and keep warm while you cook the remaining pancakes, adding more ghee as required. Divide the filling between the pancakes and fold in half. Return them to the frying pan, in batches, and fry for 30 seconds on each side. Garnish with fresh coriander sprigs and serve with chutney.

dal fritters

serves 4 | **prep: 20 mins, plus 4 hrs soaking/standing** | **cook: 15–20 mins**

Although they don't look very pretty, these crisp little bites smell and taste absolutely irresistible. They are a popular snack in northern India, where they are sold on street stalls.

INGREDIENTS

115 g/4 oz moong dal, soaked for 2–3 hours, then drained
115 g/4 oz urid dal, soaked for 2–3 hours, then drained
1–2 tbsp water
1 onion, finely chopped
1 fresh green chilli, chopped
2.5-cm/1-inch piece fresh root ginger, finely chopped
1 tbsp chopped fresh coriander
¼ tsp bicarbonate of soda
salt
ghee or vegetable oil, for deep-frying
chutney, to serve

NUTRITIONAL INFORMATION	
Calories	263
Protein	16g
Carbohydrate	30g
Sugars	3g
Fat	9g
Saturates	1g

1 Place the dals in a food processor with the water and process to make a thick paste. Transfer to a large bowl and stir in the onion, chilli, ginger, coriander and bicarbonate of soda. Season with salt to taste, mix thoroughly and leave to stand for 5 minutes.

2 Heat the ghee in a deep-fat fryer or large, heavy-based saucepan to 180–190°C/ 350–375°F, or until a cube of bread browns in 30 seconds. Drop small spoonfuls of the mixture into the hot oil and deep-fry for 3–4 minutes, or until golden.

3 Remove the fritters with a slotted spoon and drain on kitchen paper. Keep warm while you cook the remaining fritters. Serve immediately with the chutney of your choice.

variation

Substitute ½–1 teaspoon of chilli powder for the fresh chilli, if you like. Serve with either Mango or Tamarind Chutney (see pages 230–31).

stuffed meatballs

cook: 10–15 mins

prep: 20 mins, plus 30 mins resting

makes 8

These delicious koftas are the Indian equivalent of Scotch eggs and can be served hot or cold, either as a snack or as part of a main meal. They also make great picnic food.

NUTRITIONAL INFORMATION	
Calories	298
Protein	22g
Carbohydrate	4g
Sugars	1g
Fat	22g
Saturates	7g

INGREDIENTS

1 onion, roughly chopped
1 garlic clove, roughly chopped
2.5-cm/1-inch piece fresh root ginger, roughly chopped
550 g/1 lb 4 oz fresh lamb mince
40 g/1½ oz gram flour
1 tsp ground cumin
1 tbsp ground coriander
½ tsp chilli powder
1 egg, lightly beaten
salt and pepper
8 hard-boiled eggs, shelled
ghee or vegetable oil, for deep-frying, plus extra for greasing

1. Place the onion, garlic and ginger in a food processor and process to make a paste. Place the lamb in a bowl and add the onion paste. Add the flour, cumin, ground coriander, chilli and beaten egg and season to taste with salt and pepper. Mix with your hands until thoroughly blended.

2. Divide the mixture into 8 equal-sized portions and form each portion into a ball by rolling between the palms of your hands. Flatten into patties and place a hard-boiled egg in the centre of each. Shape the meat mixture to enclose the eggs completely. Place the balls in a single layer in a lightly greased dish, cover with clingfilm and leave to rest in the refrigerator for 30 minutes.

3. Heat the ghee in a deep-fat fryer or large, heavy-based saucepan to 180–190°C/ 350–375°F, or until a cube of bread browns in 30 seconds. Cook the meatballs, in batches, for 2–3 minutes, or until golden brown. Remove with a slotted spoon and drain on kitchen paper. If serving hot, keep warm while you deep-fry the remaining batches.

variation

Instead of using hard-boiled eggs, you could use 500 g/1 lb 2 oz ricotta cheese, or the same amount of paneer cut into 8 cubes.

sweet & sour fruit

serves 4 | **prep: 5 mins** | **cook: 0 mins**

This mixture of fresh and canned fruit, which has a sweet and sour flavour, is very cooling, especially in the summer months. You could serve tea or fresh fruit juices with this dish.

INGREDIENTS

400 g/14 oz canned mixed fruit cocktail
400 g/14 oz canned guavas
2 large bananas
3 apples
1 tsp pepper
1 tsp salt
2 tbsp lemon juice
½ tsp ground ginger
fresh mint leaves, to garnish

NUTRITIONAL INFORMATION	
Energy	240
Protein	2g
Carbohydrate	60g
Sugars	58g
Fat	0.4g
Saturates	0g

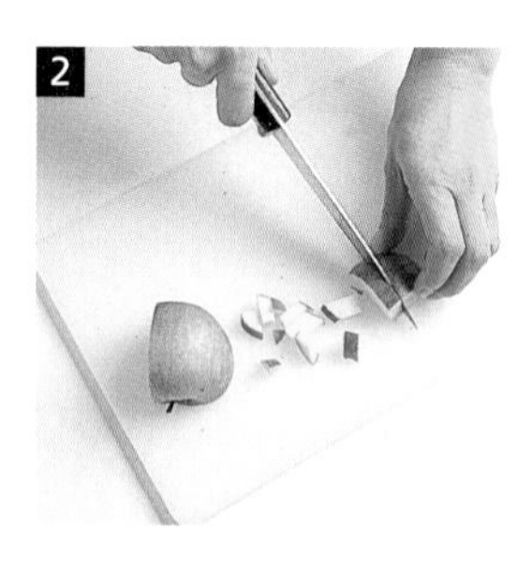

1 Drain the fruit cocktail and place the fruit in a deep bowl. Mix the guavas and their syrup with the drained fruit cocktail.

2 Peel the bananas and cut into slices. Peel the apples and cut into dice.

3 Add the fresh fruit to the bowl and mix with the canned fruit.

4 Add the pepper, salt, lemon juice and ginger and stir to mix well.

5 Transfer to a serving bowl and garnish with a few fresh mint leaves. Serve as a snack.

cook's tip

The lemon juice in this recipe serves to add a sharp flavour to the dish, but it also prevents the banana and apple discolouring when the flesh is exposed to the air.

indian-style omelette

cook: 20 mins **prep: 10 mins** **serves 2–4**

Omelettes are very versatile: they go with almost anything and you can also serve them at any time of the day. For an informal lunch you could serve this omelette with chips.

NUTRITIONAL INFORMATION	
Energy	132
Protein	7g
Carbohydrate	2g
Sugars	1g
Fat	11g
Saturates	2g

INGREDIENTS

1 small onion, very finely chopped
2 fresh green chillies, finely chopped
fresh coriander leaves, finely chopped
4 medium eggs
1 tsp salt
2 tbsp vegetable oil
fresh coriander sprigs, to garnish

TO SERVE

mixed salad leaves
chutney

1 Place the onion, chillies and coriander in a large bowl and mix together.

2 Place the eggs in a separate bowl and whisk together.

3 Add the onion mixture to the eggs and mix together well. Add the salt to the mixture and whisk together well.

4 Heat 1 tablespoon of the vegetable oil in a large frying pan. Place a ladleful of the omelette batter into the frying pan.

5 Fry the omelette, turning once, pressing down with a flat spoon to make sure that the egg is cooked right through, until the omelette is golden brown. Transfer to a plate and keep warm while you make the remaining omelettes, using the remaining vegetable oil as necessary.

6 Serve the omelettes with mixed salad leaves and a chutney of your choice, garnished with coriander.

cook's tip

Serve this omelette with a chutney of your choice, such as Mango Chutney (see page 230), or a cooling Cucumber Raita (see page 228) and Parathas (see page 215).

omelette with spicy vegetable filling

cook: 6–7 mins

prep: 25 mins

serves 4

NUTRITIONAL INFORMATION	
Calories	176
Protein	9g
Carbohydrate	4g
Sugars	3g
Fat	14g
Saturates	4g

variation

Substitute thawed frozen or drained canned sweetcorn for all or some of the cooked peas, if you prefer.

The Indian equivalent of Italian frittata, this quick and easy omelette makes a good lunch dish, although it can be served at any time of day – even at breakfast.

INGREDIENTS

- 2 tbsp ghee or vegetable oil
- 1 garlic clove, finely chopped
- 1 onion, finely chopped
- 1 tomato, peeled and finely chopped
- 1 cooked potato, diced
- 55 g/2 oz cooked peas
- 1 fresh green chilli, deseeded and finely chopped
- ½ tsp ground coriander
- ½ tsp ground cumin
- 1 tbsp chopped fresh coriander
- salt and pepper
- 2 eggs, lightly beaten
- 4 tbsp grated Cheddar cheese
- fresh coriander sprigs, to garnish

1 Preheat the grill to medium. Heat the ghee in a large, heavy-based frying pan. Add the garlic and onion and fry gently over a medium heat. Then add the tomato, potato, peas, chilli, ground coriander, cumin and chopped fresh coriander and continue to cook over a medium heat, stirring frequently, until the onion has softened and the mixture is well blended. Season to taste with salt and pepper.

2 Add the eggs, cover and cook over a low heat for 4–5 minutes, or until the underside is golden brown.

3 Sprinkle the cheese over the omelette and cook briefly under the preheated grill until the cheese has melted and the top of the omelette is set. Slide out of the frying pan, garnish with coriander sprigs and serve immediately.

cook's tip

If you don't have a frying pan that can safely be used under the grill, protect the handle by covering it with foil.

samosas

makes 10–12

prep: 40 mins, plus 1 hr standing

cook: 40 mins

These traditional, savoury, deep-fried pastries are filled with a spiced potato mixture and perfectly complemented by a squeeze of lemon juice. They are suitable for vegetarians.

NUTRITIONAL INFORMATION	
Calories	261
Protein	2g
Carbohydrate	13g
Sugars	0.4g
Fat	23g
Saturates	4g

INGREDIENTS

PASTRY

100 g/3½ oz self-raising flour
½ tsp salt
40 g/1½ oz butter, cut into small pieces
4 tbsp water

FILLING

3 potatoes
1 tsp finely chopped fresh root ginger
1 tsp crushed fresh garlic
½ tsp white cumin seeds
½ tsp mixed onion and mustard seeds
1 tsp salt
½ tsp crushed red chillies
2 tbsp lemon juice
2 small fresh green chillies, finely chopped
ghee or vegetable oil, for deep-frying
lemon wedges, to serve

variation

Substitute the green chillies with 2 red chillies, and if you don't like it too spicy, deseed the chillies before using.

1

2

3

cook's tip

When deep-frying the samosas, do not overcrowd the saucepan because you need room to turn them. Remove the cooked samosas with a slotted spoon to allow some of the oil to drain off.

1. Sift the flour and salt into a large bowl. Add the butter and rub it into the flour until the mixture resembles fine breadcrumbs. Pour in the water and mix with a fork to form a dough. Pat the dough into a ball and knead for 5 minutes or until smooth. Add a little flour if the dough is sticky. Cover and leave to stand for 1 hour.

2. Meanwhile, to make the filling, cook the potatoes in a saucepan of lightly salted boiling water for 20–25 minutes, until tender. Drain and gently mash the potatoes, then add the ginger, garlic, white cumin seeds, onion and mustard seeds, salt, crushed red chillies, lemon juice and green chillies and stir well to mix.

3. Break small balls off the dough and roll each out very thinly to form a round. Cut in half, dampen the edges and form into cones. Fill the cones with a little of the filling, dampen the open edges and pinch together to seal. Reserve.

4. Fill a deep-fat fryer or large, heavy-based saucepan one-third full with vegetable oil and heat to 180–190°C/350–375°F, or until a cube of bread browns in 30 seconds. Carefully lower the samosas into the hot oil, in batches, and fry for 2–3 minutes, or until golden brown. Remove with a slotted spoon and drain thoroughly on kitchen paper. Serve hot or cold with lemon wedges.

samosas with meat filling

cook: 30 mins | **prep: 20 mins, plus 30 mins cooling** | **makes: 10–12**

NUTRITIONAL INFORMATION	
Calories	252
Protein	9g
Carbohydrate	8g
Sugars	1g
Fat	21g
Saturates	6g

variation

If you don't want to go to the bother of making the samosa pastry yourself, you can use spring roll wrappers instead.

These spicy snacks are served throughout India and are immensely popular. They make terrific party food and can be prepared in advance and frozen either half-fried or uncooked.

INGREDIENTS

1 quantity Samosa Pastry (see page 26)
vegetable oil, for deep-frying
fresh coriander sprigs, to garnish

FILLING

2 tbsp ghee or vegetable oil
1 onion, chopped
450 g/1 lb fresh lamb mince
1 tsp Garlic Paste (see page 12)
1 tsp Ginger Paste (see page 12)
salt and pepper

1

2

3

cook's tip

Frozen samosas do not need to be thawed before deep-frying. However, if you prefer to thaw them, this will not adversely affect them.

1 To make the filling, heat the ghee in a large, heavy-based frying pan. Add the onion and cook over a low heat, stirring frequently, for 10 minutes, or until golden. Add the lamb, Garlic Paste and Ginger Paste and season to taste with salt and pepper. Cook, breaking up the meat with a wooden spoon, for 10 minutes, or until the mixture is fairly dry. Transfer to a bowl with a slotted spoon and leave to cool.

2 Break small balls off the dough and roll each out very thinly to form a round. Cut in half, dampen the edges and form into cones. Fill the cones with a little of the filling, then dampen the top and bottom edges and pinch together to seal. Reserve.

3 Fill a deep-fat fryer or large, heavy-based saucepan one-third full with vegetable oil and heat to 180–190°C/350–375°F, or until a cube of bread browns in 30 seconds. Carefully lower the samosas into the hot oil, in batches, and deep-fry for 2–3 minutes, or until golden brown. Remove with a slotted spoon and drain on kitchen paper. Keep warm while you cook the remaining samosas. Serve hot or cold, garnished with fresh coriander sprigs.

chickpea snack

serves 2–4 **prep: 5 mins** **cook: 5–10 mins**

Though you may use fresh chickpeas, soaked overnight, for this popular snack, which is eaten all over India, the canned sort are quick and easy to use without sacrificing much flavour.

NUTRITIONAL INFORMATION	
Calories	190
Protein	9g
Carbohydrate	34g
Sugars	4g
Fat	3g
Saturates	0.3g

INGREDIENTS

- **400 g/14 oz canned chickpeas, drained and rinsed**
- **2 potatoes**
- **1 onion**
- **2 tbsp tamarind paste**
- **6 tbsp water**
- **1 tsp chilli powder**
- **2 tsp sugar**
- **1 tsp salt**

TO GARNISH

- **1 tomato, quartered**
- **1 fresh green chilli, finely sliced**
- **fresh coriander leaves**

variation

Deseed the fresh green chilli before garnishing, otherwise serve with a cooling Mint Raita (see page 228).

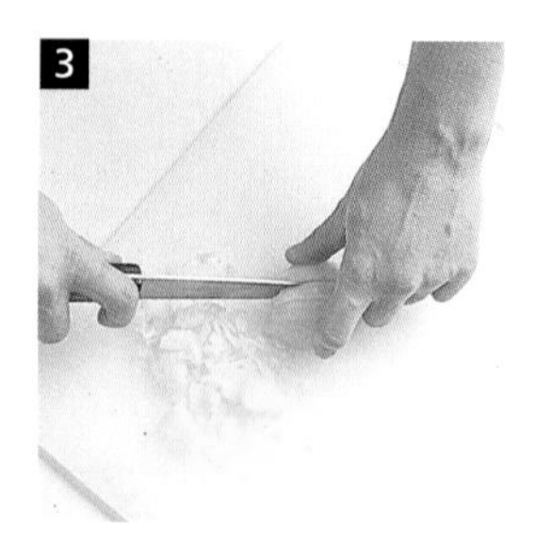

cook's tip

Chickpeas have a nutty flavour and slightly crunchy texture. Indian cooks grind these to make gram flour, which is used to make breads, thicken sauces, and to make batters for deep-fried dishes.

1. Place the chickpeas in a small bowl and reserve until required.

2. Using a sharp knife, cut the potatoes into dice, then cook in a saucepan of boiling water for 5–10 minutes until cooked through. Test by inserting the point of a knife into the potatoes – they should feel soft and tender. Drain and reserve.

3. Using a sharp knife, finely chop the onion. Reserve until required.

4. Mix the tamarind paste and water together in a small bowl, then add the chilli powder, sugar and salt and mix together thoroughly. Pour the mixture over the chickpeas.

5. Add the onion and the diced potatoes and stir to mix. Season with a little extra salt to taste. Transfer to a serving bowl, garnish with the tomatoes, chillies and coriander leaves and serve.

soft dumplings in yogurt with masala

cook: 20 mins **prep: 15 mins** **serves 4**

NUTRITIONAL INFORMATION	
Calories	476
Protein	11g
Carbohydrate	64g
Sugars	29g
Fat	21g
Saturates	3g

These little dumplings are very easy to prepare and are ideal to serve as a delicious snack at any time of the day.

INGREDIENTS

200 g/7 oz urid dal powder
1 tsp baking powder
½ tsp ground ginger
700 ml/1¼ pints water
vegetable oil, for deep-frying
400 ml/14 fl oz natural yogurt
75 g/2¾ oz sugar
sliced fresh red chillies, to garnish

MASALA

50 g/1¾ oz coriander seeds
50 g/1¾ oz white cumin seeds
25 g/1 oz crushed red chillies
100 g/3½ oz citric acid

variation

If you prefer, use low-fat natural yogurt, or rich, Greek-style yogurt for a special occasion.

cook's tip

The masala spice mixture for the dumplings is usually made in a large quantity. It can be stored in an airtight container in a dark cool place.

1. Place the powdered urid dal in a large bowl. Add the baking powder and ground ginger and stir to mix well. Add 300 ml/10 fl oz of the water and mix to form a paste.

2. Heat the vegetable oil in a deep-fat fryer or large, heavy-based saucepan to 180–190°C/350–375°F, or until a cube of bread browns in 30 seconds. Add the batter, 1 teaspoon at a time, and deep-fry the dumplings until golden brown, lowering the heat when the oil gets too hot. Remove the dumplings with a slotted spoon and reserve.

3. Place the yogurt in a separate bowl. Add the remaining water and the sugar and mix together with a whisk or fork. Reserve.

4. To make the masala, roast the coriander and white cumin seeds in a small saucepan until a little darker in colour. Transfer to a food processor and process until roughly ground. Alternatively, use a mortar and pestle. Add the crushed red chillies and citric acid and blend well together.

5. Sprinkle 1 tablespoon of the masala over the dumplings and garnish with chopped red chillies. Serve with the reserved yogurt mixture.

prawn patties

makes: 8 **prep: 15 mins** **cook: 20–25 mins**

Lightly spiced, rather than searingly hot, these tasty, sophisticated little nibbles go extremely well with pre-dinner drinks, and also make a very speedy lunchtime snack.

NUTRITIONAL INFORMATION	
Calories	105
Protein	10g
Carbohydrate	10g
Sugars	2g
Fat	3g
Saturates	0.5g

INGREDIENTS

- 280 g/10 oz cooked prawns, peeled, deveined and chopped
- 1 onion, finely chopped
- 1 fresh green chilli, deseeded and finely chopped
- 1-cm/½-inch piece fresh root ginger, finely chopped
- 1 tbsp chopped fresh coriander
- 2 tbsp fresh white breadcrumbs
- ¼ tsp ground turmeric
- 1 tbsp lime juice
- 1 egg, lightly beaten
- 85 g/3 oz dried breadcrumbs
- 3 tbsp ghee or vegetable oil
- fresh coriander sprigs, to garnish

variation

To make chicken patties, substitute the same quantity of minced cooked chicken for the prawns.

1. Mix the prawns, onion, chilli, ginger, coriander, fresh breadcrumbs, turmeric, lime juice and beaten egg in a large bowl, kneading well with your hands until thoroughly blended.

2. Divide the mixture into 8 equal-sized portions, then form each portion into a ball between the palms of your hands and flatten into patties. Place the dried breadcrumbs on a large plate and dip each patty, in turn, into the breadcrumbs to coat evenly.

3. Heat the ghee in a large, heavy-based frying pan. Add the patties, in 2 batches if necessary, and cook for 5–6 minutes on each side, until golden brown. Remove with a spatula and drain on kitchen paper. Keep each batch warm while you cook the remainder. Garnish with fresh coriander sprigs and serve immediately.

cook's tip

If possible, use natural dried breadcrumbs for coating the patties rather than coloured breadcrumbs. You may need to press the breadcrumbs on to the patties to coat.

onion bhajias

makes about 24 **prep: 10 mins** **cook: 12 mins**

These crisp fritters are a popular snack all over India and are served by just about every Indian restaurant in the world.

INGREDIENTS

- **½ tsp onion seeds**
- **½ tsp cumin seeds**
- **½ tsp fennel seeds**
- **½ tsp kalonji seeds**
- **225 g/8 oz gram flour**
- **1 tsp baking powder**
- **1 tsp ground turmeric**
- **½ tsp chilli powder**
- **pinch of asafoetida**
- **salt**
- **3 onions, thinly sliced**
- **2 fresh green chillies, deseeded and finely chopped**
- **3 tbsp chopped fresh coriander**
- **vegetable oil, for deep-frying**

NUTRITIONAL INFORMATION	
Calories	127
Protein	2g
Carbohydrate	6g
Sugars	1g
Fat	11g
Saturates	1g

variation

You can use this batter to make bhajias with a variety of other vegetables, such as cauliflower florets or sliced mushrooms.

cook's tip

Do not overcrowd the fryer or saucepan when deep-frying, as you need room to turn the bhajias over. Lower the bhajias slowly into the hot oil to prevent any splashes.

1. Heat a large, heavy-based frying pan and dry-fry the onion, cumin, fennel and kalonji seeds for a few seconds, stirring constantly, until they give off their aroma. Remove from the heat and tip into a mortar. Crush lightly with a pestle and tip into a large bowl.

2. Sift the flour, baking powder, turmeric, chilli powder, asafoetida and a pinch of salt into the bowl and add the onions, chillies and chopped coriander. Mix thoroughly, then gradually stir in enough cold water to make a thick batter.

3. Heat the vegetable oil in a deep-fat fryer or large, heavy-based saucepan to 180–190°C/350–375°F, or until a cube of bread browns in 30 seconds. Drop spoonfuls of the mixture into the hot oil and cook until golden brown, turning once. Remove with a slotted spoon and drain on kitchen paper. Serve hot.

deep-fried potato balls

cook: 15 mins | **prep: 20 mins** | **serves 4**

This is a great way to use up left-over boiled potatoes. The crisp batter contrasts beautifully with the tender filling.

NUTRITIONAL INFORMATION	
Calories	288
Protein	8g
Carbohydrate	37g
Sugars	4g
Fat	13g
Saturates	1g

variation

Substitute chopped fresh mint for the coriander for a refreshing change and replace the lemon juice with lime.

INGREDIENTS

450 g/1 lb potatoes, boiled and diced
1 onion, chopped
2.5-cm/1-inch piece fresh root ginger, finely chopped
1 fresh green chilli, deseeded and finely chopped
1 tbsp chopped fresh coriander
1 tbsp lemon juice
2 tsp aamchoor (dried mango powder)
salt
vegetable oil, for deep-frying
chutney, to serve

BATTER

115 g/4 oz gram flour
¼ tsp baking powder
¼ tsp chilli powder
salt
about 150 ml/5 fl oz water

1

2

3

cook's tip

These potato balls are also delicious served cold. Hot or cold, serve with Mango or Tamarind Chutney (see pages 230–231) for extra flavour.

1. To make the batter, sift the flour, baking powder, chilli powder and a pinch of salt into a bowl. Gradually, stir in enough cold water to make a smooth batter. Cover with clingfilm and reserve.

2. Place the potatoes, onion, ginger, chilli, coriander, lemon juice and aamchoor into a separate bowl. Mix together well with a wooden spoon, breaking up the potatoes. Season with salt to taste.Break off small pieces of the mixture and form into balls between the palms of your hands.

3. Heat the vegetable oil in a deep-fat fryer or heavy-based saucepan to 180–190°C/350–375°F, or until a cube of bread browns in 30 seconds. When the oil is hot, dip the potato balls in the batter, using a fork, and add to the oil, in batches. Deep-fry for 3–4 minutes, until golden brown. Remove with a slotted spoon and drain on kitchen paper. Keep each batch warm while you cook the remainder. Serve hot, with chutney.

spicy potato cakes

makes 8 **prep: 10 mins** **cook: 25 mins**

These are firm favourites with children who enjoy them as an after-school snack, cold or hot with tomato ketchup.

INGREDIENTS

450 g/1 lb potatoes, diced
1 onion, grated
1 tsp Garam Masala (see page 12)
¼ tsp chilli powder (optional)
1 tbsp lemon juice
2 tbsp chopped fresh coriander
salt
4 tbsp ghee or butter
fresh coriander sprigs, to garnish

NUTRITIONAL INFORMATION	
Calories	106
Protein	2g
Carbohydrate	11g
Sugars	1g
Fat	6g
Saturates	4g

1 Cook the potatoes in a saucepan of lightly salted boiling water for 10–15 minutes, or until tender, but still firm. Meanwhile, place the grated onion in a clean tea towel and wring well to squeeze out the excess moisture. Transfer the onion to a large bowl and stir in the Garam Masala, chilli powder (if using), lemon juice and chopped coriander. Season with salt to taste.

2 Drain the potatoes and add to the bowl. Mash roughly with a fork or potato masher. Divide the mixture into 8 equal-sized portions, then form each portion into a ball between the palms of your hands and flatten into a cake.

3 Heat the ghee in a large, heavy-based frying pan. Add the potato cakes, in batches, if necessary, and fry for 2 minutes on each side, until golden brown and crisp. Remove from the frying pan with a spatula and drain on kitchen paper. Serve warm or cold garnished with sprigs of fresh coriander.

variation

For a filling cake, cook 225 g/8 oz beef mince until brown. Cool and add to the potatoes. Add 115 g/4 oz cooked peas, mash, shape and cook.

cauliflower soup

cook: 40 mins **prep: 10 mins** **serves 6**

The flavour of cauliflower is transformed by Indian spices, and this smooth soup is no exception.

NUTRITIONAL INFORMATION	
Calories	111
Protein	6g
Carbohydrate	15g
Sugars	6g
Fat	4g
Saturates	1g

INGREDIENTS

1 tbsp ghee or vegetable oil
1 small cauliflower, broken into florets
2 potatoes, diced
3 tbsp water
1 tsp Garlic Paste (see page 12)
1 tbsp Ginger Paste (see page 12)
2 tsp ground turmeric
1 tsp black mustard seeds
1 tsp cumin seeds
1 tbsp coriander seeds, lightly crushed
1 litre/1¾ pints Basic Vegetable Stock (see page 13)
salt and pepper
300 ml/10 fl oz natural yogurt

1 Heat the ghee in a large, heavy-based saucepan. Add the cauliflower, potatoes and water and bring to the boil, then reduce the heat, cover and simmer for 10 minutes.

2 Stir in the Garlic Paste, Ginger Paste, turmeric, mustard seeds, cumin seeds and coriander seeds and cook, stirring frequently, for 3 minutes. Add the Stock and season to taste with salt and pepper. Bring to the boil, cover and simmer for 20 minutes.

3 Remove the saucepan from the heat and leave to cool slightly. Ladle the mixture into a food processor or blender and process until smooth. Return to the saucepan and stir in the yogurt. Reheat gently until piping hot. Taste and adjust the seasoning, if necessary, and serve immediately.

variation

For a more subtle flavour and colour, you can substitute ½ teaspoon of saffron threads for the ground turmeric.

spinach soup

serves 6 **prep: 15 mins** **cook: 35 mins**

This creamy, colourful soup is very easy to make. It would make an unusual first course for a dinner party on a cold winter's evening.

NUTRITIONAL INFORMATION	
Calories	245
Protein	15g
Carbohydrate	37g
Sugars	9g
Fat	6g
Saturates	1g

INGREDIENTS

- 2 tsp coriander seeds
- 2 tsp cumin seeds
- 1 tbsp ghee or vegetable oil
- 2 onions, chopped
- 1 tbsp Ginger Paste (see page 12)
- 2 tsp Garlic Paste (see page 12)
- 6 curry leaves, roughly torn
- 2 dried red chillies, crushed
- 2 tsp black mustard seeds
- ½ tsp fenugreek seeds
- 1 tsp ground turmeric
- 200 g/7 oz masoor dal
- 2 potatoes, diced
- 1.2 litres/2 pints Basic Vegetable Stock (see page 13)
- 1 kg/2 lb 4 oz fresh spinach, tough stalks removed, plus extra to garnish
- 2 tbsp lemon juice
- 300 ml/10 fl oz coconut milk
- salt and pepper

variation

If you can bear the smell, add a pinch of asafoetida with the ground turmeric in Step 2.

cook's tip

You can prepare this soup the day before and when cool, cover with clingfilm and store in the refrigerator until required. Make sure that it is piping hot before serving.

1. Heat a heavy-based frying pan and dry-fry the coriander and cumin seeds, stirring constantly, until they give off their aroma. Tip into a mortar and grind with a pestle. Alternatively, grind in a spice mill or blender.

2. Heat the ghee in a large saucepan. Add the onions, Ginger Paste, Garlic Paste, curry leaves, chillies, mustard seeds and fenugreek seeds and cook over a low heat, stirring frequently, for 8 minutes, or until the onions are softened and golden. Stir in the ground, dry-fried spices and turmeric and cook for a further 1 minute. Add the masoor dal, potatoes and Stock and bring to the boil, then reduce the heat and simmer for 15 minutes, or until the potatoes are tender. Stir in the spinach and cook for a further 2–3 minutes, or until wilted.

3. Remove the saucepan from the heat and leave to cool slightly. Ladle the soup into a food processor or blender and process until smooth. Return to the saucepan and stir in the lemon juice and coconut milk and season to taste with salt and pepper. Reheat gently, stirring occasionally, but do not boil. Ladle into warmed soup bowls, garnish with fresh spinach leaves and serve immediately.

lentil soup

serves 4 **prep: 5 mins** **cook: 40 mins**

This is a very substantial soup that would make a meal-in-a-bowl served with freshly cooked Parathas (see page 215).

INGREDIENTS

- 1 litre/1¾ pints water
- 250 g/9 oz toor dal or chana dal
- 1 tsp paprika
- ½ tsp chilli powder
- ½ tsp ground turmeric
- 2 tbsp ghee or vegetable oil
- 1 fresh green chilli, deseeded and finely chopped
- 1 tsp cumin seeds
- 3 curry leaves, roughly torn
- 1 tsp sugar
- salt
- 1 tsp Garam Masala (see page 12), to garnish

NUTRITIONAL INFORMATION	
Calories	264
Protein	14g
Carbohydrate	38g
Sugars	2g
Fat	7g
Saturates	1g

2

3

4

variation

For a fuller flavour, cook the dal in Basic Vegetable Stock (see page 13) instead of water.

1 Bring the water to the boil in a large, heavy-based saucepan. Add the dal, cover and simmer, stirring occasionally, for 25 minutes.

2 Stir in the paprika, chilli powder and turmeric, re-cover and cook for a further 10 minutes, or until the dal is tender.

3 Meanwhile, heat the ghee in a small frying pan. Add the chilli, cumin seeds and curry leaves and cook, stirring constantly, for 1 minute.

4 Add the spice mixture to the dal. Stir in the sugar and season with salt to taste. Ladle into warmed soup bowls, sprinkle with Garam Masala and serve immediately.

pepper water soup

cook: 20 mins **prep: 5 mins** **serves 6**

This flavoursome, southern Indian soup is the forerunner of the famous Anglo-Indian mulligatawny soup.

NUTRITIONAL INFORMATION	
Calories	45
Protein	1g
Carbohydrate	2g
Sugars	2g
Fat	4g
Saturates	0.5g

INGREDIENTS

2 tbsp ghee or vegetable oil
2 dried red chillies
4 curry leaves, roughly torn
1 tsp Garlic Paste (see page 12)
1 tsp cumin seeds
½ tsp ground turmeric
½ tsp mustard seeds
pinch of asafoetida
salt and pepper
300 ml/10 fl oz tomato juice
6 tbsp lemon juice
150 ml/5 fl oz water
chopped fresh coriander, to garnish

1 Heat the ghee in a large, heavy-based saucepan. Add the chillies, curry leaves, Garlic Paste, cumin seeds, turmeric, mustard seeds, asafoetida and ½ teaspoon pepper. Cook over a medium heat, stirring frequently, for 5–8 minutes, or until the chillies are charred.

2 Add the tomato juice, lemon juice and water and season with salt to taste. Bring to the boil, then reduce the heat and simmer for 10 minutes.

3 Remove the chillies, taste and adjust the seasoning, if necessary. Ladle into warmed bowls, sprinkle with chopped fresh coriander and serve immediately.

variation

Poach 900 g/2 lb diced chicken in 600 ml/1 pint water until tender. Proceed as in main recipe, adding the chicken to reheat at the last moment.

seafood soup

cook: 40 mins | prep: 15 mins | serves 4

NUTRITIONAL INFORMATION	
Calories	187
Protein	20g
Carbohydrate	17g
Sugars	9g
Fat	5g
Saturates	1g

variation

You could substitute 16 freshly cooked, shelled mussels for the scallops or, if you are feeling extravagant, 8 shucked oysters.

Although small, the district of Goa on the south-west coast of India has its own, quite distinctive style of cooking, which frequently features various different types of fish and seafood.

INGREDIENTS

- 225 ml/8 fl oz Basic Vegetable Stock (see page 13)
- 2 carrots, diced
- 3 garlic cloves, finely chopped
- 3 tbsp chopped fresh coriander, plus extra to garnish
- 1 tsp cumin seeds
- 1 tsp black peppercorns
- 1-cm/½-inch piece fresh root ginger, chopped
- 1 tbsp ghee or vegetable oil
- 1 onion, chopped
- 1 fresh green chilli, deseeded and chopped
- 1 potato, diced
- 2 tsp ground coriander
- 200 g/7 oz cooked prawns, peeled and deveined
- 75 ml/2½ fl oz natural yogurt
- 150 ml/5 fl oz milk
- 3 tbsp dry white wine
- 8 scallops, shelled
- salt and pepper

cook's tip

If you are buying shelled scallops, check whether they are fresh or previously frozen. Fresh ones are a translucent, creamy colour and have a better texture; frozen scallops are white and opaque.

1. Pour the stock into a large saucepan and add the carrots, 2 of the garlic cloves, the chopped coriander, cumin seeds, peppercorns and ginger. Bring to the boil, then reduce the heat, cover and simmer for 20 minutes. Sieve the Stock into a measuring jug and make up to 700 ml/1¼ pints with water, if necessary.

2. Heat the ghee in a separate saucepan. Add the onion, chilli and remaining garlic and cook for 5 minutes. Add the potato and ground coriander and cook for a further 2 minutes. Add the reserved Stock, bring to the boil, then cover and simmer for 5 minutes, or until the potato is tender.

3. Remove the saucepan from the heat and leave to cool slightly. Ladle the contents into a food processor, add half the prawns and process until smooth. Return the soup to the saucepan and add the remaining prawns with the yogurt and milk. Reheat gently. Stir in the wine and scallops, season to taste with salt and pepper and simmer for 2–3 minutes, or until the scallops are just cooked. Ladle into warmed bowls, garnish with chopped fresh coriander and serve.

meat, poultry & fish

From kebabs to curries and from chicken to prawns, the choice is huge. There are richly flavoured stews, quick stir-fries, succulent roasts, colourful tandoori dishes and tempting parcels of steamed fish. Whether you want an easy, but tasty dish for a midweek family supper or something special for entertaining guests, you are sure to find exactly the right recipe here. Lamb is undoubtedly India's favourite meat, and this chapter includes such classics as Rogan Josh (see page 67) and Lamb Koftas (see page 60). However, both pork and beef also feature.

Chicken is an economical choice, but the problem is that it is so often disappointingly bland and almost tasteless – but not in the hands of Indian cooks. It is the perfect partner for subtle spices and is transformed when served, southern-Indian-style, in a combination of coconut milk, lime juice and fresh coriander. Favourites among the recipes here include Chicken Dhansak (see page 112) and Chicken Dopiaza (see page 98), as well as some mouthwatering Balti curries.

Fish is one of the most versatile ingredients and is equally delicious in spicy curries, creamy stews and presented as fragrantly marinated kebabs. There are recipes for both freshwater and sea fish, as well as many great ways of cooking prawns.

saffron & almond lamb

serves 6 **prep: 20 mins, plus 1 hr 10 mins infusing/marinating** **cook: 1 hr 25 mins**

This is a very rich, mildly spiced dish – saffron threads and ground almonds ensure that it looks and smells extremely appetizing. Serve it with plain boiled rice or Naan Bread (see page 194).

NUTRITIONAL INFORMATION	
Calories	827
Protein	55g
Carbohydrate	12g
Sugars	11g
Fat	63g
Saturates	21g

INGREDIENTS

- large pinch of saffron threads
- 4 tbsp boiling water
- 25 g/1 oz dark muscovado or raw sugar
- 15 g/½ oz fresh mint leaves
- 175 ml/6 fl oz cold water
- 1.5 kg/3 lb 5 oz lean, diced lamb
- 225 ml/8 fl oz natural yogurt
- 3 tbsp vegetable oil
- 2 onions, sliced
- 2 tsp Garlic Paste (see page 12)
- 2 tsp Ginger Paste (see page 12)
- 1 cinnamon stick
- 6 cardamom pods, lightly crushed
- 1 tbsp ground cumin
- 55 g/2 oz ground almonds
- 1 tbsp lemon juice
- 1 tbsp chopped fresh coriander

TO GARNISH

- 4 tbsp natural yogurt
- 2 tbsp chopped fresh mint

variation

This recipe would also work well with chicken, but substitute fresh coriander for the mint in the paste.

2

3

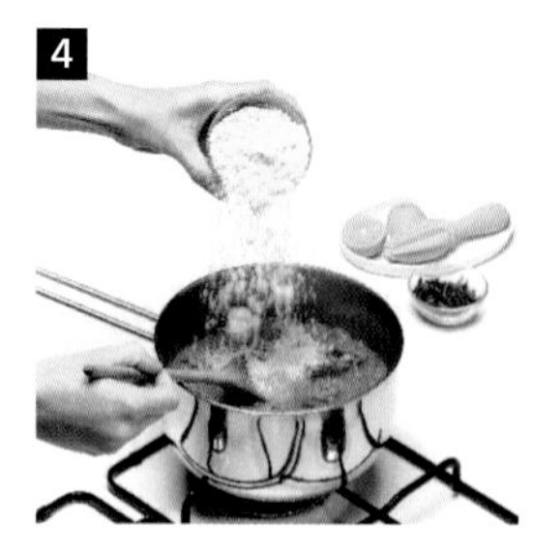

4

cook's tip

Raw sugar, known in India as jaggery, is a sticky residue left after cane sugar juice has been boiled. It may still include the molasses, or have been separated to produce lumps.

1 Place the saffron threads in a small bowl and pour in the boiling water. Leave to infuse for 10 minutes. Place the sugar, mint leaves and cold water in a food processor and process to make a smooth paste. Reserve.

2 Place the lamb in a bowl and add the yogurt. Pour in the saffron and soaking water, cover with clingfilm and leave to marinate in the refrigerator for 1 hour.

3 Heat the vegetable oil in a large saucepan or flameproof casserole. Add the onion and cook over a low heat, stirring occasionally, for 10 minutes, or until golden. Stir in the Garlic Paste, Ginger Paste, cinnamon, cardamoms and cumin and cook, stirring constantly, for a further 2 minutes. Add the lamb, together with its marinade, and the mint and sugar paste. Stir well, cover and simmer for 1 hour, or until the lamb is tender.

4 Stir in the ground almonds, lemon juice and chopped coriander and cook, stirring occasionally, for a further 10–15 minutes, or until thickened. Ladle into a warmed serving dish and garnish with the yogurt and chopped mint.

lamb & apricots

serves 6 **prep: 10 mins** **cook: 1 hr 30 mins**

Lamb goes particularly well with dried fruit, such as apricots, which cut through the richness, but complement the sweetness of the meat. Serve with plain boiled rice for a filling supper dish.

INGREDIENTS

2 tbsp ghee or vegetable oil
4 cardamom pods, lightly crushed
1 cinnamon stick
1 large onion, chopped
1 tbsp Curry Paste (see page 12)
200 g/7 oz ready-to-eat dried apricots
1 kg/2 lb 4 oz diced lamb
400 ml/14 fl oz chicken Basic Meat Stock (see page 13)
salt
chopped fresh coriander, to garnish

NUTRITIONAL INFORMATION	
Calories	449
Protein	35g
Carbohydrate	16g
Sugars	15g
Fat	28g
Saturates	11g

1 Heat the ghee in a large, heavy-based saucepan. Add the cardamoms and cinnamon stick and cook over a low heat, stirring constantly, for 2 minutes, or until they give off their aroma. Add the onion and cook, stirring occasionally, for 10 minutes, until light golden.

2 Add the Curry Paste and cook, stirring constantly, for 2 minutes. Add the apricots, lamb and Stock and season with salt to taste. Bring to the boil, then cover and simmer for 1¼ hours, or until the lamb is tender.

3 Taste and adjust the seasoning, if necessary. Ladle the curry into a warmed serving dish, sprinkle with the chopped coriander and serve immediately.

cook's tip

If the curry seems a bit too runny, remove the lid for the last 15 minutes of the cooking time to allow some of the liquid to evaporate.

marinated roast lamb

cook: 2hrs–2 hrs 15 mins | **prep: 20 mins, plus 8 hrs 10 mins marinating/resting** | **serves 6**

Spicing up the Sunday roast couldn't be simpler or more delicious. Serve this succulent lamb, marinated in yogurt and spices, with Pulao Rice (see page 197) and Onion Dal (see page 211).

NUTRITIONAL INFORMATION	
Calories	361
Protein	50g
Carbohydrate	6g
Sugars	6g
Fat	15g
Saturates	6g

INGREDIENTS

425 ml/15 fl oz natural yogurt
125 ml/4 fl oz lemon juice
3 tbsp malt vinegar
2 tsp chilli powder
2 tsp Ginger Paste (see page 12)
2 tsp Garlic Paste (see page 12)
1 tsp brown sugar
1 tsp salt
few drops red food colouring (optional)
2.5 kg/5 lb 8 oz leg of lamb
vegetable oil, for brushing
fresh coriander sprigs, to garnish

1

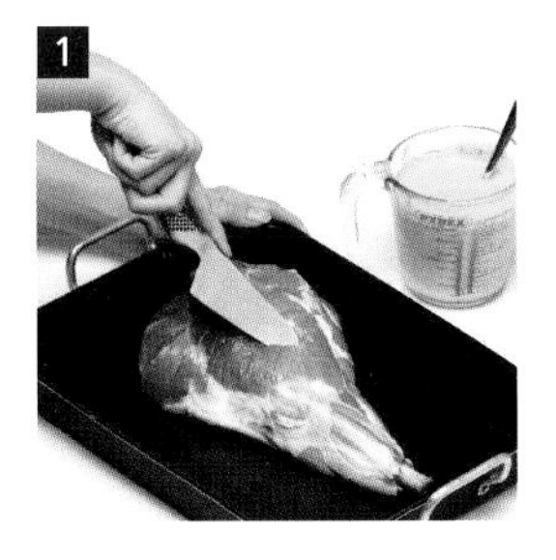

1

3

cook's tip

Red food colouring gives the lamb an attractive appearance. However, some synthetic colouring agents have been associated with allergies and other effects, so you may wish to omit it.

1 Mix the yogurt, lemon juice, vinegar, chilli powder, Ginger Paste, Garlic Paste, sugar, salt and food colouring (if using) together in a bowl. Make several deep gashes all over the lamb and place in a large, roasting tin. Pour over the yogurt mixture, turning to coat and pressing it well into the gashes. Cover with clingfilm and leave to marinate in the refrigerator for 8 hours or overnight.

2 Preheat the oven to 190°C/375°F/Gas Mark 5. Remove the lamb from the refrigerator and bring to room temperature. Roast the lamb in the preheated oven for 1¼ hours, basting occasionally with the marinade.

3 Remove the lamb from the oven and reduce the oven temperature to 160°C/325°F/Gas Mark 3. Place the lamb on a large sheet of foil, brush with vegetable oil, then wrap the foil around the meat to enclose it completely. Return to the oven and roast for a further 45–60 minutes, or until tender.

4 Leave the lamb to rest for 10 minutes before carving and serving, garnished with fresh coriander sprigs.

lamb with onions & dried mango powder

cook: 1 hr **prep: 20 mins** **serves 4**

NUTRITIONAL INFORMATION	
Calories	968
Protein	24g
Carbohydrate	14g
Sugars	10g
Fat	91g
Saturates	16g

variation

You can substitute the chopped fresh root ginger with the same amount of ground ginger.

This dish originates from Hyderabad, in central southern India. Serve with poppadums and Pulao Rice (see page 197).

INGREDIENTS

- 4 medium onions
- 300 ml/10 fl oz vegetable oil
- 1 tsp finely chopped fresh root ginger
- 1 tsp crushed fresh garlic
- 1 tsp chilli powder
- 1 pinch of ground turmeric
- 1 tsp salt
- 1 tomato, finely chopped
- 3 fresh green chillies, sliced
- 450 g/1 lb leg of lamb, cubed
- 600 ml/1 pint water
- 1½ tsp aamchoor (dried mango powder)
- 2–3 tbsp fresh coriander leaves
- freshly cooked rice, to serve

2

2

3

1 Using a sharp knife, chop 3 of the onions.

2 Heat half the vegetable oil in a frying pan, add the onions and fry until golden. Reduce the heat and add the ginger, garlic, chilli powder, turmeric and salt to the frying pan. Stir-fry the mixture for 5 minutes, then add the tomato and 2 of the green chillies.

3 Add the meat to the frying pan and stir-fry the mixture for a further 7 minutes. Add the water, cover and cook over a low heat for 35–45 minutes, stirring occasionally.

4 Meanwhile, slice the remaining onion. Heat the remaining vegetable oil in a separate frying pan and fry the onion until golden. Reserve until required. Once the meat is tender, add the aamchoor (dried mango powder), the remaining green chilli and the fresh coriander leaves and stir-fry for 3–5 minutes.

5 Transfer the curry to warmed serving plates and pour the fried onion slices and vegetable oil along the centre. Serve hot with freshly cooked rice.

cook's tip

Aamchoor (dried mango powder) is made from dried unripe mangoes, and has a sour taste. It can be bought in jars from Asian food shops.

grilled minced lamb

serves 4 **prep: 10 mins** **cook: 25–35 mins**

This is rather an unusual, but easy way of cooking mince. In India this dish is cooked over a naked flame, but you can use the grill instead – you will find that it works just as well!

NUTRITIONAL INFORMATION	
Calories	341
Protein	25g
Carbohydrate	8g
Sugars	5g
Fat	24g
Saturates	6g

INGREDIENTS

5 tbsp vegetable oil
2 onions, sliced
450 g/1 lb fresh lamb mince
2 tbsp natural yogurt
1 tsp chilli powder
1 tsp finely chopped fresh root ginger
1 tsp crushed fresh garlic
1 tsp salt
1½ tsp Garam Masala (see page 12)
½ tsp ground mixed spice
2 fresh green chillies
2–3 tbsp fresh coriander leaves

TO GARNISH

1 fresh red chilli, finely sliced
fresh coriander leaves
1 lemon, cut into wedges

TO SERVE

lettuce leaves
Naan Bread (see page 194)

variation

If you don't like it too spicy, then deseed the fresh green and red chillies before using.

1

2

3
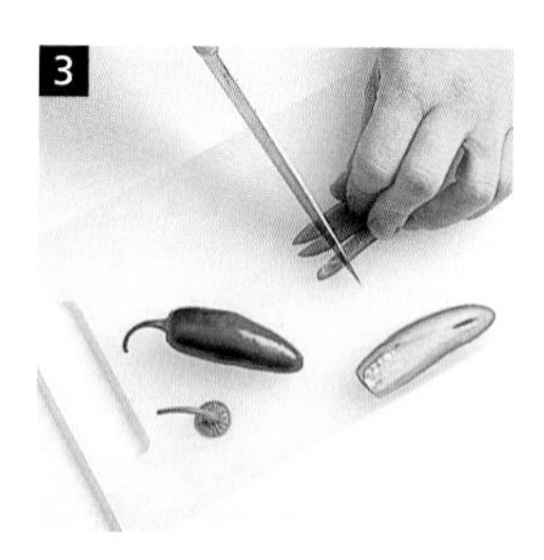

cook's tip

When the lamb mixture is cooking under the hot grill, move it around with a fork and watch it very carefully to prevent it burning.

1 Preheat the grill to medium. Heat the vegetable oil in a saucepan. Add the onions and fry until golden. Place the lamb mince in a large bowl. Add the yogurt, chilli powder, ginger, garlic, salt, Garam Masala and mixed spice and mix well.

2 Add the lamb mixture to the fried onions and stir-fry for 10–15 minutes. Remove the saucepan from the heat and reserve.

3 Meanwhile, place the green chillies and half of the coriander leaves in a processor and grind. Alternatively, finely chop the green chillies and coriander with a sharp knife. Reserve until required.

4 Place the lamb mixture in a food processor and process until smooth. Alternatively, place in a large bowl and mash with a fork. Mix the lamb mixture with the chopped chillies and coriander and blend well.

5 Transfer the mixture to a shallow heatproof dish. Cook under the preheated grill for 10–15 minutes, moving the mixture about with a fork. Transfer to serving plates and garnish with sliced red chilli, coriander leaves and lemon wedges. Serve with lettuce leaves and Naan Bread.

lamb keema

cook: 35–45 mins **prep: 20 mins** **serves 4**

NUTRITIONAL INFORMATION	
Calories	298
Protein	24g
Carbohydrate	3g
Sugars	3g
Fat	22g
Saturates	8g

variation

You could add 115 g/4 oz frozen peas 10 minutes before the end of the cooking time, if you like.

This is a very quick and easy dish to prepare and cook and requires nothing more than a serving of Naan Bread (see page 194) or a Chapati (see page 195) as an accompaniment.

INGREDIENTS

- 2 tbsp ghee or vegetable oil
- 1 onion, chopped
- 1 cinnamon stick
- 4 cardamom pods, lightly crushed
- 1 curry leaf
- 4 cloves
- 1 tsp Ginger Paste (see page 12)
- 1 tsp Garlic Paste (see page 12)
- 450 g/1 lb fresh lamb mince
- 2 tsp ground coriander
- 2 tsp ground cumin
- 1 tsp chilli powder
- 150 ml/5 fl oz natural yogurt
- 1 tbsp dried fenugreek
- salt
- chopped fresh coriander, to garnish

2

3

4

cook's tip

In India, this dish would be flavoured with fresh fenugreek leaves, known as methi. You will need 1 bunch of fresh leaves. Always remove and discard the bitter stems.

1 Heat the ghee in a karahi, wok or large, heavy-based saucepan. Add the onion and cook over a low heat, stirring occasionally, for 5 minutes, or until softened.

2 Add the cinnamon stick, cardamoms, curry leaf and cloves and cook, stirring constantly, for 1 minute, then add the Ginger Paste and Garlic Paste and cook, stirring constantly, for a further 1 minute.

3 Add the lamb mince and sprinkle over the ground coriander, cumin and chilli powder. Cook for 5 minutes, or until the lamb is lightly browned, stirring and breaking up the meat with a wooden spoon.

4 Stir in the yogurt and fenugreek and season with salt to taste. Cover and cook over a low heat for 20–30 minutes, or until the lamb is tender and the liquid has been absorbed. Ladle into a warmed serving dish and discard the curry leaf. Garnish with chopped coriander and serve immediately.

lamb koftas

serves 4 **prep: 20 mins** **cook: 25 mins**

These delicious spicy lamb koftas are cooked throughout northern India. Serve with Oil-dressed Dal (see page 212) and Bombay Potatoes (see page 220) for a filling supper.

NUTRITIONAL INFORMATION	
Calories	766
Protein	30g
Carbohydrate	11g
Sugars	6g
Fat	68g
Saturates	13g

variation

You can use any mixture of vegetables you have to hand, such as red pepper, broccoli, chopped green beans or mangetout.

INGREDIENTS

- **450 g/1 lb fresh lamb mince**
- **1 small onion, finely chopped**
- **1 tsp ground cumin**
- **1 tsp ground coriander**
- **1 tsp chilli powder**
- **1 tsp Garam Masala (see page 12)**
- **1 tsp Garlic Paste (see page 12)**
- **2 tbsp chopped fresh coriander**
- **salt**
- **200 ml/7 fl oz vegetable oil**
- **6 spring onions, chopped**
- **1 green pepper, deseeded and chopped**
- **175 g/6 oz broad beans, thawed if frozen**
- **12 baby corn cobs, thawed if frozen**
- **1 small cauliflower, cut into florets**
- **3 fresh green chillies, deseeded and chopped**
- **1 tbsp lime juice**
- **1 tbsp fresh mint leaves**

cook's tip

The lamb must be finely minced for making koftas. If necessary, process in a food processor for 1 minute before mixing with the other ingredients.

1. Place the lamb, onion, cumin, ground coriander, chilli powder, Garam Masala, Garlic Paste and half the fresh coriander in a bowl and mix well with your hands. Season with salt to taste. Cover with clingfilm and leave to chill in the refrigerator for a few minutes.

2. Heat 3 tablespoons of the vegetable oil in a preheated wok or large frying pan. Add the spring onions and cook, stirring frequently, for 1 minute. Add the green pepper, broad beans, corn cobs, cauliflower and chillies and cook over a high heat, stirring, for 3 minutes, or until crisp-tender. Reserve.

3. Heat the remaining vegetable oil in a separate preheated wok or large frying pan. Meanwhile, form the lamb mixture into small balls or ovals between the palms of your hands. Add the koftas, in batches, to the hot oil and fry, turning them frequently, until golden brown. Remove with a slotted spoon and drain on kitchen paper. When they are all cooked, return the vegetables to the heat and stir in the koftas. Cook over a low heat, stirring frequently, for 5 minutes, or until heated through. Sprinkle with the lime juice and serve garnished with the remaining coriander and the mint leaves.

lamb curry in a thick sauce

cook: 55 mins **prep: 15 mins** **serves 6**

NUTRITIONAL INFORMATION	
Calories	797
Protein	33g
Carbohydrate	12g
Sugars	9g
Fat	69g
Saturates	11g

variation

If you can't find canned chopped tomatoes, use 400 g/14 oz canned whole tomatoes and chop them before adding in Step 4.

Originally a Kashmiri dish, this lamb stew is now made all over India and is popular wherever Indian food is eaten. Noted for its delicious tomato-flavoured sauce, it is ideal for a dinner party.

INGREDIENTS

1 kg/2 lb 4 oz lean lamb, with or without bone
200 ml/7 fl oz natural yogurt
75 g/2¾ oz almonds
2 tsp Garam Masala (see page 12)
2 tsp finely chopped fresh root ginger
2 tsp crushed fresh garlic
1½ tsp chilli powder
1½ tsp salt
300 ml/10 fl oz vegetable oil
3 onions, finely chopped
4 green cardamoms
2 bay leaves
3 fresh green chillies, chopped
2 tbsp lemon juice
400 g/14 oz canned chopped tomatoes
300 ml/10 fl oz water
1 tbsp chopped fresh coriander leaves
freshly cooked rice, to serve

cook's tip

If the sauce is too watery, then remove the lid, increase the heat slighly and cook until the sauce has thickened to the correct consistency.

1 Using a very sharp knife, cut the lamb into small, even-sized pieces. Reserve until required

2 Mix the yogurt, almonds, Garam Masala, ginger, garlic, chilli powder and salt together in a large bowl, stirring to mix well. Reserve until required.

3 Heat the vegetable oil in a large saucepan, add the onions, cardamoms and bay leaves and fry until golden, stirring constantly. Add the meat and the yogurt mixture to the saucepan and stir-fry for 3–5 minutes.

4 Add 2 green chillies, the lemon juice and the canned tomatoes to the mixture in the saucepan and stir-fry for a further 5 minutes. Add the water, cover and simmer over a low heat for 35–40 minutes.

5 Add the remaining green chilli and the coriander and stir until the sauce has thickened. Transfer the curry to warmed serving plates and serve hot, with rice.

lamb vindaloo

serves 6 **prep: 25 mins** **cook: 1 hr**

The classic version of this fiery curry is made with pork (see page 91). It is flavoured with a unique blend of spices and vinegar.

NUTRITIONAL INFORMATION	
Calories	463
Protein	35g
Carbohydrate	12g
Sugars	9g
Fat	34g
Saturates	12g

INGREDIENTS

- 4 onions, roughly chopped
- 5 tbsp ghee or vegetable oil
- 1 kg/2 lb 4 oz diced lamb
- 2 tsp Garlic Paste (see page 12)
- 2 tsp Ginger Paste (see page 12)
- 1 tsp ground coriander
- 2 tsp paprika
- 2 tsp ground turmeric
- 1 tsp chilli powder
- 2 tbsp tomato purée
- salt
- 300 ml/10 fl oz water

VINDALOO PASTE

- 2 dried chillies
- 2 tsp cumin seeds
- 1 tsp black mustard seeds
- ½ tsp cardamom seeds
- 1 tsp fenugreek seeds
- 1 tsp black peppercorns
- 1 tsp ground cinnamon
- 1 tsp salt
- 4 tbsp white wine vinegar
- 2 tsp muscovado sugar

TO SERVE

- freshly cooked rice
- Naan Bread (see page 194)

variation

For a beef vindaloo, substitute the same quantity of diced stewing or braising steak and simmer for 1¼–1½ hours, or until tender.

cook's tip

As this is such a hot dish, it would be good served with a cooling Cucumber or Mint Raita (see page 228) and Naan Bread (see page 194).

1. To make the vindaloo paste, grind the chillies, cumin seeds, mustard seeds, cardamom seeds, fenugreek seeds and peppercorns in a mortar with a pestle. Alternatively, use a spice grinder or food processor. Transfer to a bowl and stir in the cinnamon, salt, vinegar, sugar and enough water to make a smooth paste.

2. Place the onions in a food processor and process until very finely chopped. Heat 3 tablespoons of the ghee in a small, heavy-based saucepan, add the onions and fry over a low heat, stirring frequently, for 8 minutes, or until browned. Stir in the vindaloo paste and remove the saucepan from the heat.

3. Heat the remaining ghee in a frying pan, add the lamb and cook in batches, stirring frequently, until browned all over. Remove with a slotted spoon and drain on kitchen paper. Stir the Garlic Paste and Ginger Paste into the frying pan and cook, stirring, for 1 minute. Add the ground coriander, paprika, turmeric, chilli powder and tomato purée and cook, stirring, for a further 1 minute. Return the lamb and vindaloo mixture to the frying pan, season with salt to taste and pour in the water. Stir well and bring to the boil, then reduce the heat, cover and simmer for 45 minutes, or until the lamb is tender. Serve immediately with rice and Naan Bread.

rogan josh

cook: 2 hrs **prep: 15 mins** **serves 6**

NUTRITIONAL INFORMATION	
Calories	454
Protein	36g
Carbohydrate	6g
Sugars	4g
Fat	33g
Saturates	12g

variation

For an aromatic garnish, heat 1 tablespoon oil and add 1 tablespoon cumin seeds and 2 bay leaves. Cook for 2 minutes. Sprinkle over and serve.

Highly popular in Indian restaurants, this dish originated in Kashmir in northern India. It is usually served with Naan Bread (see page 194) or Parathas (see page 215), rather than rice.

INGREDIENTS

- **225 ml/8 fl oz natural yogurt**
- **½ tsp cayenne pepper**
- **¼ tsp asafoetida**
- **1 kg/2 lb 4 oz diced lamb**
- **1 tbsp coriander seeds**
- **1 tbsp cardamom seeds**
- **1 tsp cumin seeds**
- **1 tsp white poppy seeds**
- **8 black peppercorns**
- **4 cloves**
- **3-cm/1¼-inch piece fresh root ginger**
- **4 garlic cloves**
- **2 tbsp almonds**
- **300 ml/10 fl oz water**
- **4 tbsp ghee or vegetable oil**
- **1 onion, chopped**
- **1 tsp ground turmeric**
- **2 tbsp chopped fresh coriander**
- **1 tsp Garam Masala (see page 12)**
- **salt**

1

3

4

cook's tip

For a richer colour, add 400 g/14 oz canned tomatoes and 2 tablespoons of tomato purée in Step 3 and omit the final quantity of water.

1 Mix the yogurt, cayenne and asafoetida together in a large, shallow dish. Add the lamb and toss well to coat. Cover and set aside.

2 Preheat the oven to 140°C/275°F/Gas Mark 1. Place the coriander seeds and the cardamom, cumin and poppy seeds in a food processor or blender with the peppercorns, cloves, ginger, garlic, almonds and 4 tablespoons of the water and process to make a paste, adding a little more water, if necessary. Reserve.

3 Heat the ghee in a flameproof casserole. Add the onion and cook over a low heat for 10 minutes, or until golden. Stir in the spice paste and turmeric and cook, stirring, for 5 minutes. Add the lamb, with its marinade, increase the heat to high and cook, stirring, for 10 minutes. Reduce the heat, cover and simmer for 45 minutes.

4 Stir 4 tablespoons of the water into the casserole and cook, stirring, until it has been incorporated. Stir in another 4 tablespoons of the water and cook until incorporated, then add the remaining water, re-cover the casserole and simmer for 15 minutes. Stir the chopped coriander and Garam Masala into the lamb and season with salt to taste. Cover, then transfer the casserole to the oven and cook for a further 25 minutes. Serve immediately.

lean lamb cooked in spinach

serves 2–4 **prep: 5 mins** **cook: 1 hr 15 mins**

This nutritious combination of lamb and spinach is perfect served with plain boiled rice and Okra Curry (see page 158).

NUTRITIONAL INFORMATION	
Calories	944
Protein	31g
Carbohydrate	11g
Sugars	8g
Fat	87g
Saturates	12g

INGREDIENTS

- 300 ml/10 fl oz vegetable oil
- 2 onions, sliced
- ¼ bunch of fresh coriander
- 2 fresh green chillies, chopped
- 1½ tsp finely chopped fresh root ginger
- 1½ tsp crushed fresh garlic
- 1 tsp chilli powder
- ½ tsp ground turmeric
- 450 g/1 lb lean lamb, with or without bone
- 1 tsp salt
- 1 kg/2 lb 4 oz fresh spinach, trimmed, washed and chopped
- 700 ml/1¼ pints water
- 1 fresh red chilli, finely chopped, to garnish

variation

If fresh spinach is unavailable, then you can substitute with 425 g/15 oz canned spinach instead.

2

2

3

1 Heat the vegetable oil in a large, heavy-based frying pan. Add the onions and fry until light golden.

2 Add the fresh coriander and green chillies to the frying pan and stir-fry for 3–5 minutes. Reduce the heat and add the ginger, garlic, chilli powder and turmeric, stirring well.

3 Add the lamb to the frying pan and stir-fry for a further 5 minutes. Add the salt and the spinach and cook, stirring occasionally with a wooden spoon, for a further 3–5 minutes.

4 Add the water, stirring, and cook over a low heat, covered, for 45 minutes. Remove the lid and check the meat. If it is not tender, turn the meat over, increase the heat and cook, uncovered, until the surplus water has been absorbed. Stir-fry the mixture for a further 5–7 minutes.

5 Transfer the lamb and spinach mixture to a serving dish and garnish with chopped red chilli. Serve hot.

cook's tip

When handling fresh chillies always remember to wash your hands, chopping board and knife thoroughly afterwards. Never let any part of the chilli go near your face.

cubed lamb kebabs

cook: 30 mins

prep: 15 mins, plus 3 hrs standing

serves 6–8

NUTRITIONAL INFORMATION	
Calories	258
Protein	27g
Carbohydrate	7g
Sugars	6g
Fat	14g
Saturates	5g

variation

Replace the green pepper with either an orange or yellow pepper and use lime wedges instead of lemon, if you prefer.

Serve these kebabs with either plain boiled rice or Pulao Rice (see page 197) accompanied with a cooling Mint Raita (see page 228).

INGREDIENTS

- 1 kg/2 lb 4 oz lean lamb, boned and cubed
- 1 tsp meat tenderizer
- 1½ tsp finely chopped fresh root ginger
- 1½ tsp crushed fresh garlic
- 1 tsp chilli powder
- ½ tsp ground turmeric
- ½ tsp salt
- 2 tbsp water
- 8 tomatoes, cut in quarters
- 8 small pickling onions
- 10 mushrooms
- 1 green pepper, cut into large pieces
- 1 red pepper, cut into large pieces
- 2 tbsp vegetable oil
- 2 lemons, quartered, to garnish

TO SERVE

- freshly cooked rice
- Mint Raita (see page 228)

2

2

3

cook's tip

If using wooden skewers, remember to soak them in a bowl of hot water for 20 minutes before using to prevent them burning during cooking.

1. Rinse the meat under cold running water and place it in a clean dish. Apply the tenderizer to the meat, using your hands. Leave to stand for 3 hours at room temperature.

2. Preheat the grill to medium. Mix the ginger, garlic, chilli powder, turmeric and salt together in a bowl. Add the water and mix to form a paste. Add the meat and mix until it is well coated with the spices.

3. Arrange the meat cubes on metal or wooden skewers, alternating with the tomatoes, pickling onions, mushrooms and pepper pieces. Brush the meat and vegetables with the vegetable oil.

4. Cook the kebabs under the preheated grill for 25–30 minutes, or until the meat is cooked through. When cooked, remove the kebabs from the grill and transfer to a serving plate. Arrange lemon wedges on the side and serve immediately with freshly cooked rice and a Mint Raita.

deep-fried lamb

serves 4 | **prep: 20 mins, plus 30 mins cooling/resting** | **cook: 50 mins**

Cubes of lamb are first cooked in a mixture of garlic, ginger and spiced yogurt, then coated in a batter and deep-fried with potatoes to make a satisfying and substantial meal.

INGREDIENTS

- 4 tbsp natural yogurt
- 2 tsp chilli powder
- 1 tsp ground turmeric
- salt
- 2 tbsp ghee or vegetable oil, plus vegetable oil for deep-frying
- 3 garlic cloves, finely chopped
- 3-cm/1¼-inch piece fresh root ginger, finely chopped
- 675 g/1½ lb diced lamb
- 450 g/1 lb potatoes
- lime wedges, to garnish

BATTER

- 225 g/8 oz gram flour
- ½ tsp chilli powder
- 1 tsp salt
- 5 tbsp natural yogurt
- 225 ml/8 fl oz water

NUTRITIONAL INFORMATION	
Calories	808
Protein	51g
Carbohydrate	55g
Sugars	9g
Fat	44g
Saturates	14g

variation

This recipe is also delicious made with diced chicken instead of lamb and sweet potatoes instead of ordinary ones.

cook's tip

The potatoes and lamb cubes must be cold before coating with the batter, otherwise they won't be crisp when they are cooked.

1. Mix the yogurt, chilli powder, turmeric and a pinch of salt together in a bowl and reserve.

2. Heat the ghee in a karahhi or large frying pan. Add the garlic and ginger and cook, stirring frequently, for 2 minutes. Add the lamb and cook, stirring frequently, until browned all over. Stir in the yogurt mixture and simmer gently, stirring occasionally, for 30 minutes, or until the lamb is tender, then leave to cool.

3. Meanwhile, cook the potatoes in a large saucepan of lightly salted boiling water for 20 minutes, or until nearly tender. Drain, leave to cool, then dice.

4. To make the batter, sift the flour, chilli powder and salt into a bowl. Stir in the yogurt, then gradually beat in the water to make a smooth batter. Leave to rest for 30 minutes.

5. Heat the vegetable oil in a deep-fat fryer or heavy-based saucepan to 180–190°C/350–375°F, or until a cube of bread browns in 30 seconds. Dip the lamb and potato cubes in the batter, then deep-fry, in batches, for 3–4 minutes, or until golden brown. Drain each batch on kitchen paper and keep warm while you cook the remainder. Serve immediately, garnished with lime wedges.

cauliflower with meat

cook: 1 hr | prep: 20 mins | serves 4

NUTRITIONAL INFORMATION	
Calories	1285
Protein	28g
Carbohydrate	10g
Sugars	8g
Fat	127g
Saturates	19g

variation

Substitute the cauliflower with broccoli, cut into florets, and replace the lemon juice with lime juice.

Vegetables cooked with meat have a lovely flavour, especially cauliflower and spinach. It is best to use only a few spices, then add a baghaar (seasoned oil dressing) at the end.

INGREDIENTS

- 1 cauliflower
- 2 fresh green chillies
- 300 ml/10 fl oz vegetable oil
- 2 onions, sliced
- 450 g/1 lb lean lamb, cubed
- 1½ tsp finely chopped fresh root ginger
- 1½ tsp crushed fresh garlic
- 1 tsp chilli powder
- 1 tsp salt
- 1 tbsp chopped fresh coriander leaves
- 850 ml/1½ pints water
- 1 tbsp lemon juice

BAGHAAR

- 150 ml/5 fl oz vegetable oil
- 4 dried red chillies
- 1 tsp mixed mustard and onion seeds

1

1

2

cook's tip

Fresh root ginger is one of the most popular spices used in Indian cooking. Buy small amounts and store in a cool dry place. Peel before using.

1 Cut the cauliflower into small florets. Chop the green chillies finely.

2 Heat the vegetable oil in a large frying pan. Add the onions and fry until golden. Reduce the heat and add the meat, stirring constantly. Add the ginger, garlic, chilli powder and salt and stir-fry for 5 minutes.

3 Add 1 green chilli and half of the coriander leaves. Stir in the water, cover and cook over a low heat for 30 minutes.

4 Add the cauliflower and simmer for a further 15–20 minutes, or until the water has evaporated completely. Stir-fry the mixture for a further 5 minutes. Remove the frying pan from the heat and sprinkle over the lemon juice sparingly.

5 To make the baghaar, heat the vegetable oil in a separate small saucepan. Add the dried red chillies and the mixed mustard and onion seeds and fry until they turn a darker colour, stirring occasionally. Remove the saucepan from the heat and pour the mixture over the cooked cauliflower. Garnish with the remaining green chilli and fresh coriander leaves. Serve immediately.

lamb & lentils

serves 6

prep: 30 mins, plus 8 hrs soaking

cook: 2 hrs

This recipe takes some time to cook as you have to cook the lamb korma separately. However, the result is truly delicious! Serve with plain boiled rice and Naan Bread (see page 194).

NUTRITIONAL INFORMATION	
Calories	1454
Protein	70g
Carbohydrate	58g
Sugars	11g
Fat	106g
Saturates	22g

variation

Replace the shredded fresh root ginger garnish with lemon or lime wedges, if you prefer.

INGREDIENTS

- 100 g/3½ oz chana dal
- 100 g/3½ oz masoor dal
- 100 g/3½ oz moong dal
- 100 g/3½ oz urid dal
- 75 g/2¾ oz porridge oats

KORMA

- 1.5 kg/3 lb 5 oz lamb, cubed
- 200 ml/7 fl oz natural yogurt
- 2 tsp finely chopped fresh root ginger
- 2 tsp crushed fresh garlic
- 1 tbsp Garam Masala (see page 12)
- 2 tsp chilli powder
- ½ tsp ground turmeric
- 3 whole green cardamom pods
- 2 cinnamon sticks
- 1 tsp black cumin seeds
- 2 tsp salt
- 450 ml/16 fl oz vegetable oil
- 5 onions, sliced
- 700 ml/1¼ pints water
- 2 fresh green chillies
- 2–3 tbsp fresh coriander leaves

TO GARNISH

- 4 tbsp fresh coriander leaves, chopped
- 5-cm/2-inch piece fresh root ginger, shredded

cook's tip

Always keep spices in airtight containers and store in a dry, dark place. The flavour deteriorates fairly quickly, so use within 4–6 months.

1. Soak the dals and oats overnight. Place in a large, heavy-based saucepan, cover with water and boil for 15 minutes, or until soft. Remove the saucepan from the heat and mash until smooth. Reserve until required.

2. Place the lamb in a large bowl. Add the yogurt, spices and salt, mix and reserve until required.

3. Heat 300 ml/10 fl oz of the vegetable oil in a frying pan, add 4 of the onions and fry until golden. Add the meat mixture and stir-fry for 7–10 minutes. Stir in the water, reduce the heat, cover and cook for 1 hour, stirring frequently. If the meat is not tender, add more water and cook for 15–20 minutes. Remove from the heat.

4. Add the dal and porridge mixture to the meat, stir and mix well. If the mixture is too thick, add 300 ml/10 fl oz water, stir and cook for 10–12 minutes. Add the chillies and the coriander. Transfer to a serving dish and reserve.

5. Heat the remaining vegetable oil in a frying pan, add the remaining onion and fry until golden. Pour over the lamb and lentils. Garnish with coriander and shredded ginger and serve.

boti kebabs

cook: 5–6 mins

prep: 20 mins, plus 4 hrs marinating

serves 4

This is a classic tandoori dish, but works well cooked under a conventional grill. It is delicious served with a mixed salad.

NUTRITIONAL INFORMATION	
Calories	201
Protein	17g
Carbohydrate	6g
Sugars	5g
Fat	12g
Saturates	5g

variation

For a creamier, less sharp flavour, substitute 150 ml/5 fl oz natural yogurt for the vinegar.

INGREDIENTS

- 1 tsp Garlic Paste (see page 12)
- 1 tsp Ginger Paste (see page 12)
- 1 tsp chilli powder
- 1 tbsp ground coriander
- 2 tbsp red wine vinegar
- 450 g/1 lb lamb, diced
- 2 tbsp lemon juice
- 1 green pepper, deseeded and cut into chunks
- 1 large onion, cut into wedges
- 4 tomatoes, quartered
- vegetable oil, for brushing
- freshly cooked rice, to serve

TO GARNISH

- fresh coriander sprigs
- lime wedges

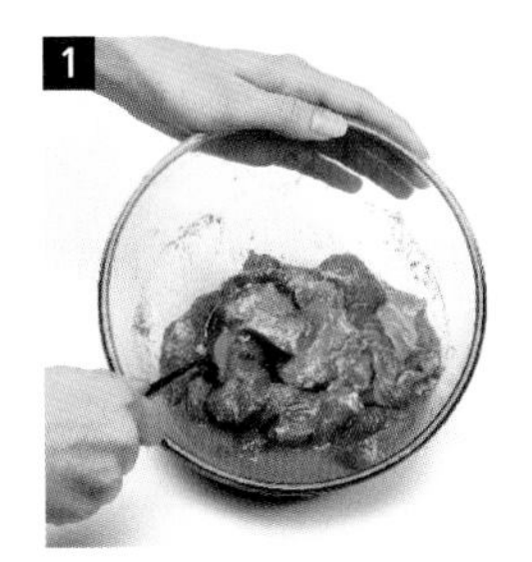

1 Mix the Garlic Paste, Ginger Paste, chilli powder, ground coriander and vinegar in a large, shallow, non-metallic dish. Add the lamb and stir to coat. Cover with clingfilm and leave to marinate in the refrigerator for 4–6 hours, stirring occasionally.

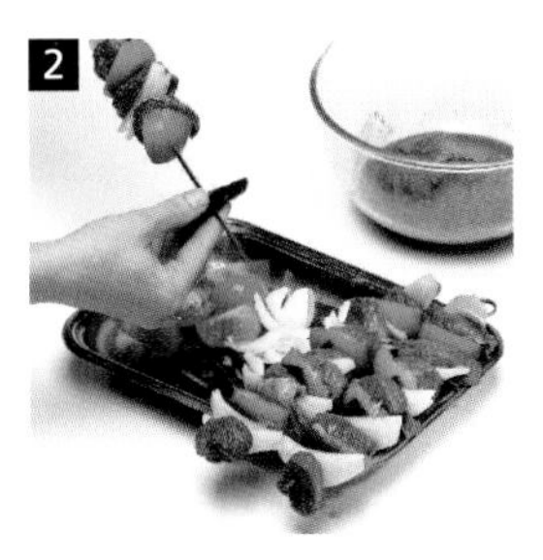

2 Preheat the grill to medium. Sprinkle the lemon juice over the meat, then thread the meat on to skewers, alternating with the chunks of green pepper, onion wedges and tomato quarters.

3 Brush with vegetable oil and grill, turning frequently and brushing with more oil as necessary, for 5–6 minutes, or until the lamb is browned all over and cooked through. Transfer to warmed serving plates, garnish with coriander sprigs and lime wedges and serve.

cook's tip

It is important to use a glass or ceramic dish while the meat is marinating, as vinegar can react with metal and will taint the flavour of the meat.

balti beef curry

serves 4 **prep: 10 mins** **cook: 25 mins**

Balti dishes are quick, stir-fried curries. They were introduced to the West by Pakistan's Multani community, but are also widely cooked in Kashmir and other northern regions of India, although no Hindu would eat beef – the dish can also be made with prawns or lamb.

NUTRITIONAL INFORMATION	
Calories	255
Protein	28g
Carbohydrate	12g
Sugars	8g
Fat	11g
Saturates	3g

INGREDIENTS

2 tbsp ghee or vegetable oil
1 onion, thinly sliced
1 garlic clove, finely chopped
3-cm/1¼-inch piece fresh root ginger, grated
2 fresh red chillies, deseeded and finely chopped
450 g/1 lb rump steak, cut into thin strips
1 green pepper, deseeded and thinly sliced
1 yellow pepper, deseeded and thinly sliced
1 tsp ground cumin
1 tbsp Garam Masala (see page 12)
4 tomatoes, chopped
2 tbsp lemon juice
1 tbsp water
salt
chopped fresh coriander, to garnish
Naan Bread (see page 194), to serve

variation

Use the same quantity of peeled and deveined raw prawns instead of the steak. Add them in Step 2 and cook until they have just changed colour.

cook's tip

The Balti equivalent of a wok is the karahi. It has a round base and carrying handles and may come with a stand so that it can easily be brought to the table for serving.

1 Heat half the ghee in a preheated wok or large, heavy-based frying pan. Add the onion and cook over a low heat, stirring occasionally, for 8–10 minutes, or until golden. Increase the heat to medium, add the garlic, ginger, chillies and steak and cook, stirring occasionally, for 5 minutes, or until the steak is browned all over. Remove with a slotted spoon, reserve and keep warm.

2 Add the remaining ghee to the wok, add the peppers and cook over a medium heat, stirring occasionally, for 4 minutes, or until softened. Stir in the cumin and Garam Masala and cook, stirring, for 1 minute.

3 Add the tomatoes, lemon juice and water, season with salt to taste and simmer, stirring constantly, for 3 minutes. Return the steak mixture to the wok and heat through. Serve immediately, garnished with chopped fresh coriander and accompanied by Naan Bread.

NIKADO AMMAM

beef korma with almonds

cooking: 1 hr 30 mins | **prep: 20 mins** | **serves 6**

NUTRITIONAL INFORMATION	
Calories	735
Protein	41g
Carbohydrate	9g
Sugars	6g
Fat	60g
Saturates	9g

variation

Substitute the cubed lean beef with the same amount of cubed lean lamb, if you prefer.

This korma, a traditional northern Indian recipe, has a thick, spicy sauce and is quite simple to cook.

INGREDIENTS

300 ml/10 fl oz vegetable oil
3 onions, finely chopped
1 kg/2 lb 4 oz lean beef, cubed
1½ tsp Garam Masala (see page 12)
1½ tsp ground coriander
1½ tsp finely chopped fresh root ginger
1½ tsp crushed fresh garlic
1 tsp salt
150 ml/5 fl oz natural yogurt
2 whole cloves
3 green cardamom pods
4 black peppercorns
600 ml/1 pint water
Chapatis (see page 195), to serve

TO GARNISH

6 soaked, peeled and chopped almonds
2 sliced fresh green chillies
few fresh coriander leaves

cook's tip

Cloves have a distinct aroma and flavour, so use sparingly as they may overpower the finished dish. Cloves are widely available, whole and ground, from supermarkets.

1. Heat the vegetable oil in a large, heavy-based frying pan. Add the onions and stir-fry for 8–10 minutes, until golden. Remove half of the onions and reserve.

2. Add the meat to the remaining onions in the frying pan and stir-fry for 5 minutes. Remove the frying pan from the heat.

3. Mix the Garam Masala, ground coriander, ginger, garlic, salt and yogurt together in a large bowl. Gradually add the meat to the yogurt and spice mixture and mix to coat the meat on all sides. Place the meat mixture in the frying pan, return to the heat, and stir-fry for 5–7 minutes, or until the mixture is nearly brown.

4. Add the cloves, green cardamoms and black peppercorns. Add the water, reduce the heat, cover and simmer for 45–60 minutes. If the water has completely evaporated, but the meat is still not tender enough, add another 300 ml/10 fl oz water and cook for a further 10–15 minutes, stirring occasionally. Just before serving, garnish with the reserved onions, chopped almonds, green chillies and fresh coriander leaves. Serve with Chapatis (see page 195).

beef dhansak

serves 6 | **prep: 15 mins** | **cook: 2 hrs 30 mins**

This is a northern Indian version of a west coast speciality – a rich-tasting mixture of meat, vegetables and lentils.

NUTRITIONAL INFORMATION	
Calories	407
Protein	49g
Carbohydrate	28g
Sugars	6g
Fat	12g
Saturates	4g

INGREDIENTS

- 2 tbsp ghee or vegetable oil
- 2 onions, chopped
- 3 garlic cloves, finely chopped
- 2 tsp ground coriander
- 2 ground cumin
- 2 tsp Garam Masala (see page 12)
- 1 tsp ground turmeric
- 450 g/1 lb courgettes, peeled and chopped, or bitter gourd or pumpkin, peeled, deseeded and chopped
- 1 aubergine, peeled and chopped
- 4 curry leaves
- 225 g/8 oz masoor dal
- 1 litre/1¾ pints water
- salt
- 1 kg/2 lb 4 oz stewing or braising steak, diced
- fresh coriander leaves, to garnish

variation

For a hotter flavour, add 1–2 chopped fresh green chillies with the spices in Step 1.

cook's tip

Bitter gourds are widely used in Indian cooking. To prepare this long, knobbly vegetable, use a sharp knife to peel the ridged skin, then scrape out and discard the seeds before chopping.

1. Heat the ghee in a large, heavy-based saucepan. Add the onions and garlic and cook over a low heat, stirring occasionally, for 8–10 minutes, or until light golden. Stir in the ground coriander, cumin, Garam Masala and turmeric and cook, stirring constantly, for 2 minutes.

2. Add the courgettes, aubergine, curry leaves, masoor dal and water. Bring to the boil, then reduce the heat, cover and simmer for 30 minutes, or until the vegetables are tender. Remove the saucepan from the heat and leave to cool slightly. Transfer the mixture to a food processor, in batches if necessary, and process until smooth. Return the mixture to the saucepan and season with salt to taste.

3. Add the steak to the saucepan and bring to the boil. Reduce the heat, cover and simmer for 1¼ hours. Remove the lid and continue to simmer for a further 30 minutes, or until the sauce is thick and the steak is tender. Serve garnished with coriander leaves.

dry beef curry with carrot sambal

cook: 2 hrs 15 mins | **prep: 20 mins** | **serves 6**

This extremely hot, but easy-to-make curry is perfectly complemented by the sweet and spicy sambal. Serve with plain boiled rice to complete a filling main course.

NUTRITIONAL INFORMATION	
Calories	460
Protein	40g
Carbohydrate	23g
Sugars	21g
Fat	25g
Saturates	7g

variation

If you prefer, substitute natural yogurt for the coconut milk and, for a less fiery flavour, reduce the quantity of Curry Paste.

INGREDIENTS

4 tbsp ghee or vegetable oil
2 fresh green chillies, deseeded and chopped
2 onions, chopped
1 kg/2 lb 4 oz stewing or braising steak, diced
200 g/7 oz canned tomatoes, drained
salt
2 tsp ground coriander
1½ tsp Garam Masala (see page 12)
1 tsp ground cumin
3 tbsp Curry Paste (see page 12)
300 ml/10 fl oz coconut milk
1 tbsp chopped fresh coriander, to garnish

CARROT SAMBAL

1 tbsp ghee or vegetable oil
40 g/1½ oz shredded coconut
1 tbsp black mustard seeds
350 g/12 oz carrots, grated
4 tbsp lemon juice
85 g/3 oz sultanas
4 tbsp chopped fresh mint

1 To make the sambal, heat the ghee in a small frying pan. Add the coconut and mustard seeds and cook over a low heat, stirring constantly, for 2 minutes, or until the coconut is beginning to brown. Transfer the mixture to a bowl and stir in the carrots, lemon juice, sultanas and mint. Mix well and reserve until required.

2 To make the curry, heat the ghee in a large, heavy-based saucepan. Add the chillies and onions and cook over a low heat, stirring occasionally, until the onions are light golden. Add the steak and cook, stirring frequently, for 10 minutes, or until browned all over. Stir in the tomatoes and season with salt to taste.

3 Mix the ground coriander, 1 teaspoon of the Garam Masala, the cumin, Curry Paste and coconut milk together in a bowl, then add to the saucepan. Stir well, half-cover and simmer over a low heat for 1½ hours. Remove the lid from the saucepan and continue to simmer for a further 30 minutes, or until the meat is tender and the sauce is very thick. If it dries out too much, add a little water. Transfer to a warmed dish, sprinkle with the remaining Garam Masala and chopped coriander and serve with the carrot sambal.

cook's tip

If you have a grater attachment on your food processor, it makes the job of grating the carrots much easier. Remember to peel the carrots first.

beef cooked in whole spices

serves 4 | **prep: 15 mins** | **cook: 1 hr 30 mins**

This is a delicious way of cooking beef. The fragrant whole spices perfectly complement the flavour of the meat.

INGREDIENTS

- 300 ml/10 fl oz vegetable oil
- 3 onions, finely chopped
- 2.5-cm/1-inch fresh root ginger, shredded
- 4 garlic cloves, shredded
- 2 cinnamon sticks
- 3 whole green cardamoms
- 3 whole cloves
- 4 whole black peppercorns
- 6 dried red chillies
- 150 ml/5 fl oz natural yogurt
- 450 g/1 lb beef, with or without bone
- 3 fresh green chillies, chopped
- 600 ml/1 pint water

NUTRITIONAL INFORMATION	
Calories	900
Protein	30g
Carbohydrate	13g
Sugars	10g
Fat	81g
Saturates	10g

variation

Substitute lamb for the beef in this recipe, if you prefer. You can also replace the green chillies with 3 fresh red chillies.

1. Heat the vegetable oil in a large, heavy-based frying pan. Add the onion and fry for 8–10 minutes, stirring, until golden.

2. Reduce the heat and add the ginger, garlic, cinnamon sticks, cardamoms, cloves, peppercorns and chillies to the frying pan and stir-fry for 5 minutes.

3. Whip the yogurt with a fork, then add to the onions in the frying pan and stir to blend. Add the meat and 2 of the green chillies and stir-fry for 5–7 minutes.

4. Gradually add the water to the frying pan, stirring. Cover and cook for 1 hour, stirring and adding more water if necessary.

5. When the meat is thoroughly cooked through, remove the frying pan from the heat and transfer the beef and spice mixture to a serving dish. Garnish with the remaining chopped green chilli.

cook's tip

Dried red chillies can be kept in a screw-top jar and should be stored in a cool, dark place. Take care when using dried red chillies as they can be very hot.

classic vindaloo

cook: 1 hr 10 mins

prep: 15 mins, plus 9 hrs marinating

serves 6

NUTRITIONAL INFORMATION	
Calories	264
Protein	37g
Carbohydrate	1g
Sugars	0.5g
Fat	13g
Saturates	3g

variation

Serve with yellow rice. Stir a pinch of ground turmeric with 1 tablespoon of boiling water until dissolved, then stir into the cooked rice until mixed.

This dish comes from Goa on the west coast of India, a former Portuguese colony. The use of both vinegar and pork reveal the Portuguese influence on the local cuisine.

INGREDIENTS

- **150 ml/5 fl oz malt vinegar**
- **2 tbsp coriander seeds**
- **1 tbsp cumin seeds**
- **2 tsp chilli powder**
- **2 tsp ground turmeric**
- **1 tsp cardamom seeds**
- **5-cm/2-inch piece fresh root ginger, roughly chopped**
- **4 garlic cloves, roughly chopped**
- **6 black peppercorns**
- **6 whole cloves**
- **1 cinnamon stick**
- **salt**
- **1 kg/2 lb 4 oz pork fillet, diced**
- **6 curry leaves**
- **3 tbsp ghee or vegetable oil**
- **1 tsp black mustard seeds**
- **150 ml/5 fl oz water**
- **freshly cooked rice, to serve**

1

1

2

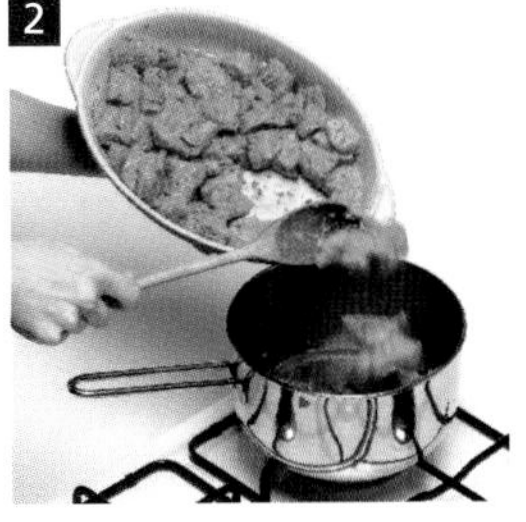

cook's tip

Remove the marinating meat from the refrigerator 30 minutes before you intend to begin cooking to bring it to room temperature.

1 Place the vinegar, coriander, cumin, chilli powder, turmeric, cardamom, ginger, garlic, peppercorns, cloves, cinnamon and a pinch of salt in a blender or food processor and process to make a paste, adding a little more vinegar if necessary. Place the pork in a large, shallow, non-metallic dish and pour over the spice paste, turning the meat to coat all over. Cover with clingfilm and leave to marinate in the refrigerator for 1 hour. Arrange the curry leaves on top of the pork, re-cover and leave to marinate for at least 8 hours or overnight.

2 Heat the ghee in a large, heavy-based saucepan. Add the mustard seeds and cook over a low heat, stirring frequently, until they begin to splutter and give off their aroma. Add the pork, with the marinade, and the water. Bring to the boil, stirring constantly, then reduce the heat, cover and simmer for 30 minutes.

3 Remove the lid from the saucepan and stir the curry. Simmer for a further 30 minutes, or until the pork is tender. Transfer to a warmed serving dish and serve with rice.

pork with tamarind

serves 6 | **prep: 15 mins, plus 30 mins soaking** | **cook: 1 hr 5 mins**

This Goan curry has a thick, smooth sauce and a hot and sour flavour, resulting from the spice mix and tamarind.

NUTRITIONAL INFORMATION	
Calories	344
Protein	38g
Carbohydrate	15g
Sugars	14g
Fat	15g
Saturates	4g

INGREDIENTS

- 55 g/2 oz dried tamarind, roughly chopped
- 500 ml/18 fl oz boiling water
- 2 fresh green chillies, deseeded and roughly chopped
- 2 onions, roughly chopped
- 2 garlic cloves, roughly chopped
- 1 lemon grass stalk, bulb end roughly chopped
- 2 tbsp ghee or vegetable oil
- 1 tbsp ground coriander
- 1 tsp ground turmeric
- 1 tsp ground cardamom
- 1 tsp chilli powder
- 1 tsp Ginger Paste (see page 12)
- 1 cinnamon stick
- 1 kg/2 lb 4 oz diced pork fillet
- 1 tbsp chopped fresh coriander

TO GARNISH

- fresh coriander sprigs
- sliced fresh red chillies

variation

If you like, add 1 tablespoon desiccated coconut to the tamarind liquid in Step 2.

2

3

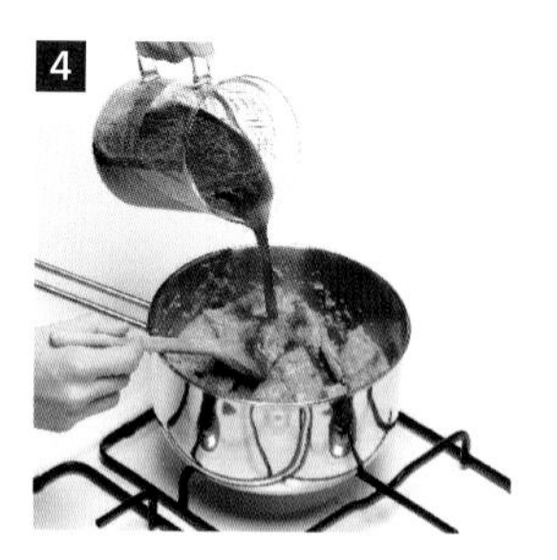
4

cook's tip

Dried tamarind is usually sold in compressed blocks from large supermarkets and Asian food shops. If you can't find it, substitute 450 ml/16 fl oz lemon juice, but the flavour will not be the same.

1 Place the dried tamarind in a small bowl, pour in the boiling water and mix well. Leave to soak for 30 minutes.

2 Sieve the soaking liquid into a clean bowl, pressing down the pulp with the back of a wooden spoon. Discard the pulp. Pour 1 tablespoon of the tamarind liquid into a food processor and add the green chillies, onions, garlic and lemon grass and process until smooth.

3 Heat the ghee in a large, heavy-based saucepan. Add the chilli and onion paste, ground coriander, turmeric, cardamom, chilli powder, Ginger Paste and cinnamon stick and cook, stirring, for 2 minutes, or until the spices give off their aroma.

4 Add the pork and cook, stirring constantly, until lightly browned and well coated in the spices mixture. Pour in the remaining tamarind liquid, bring to the boil, then reduce the heat, cover and simmer for 30 minutes. Remove the lid from the saucepan and simmer for a further 30 minutes, or until the pork is tender. Stir in the chopped coriander and serve garnished with coriander sprigs and sliced red chillies.

pork with cinnamon & fenugreek

cook: 40–50 mins

prep: 15 mins, plus 30 mins marinating

serves 4

NUTRITIONAL INFORMATION	
Calories	317
Protein	28g
Carbohydrate	9g
Sugars	6g
Fat	19g
Saturates	4g

This is a dry dish, that is, one served without an integral sauce. It would go well with Bombay Potatoes (see page 220) and a vegetable curry, such as Mixed Vegetable Curry (see page 153).

variation

This recipe would also work well with lean lamb or rump steak instead of the pork, if you prefer.

INGREDIENTS

- 1 tsp ground coriander
- 1 tsp ground cumin
- 1 tsp chilli powder
- 1 tbsp dried fenugreek
- 1 tsp ground fenugreek
- 150 ml/5 fl oz natural yogurt
- 450 g/1 lb diced pork fillet
- 4 tbsp ghee or vegetable oil
- 1 large onion, sliced
- 5-cm/2-inch piece fresh root ginger, finely chopped
- 4 garlic cloves, finely chopped
- 1 cinnamon stick
- 6 cardamom pods
- 6 whole cloves
- 2 bay leaves
- 175 ml/6 fl oz water
- salt

cook's tip

Look for kasuri dry methi leaves in Asian food shops, as these are dried fenugreek leaves. Use fenugreek sparingly because it has a strong flavour and may overpower the finished dish.

1. Mix the ground coriander, cumin, chilli powder, dried fenugreek, ground fenugreek and yogurt together in a small bowl. Place the diced pork in a large, shallow, non-metallic dish and add the spice mixture, turning well to coat. Cover with clingfilm and leave to marinate in the refrigerator for 30 minutes.

2. Heat the ghee in a large, heavy-based saucepan. Cook the onion over a low heat, stirring occasionally, for 5 minutes, or until softened. Add the ginger, garlic, cinnamon stick, cardamom, cloves and bay leaves and cook, stirring constantly, for 2 minutes, or until the spices give off their aroma. Add the meat with its marinade and the water, and season with salt to taste. Bring to the boil, reduce the heat, cover and simmer for 30 minutes.

3. Transfer the meat to a preheated wok or large, heavy-based frying pan and cook over a low heat, stirring constantly, until dry and tender. If necessary, occasionally sprinkle with a little water to prevent it sticking to the wok. Serve immediately.

chicken tikka

cook: 30 mins

prep: 15 mins, plus 3 hrs marinating

serves 6

NUTRITIONAL INFORMATION	
Calories	783
Protein	4g
Carbohydrate	58g
Sugars	3g
Fat	58g
Saturates	7g

variation

Replace the vegetable oil with sunflower oil and substitute the lemon wedges with lime, if you prefer.

For this very popular dish, small pieces of chicken are marinated for a minimum of 3 hours in yogurt and spices. Serve with lettuce leaves and Naan Bread (see page 194) for a filling supper dish.

INGREDIENTS

1 tsp finely chopped fresh root ginger
1 tsp crushed fresh garlic
½ tsp ground coriander
½ tsp ground cumin
1 tsp chilli powder
3 tbsp natural yogurt
1 tsp salt
2 tbsp lemon juice
few drops of red food colouring (optional)
1 tbsp tomato purée
1.5 kg/3 lb 5 oz chicken breast
1 onion, sliced
3 tbsp vegetable oil
Naan Bread (see page 194), to serve

TO GARNISH

lettuce leaves
1 lemon, cut into wedges

1

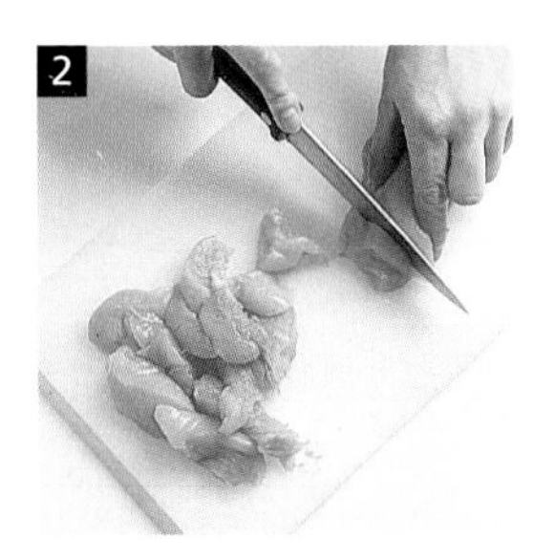

2

2

1 Blend the ginger, garlic, ground coriander, cumin and chilli powder together in a large bowl. Add the yogurt, salt, lemon juice, red food colouring (if using) and tomato purée to the spice mixture.

2 Using a sharp knife, cut the chicken into pieces. Add the chicken to the spice mixture and toss to coat well. Cover and leave to marinate in the refrigerator for at least 3 hours, preferably overnight.

3 Preheat the grill to medium. Arrange the onion in the base of a large, heatproof dish. Carefully drizzle half the vegetable oil over the onions.

4 Arrange the marinated chicken pieces on top of the onions and cook under the preheated grill, turning once and basting with the remaining oil, for 25–30 minutes. Serve the chicken on a bed of lettuce, garnished with lemon wedges, with a helping of Naan Bread.

cook's tip

Chicken Tikka can also be served with a cooling Cucumber Raita (see page 228) and Mango Chutney (see page 230). Alternatively, serve as a starter.

chicken dopiaza

serves 4 **prep: 10 mins** **cook: 55 mins**

The defining characteristic of this dish is that two types of onions are cooked at different stages in the preparation. Dopiaza means two onions. The dish is best served with plain boiled rice.

INGREDIENTS

- 3 tbsp ghee or vegetable oil
- 8 baby onions or shallots, halved
- 3 dried red chillies
- 6 cardamom pods
- 6 black peppercorns
- 2 whole cloves
- 2 bay leaves
- 2 onions, finely chopped
- 1 tsp Garlic Paste (see page 12)
- 1 tsp Ginger Paste (see page 12)
- 1 tsp ground cumin
- 1 tsp ground coriander
- 1 tsp chilli powder
- ½ tsp ground turmeric
- 200 g/7 oz canned tomatoes
- 4 tbsp water
- 8 skinless chicken thighs
- fresh coriander leaves, to garnish
- freshly cooked rice, to serve

NUTRITIONAL INFORMATION	
Calories	241
Protein	18g
Carbohydrate	11g
Sugars	8g
Fat	15g
Saturates	2g

variation

You could use 8 skinless chicken drumsticks or 4 larger chicken portions. Increase the cooking time by 15 minutes for chicken portions.

cook's tip

This dish can be prepared a day in advance, cooled, covered and stored in the refrigerator. It is, however, not suitable for freezing.

1. Heat 2 tablespoons of the ghee in a large, heavy-based saucepan or flameproof casserole. Add the baby onions and cook over a low heat, stirring occasionally, for 10 minutes, until golden. Remove with a slotted spoon and reserve until required.

2. Add the remaining vegetable oil to the saucepan and cook the chillies, cardamom pods, peppercorns, cloves and bay leaves, stirring constantly, for 2 minutes, or until they give off their aroma. Add the chopped onions and cook, stirring frequently, for 5 minutes, or until softened.

3. Stir in the Garlic Paste, Ginger Paste, cumin, ground coriander, chilli powder and turmeric and cook, stirring constantly, for 2 minutes. Add the tomatoes and their can juices and the water. Stir well and simmer gently for 5 minutes, or until slightly thickened.

4. Add the chicken thighs and simmer for 20 minutes. Return the baby onions or shallots to the saucepan and cook for a further 10 minutes, or until the chicken is tender and cooked through. Serve immediately with rice, garnished with fresh coriander leaves.

chicken korma

cook: 40 mins

prep: 15 mins, plus 3 hrs marinating

serves 8

NUTRITIONAL INFORMATION	
Calories	764
Protein	49g
Carbohydrate	24g
Sugars	8g
Fat	54g
Saturates	6g

variation

Chicken thighs and drumsticks may be used instead of breasts, if you prefer, and should be cooked for 10 minutes longer in Step 3.

This delicious creamy curry is perfect for informal entertaining or as a midweek supper dish for the whole family. Serve with either plain boiled rice or Pulao Rice (see page 197).

INGREDIENTS

- 1½ tsp finely chopped fresh root ginger
- 1½ tsp crushed fresh garlic
- 2 tsp Garam Masala (see page 12)
- 1 tsp chilli powder
- 1 tsp salt
- 1 tsp black cumin seeds
- 3 green cardamom pods, husks removed and seeds crushed
- 1 tsp ground coriander
- 1 tsp ground almonds
- 150 ml/5 fl oz natural yogurt
- 8 whole chicken breasts, skinned
- 300 ml/10 fl oz vegetable oil
- 2 onions, sliced
- 150 ml/5 fl oz water
- 2–3 tbsp fresh coriander leaves, plus extra to garnish
- fresh green chillies, chopped
- freshly cooked rice, to serve

1

2

3

cook's tip

Cardamoms are widely used in Indian cooking. Both ground cardamoms and cardamom pods are available from most supermarkets. Store the pods in an airtight container in a cool, dark place.

1 Mix the ginger, garlic, Garam Masala, chilli powder, salt, black cumin seeds, crushed cardamom, ground coriander, almonds and yogurt together in a bowl.

2 Spoon the yogurt and spice mixture over the chicken breasts, then cover and leave in the refrigerator for 3 hours to marinate.

3 Heat the vegetable oil in a large, heavy-based frying pan. Add the onions and fry until golden. Add the chicken breasts to the frying pan and stir-fry for 5–7 minutes. Add the water, cover and leave to simmer for 20–25 minutes.

4 Add the coriander and green chillies and cook for a further 10 minutes, stirring gently occasionally. Transfer to serving plates, garnish with coriander leaves and serve immediately with freshly cooked rice.

butter chicken

serves 6 | **prep: 15 mins, plus 8 hrs marinating** | **cook: 25 mins**

Also known as chicken makhani, this rich and flavoursome dish from northern India is cooked with aromatic spices and almonds.

INGREDIENTS

- 150 ml/5 fl oz natural yogurt
- 1 tsp Ginger Paste (see page 12)
- salt
- 6 skinless, boneless chicken breasts
- 55 g/2 oz butter
- 1 cinnamon stick
- 6 cardamom pods
- 6 cloves
- 2 bay leaves
- 150 ml/5 fl oz soured cream
- 150 ml/5 fl oz single cream
- large pinch of saffron threads, crushed
- 1 tbsp ground almonds
- ¼ tsp cornflour

NUTRITIONAL INFORMATION	
Calories	315
Protein	33g
Carbohydrate	5g
Sugars	4g
Fat	18g
Saturates	11g

1 Mix the yogurt, Ginger Paste and 1 teaspoon of salt in a large, shallow dish. Cut each chicken breast into 3 pieces and add to the dish. Rub the yogurt mixture into the chicken, then cover with clingfilm and leave to marinate in the refrigerator overnight.

2 Remove the chicken from the dish, reserving any marinade. Melt the butter in a large, heavy-based frying pan, add the chicken and cook over a low heat, turning occasionally, for 10 minutes, or until browned and nearly cooked through. Remove with a slotted spoon and reserve.

3 Add the cinnamon, cardamoms, cloves and bay leaves to the frying pan and cook, stirring constantly, for 1 minute, or until they give off their aroma. Add the reserved marinade, soured cream, single cream and saffron, stir well, cover and simmer for 5 minutes.

4 Return the chicken pieces to the frying pan and stir in the ground almonds. Mix the cornflour with enough water to make a smooth paste and stir into the saucepan. Cover and simmer for 5 minutes, or until the chicken is tender and cooked through. Taste and add more salt, if necessary, and serve immediately.

cook's tip

For a special occasion, you can add a few drops of red food colouring to the yogurt marinade before rubbing it into the chicken.

chicken masala

cook: 55 mins

prep: 15 mins, plus 8 hrs marinating

serves 4

These aromatic, spicy chicken bites can be served as part of an Indian meal, or on their own as an interesting snack.

NUTRITIONAL INFORMATION	
Calories	189
Protein	18g
Carbohydrate	4g
Sugars	3g
Fat	12g
Saturates	2g

INGREDIENTS

150 ml/5 fl oz natural yogurt
4 tbsp lemon juice
2 tbsp sunflower oil
2 tsp Garam Masala (see page 12)
2 tsp ground cumin
1 tsp chopped fresh root ginger
1 tsp chopped fresh garlic
salt
8 skinless, boneless chicken thighs
1 tsp dried fenugreek
2 tsp aamchoor (dried mango powder)
1 tsp dried mint
fresh coriander sprigs, to garnish
lime and tomato wedges, to serve

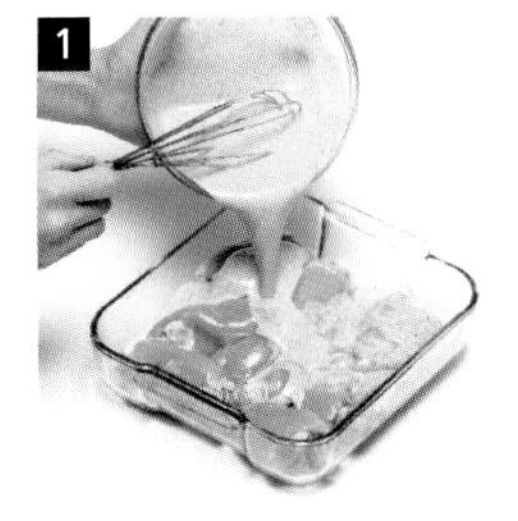

1 Mix the yogurt, lemon juice, sunflower oil, Garam Masala, cumin, ginger, garlic and a pinch of salt together in a bowl. Place the chicken thighs in a large, shallow, ovenproof dish, pour over the yogurt mixture and turn the chicken to coat well. Cover with clingfilm and leave to marinate in the refrigerator overnight.

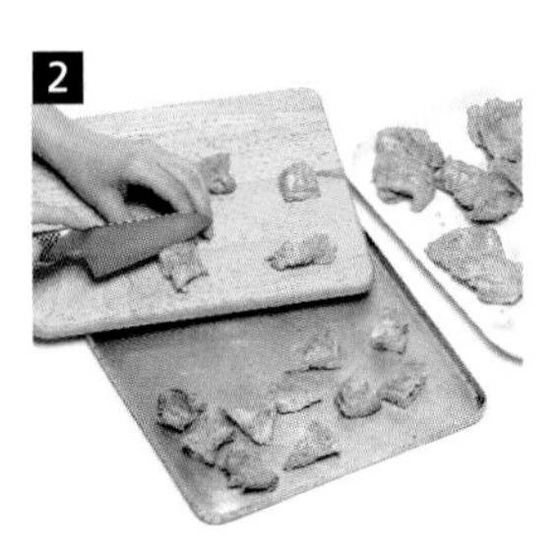

2 Preheat the oven to 190°C/375°F/Gas Mark 5. Remove the clingfilm from the chicken and cover the dish with foil. Bake the chicken in its marinade in the preheated oven for 45 minutes. Remove the chicken from the dish with a slotted spoon, cut into bite-sized pieces and spread out on a baking tray.

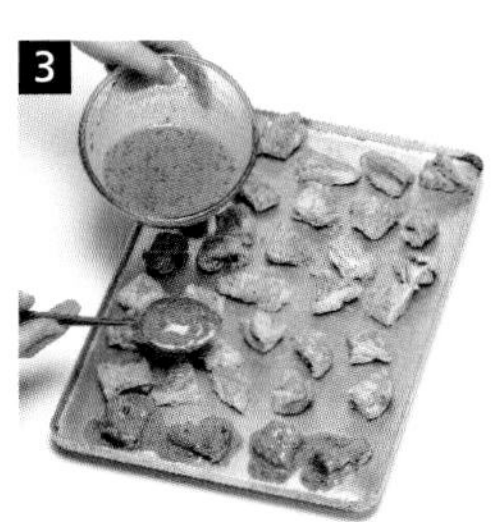

3 Stir the fenugreek, aamchoor and mint into the remaining marinade, then pour over the chicken. Return to the oven and bake for a further 10 minutes. Transfer to a warmed dish, garnish with fresh coriander and serve with lime and tomato wedges.

cook's tip

Fresh garlic adds a wonderful flavour to many dishes, including spicy curries. Store garlic bulbs in a cool, dark place. They will last up to 6 months if kept correctly.

balti chicken

serves 6 **prep: 15 mins** **cook: 30 mins**

This highly popular dish has a wonderful flavour and is very easy to prepare. Serve with Naan Bread (see page 194) and a mixed salad.

NUTRITIONAL INFORMATION	
Calories	228
Protein	30g
Carbohydrate	11g
Sugars	8g
Fat	7g
Saturates	1g

INGREDIENTS

- 3 tbsp ghee or vegetable oil
- 2 large onions, sliced
- 3 tomatoes, sliced
- ½ tsp kalonji seeds
- 4 black peppercorns
- 2 cardamom pods
- 1 cinnamon stick
- 1 tsp chilli powder
- 1 tsp Garam Masala (see page 12)
- 1 tsp Garlic Paste (see page 12)
- 1 tsp Ginger Paste (see page 12)
- salt
- 700 g/1 lb 9 oz skinless, boneless chicken breasts or thighs, diced
- 2 tbsp natural yogurt
- 2 tbsp chopped fresh coriander, plus extra to garnish
- 2 fresh green chillies, deseeded and finely chopped
- 2 tbsp lime juice

variation

This recipe would also work well with firm-fleshed fish, such as monkfish, cod or hake.

1 Heat the ghee in a large, heavy-based frying pan. Add the onions and cook over a low heat, stirring occasionally, for 10 minutes, or until golden. Add the sliced tomatoes, kalonji seeds, peppercorns, cardamoms, cinnamon stick, chilli powder, Garam Masala, Garlic Paste and Ginger Paste and season with salt to taste. Cook, stirring constantly, for 5 minutes.

2 Add the chicken and cook, stirring constantly, for 5 minutes, or until well coated in the spice paste. Stir in the yogurt. Cover and simmer, stirring occasionally, for 10 minutes.

3 Stir in the chopped coriander, chillies and lime juice. Transfer to a warmed serving dish, sprinkle with more chopped coriander and serve immediately.

cook's tip

Kalonji seeds, also known as nigella, are very tiny and black, resembling onion seeds in appearance. They are sometimes known as black cumin, but are a different spice with a peppery flavour.

tandoori-style chicken

cook: 35 mins

prep: 15 mins, plus 6 hrs marinating

serves 4

In India, tandoori chicken is traditionally cooked in a tandoor (clay) oven. Alternatively, this popular dish can be cooked just as well under a hot grill.

NUTRITIONAL INFORMATION	
Calories	549
Protein	43g
Carbohydrate	7g
Sugars	7g
Fat	65g
Saturates	7g

variation

Use low-fat natural yogurt and serve with plain boiled rice instead of Naan Bread, if you prefer.

INGREDIENTS

- 8 chicken drumsticks, skinned
- 150 ml/5 fl oz natural yogurt
- 1½ tsp finely chopped fresh root ginger
- 1½ tsp crushed fresh garlic
- 1 tsp chilli powder
- 2 tsp ground cumin
- 2 tsp ground coriander
- 1 tsp salt
- ½ tsp red food colouring
- 1 tbsp tamarind paste
- 150 ml/5 fl oz water
- 150 ml/5 fl oz vegetable oil
- lettuce leaves
- Naan Bread (see page 194), to serve

TO GARNISH

- onion rings
- sliced tomatoes
- lemon wedges

2

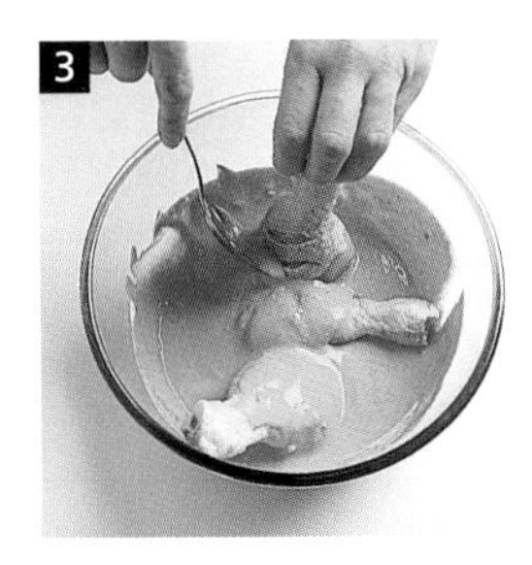

3

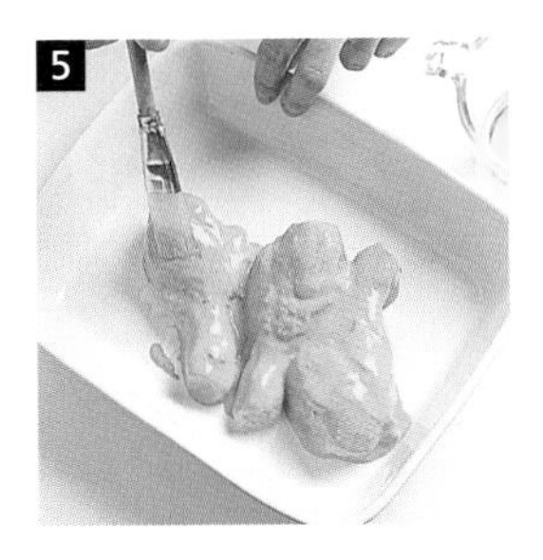

5

1 Using a sharp knife, make 2–3 slashes in each piece of chicken.

2 Place the yogurt in a large bowl. Add the ginger, garlic, chilli powder, ground cumin, ground coriander, salt and red food colouring and blend together until well mixed.

3 Add the chicken to the yogurt and spice mixture and mix to coat well. Cover and leave the chicken to marinate in the refrigerator for a minimum of 3 hours.

4 Mix the tamarind paste with the water in a separate bowl and fold into the yogurt and spice mixture. Toss the chicken pieces in the mixture again, cover and leave to marinate in the refrigerator for a further 3 hours.

5 Preheat the grill to medium. Transfer the chicken pieces to a heatproof dish and brush with vegetable oil. Cook under the preheated grill for 30–35 minutes, turning the pieces occasionally and basting with any remaining oil, until the meat is tender and cooked through.

6 Arrange the chicken on a bed of lettuce, garnish with onion rings, sliced tomatoes and lemon wedges and serve.

cook's tip

Suitable accompaniments include Naan Bread (see page 194) and Mint Raita (see page 228), which complement the dish perfectly.

chicken jalfrezi

serves 4 **prep: 15 mins** **cook: 20 mins**

This is a quick and tasty way to use leftover roast chicken. The sauce can also be used for any cooked poultry, lamb or beef.

NUTRITIONAL INFORMATION	
Calories	343
Protein	42g
Carbohydrate	13g
Sugars	8g
Fat	14g
Saturates	2g

INGREDIENTS

- 1 tsp mustard oil
- 3 tbsp vegetable oil
- 1 large onion, finely chopped
- 3 garlic cloves, crushed
- 1 tbsp tomato purée
- 2 tomatoes, peeled and chopped
- 1 tsp ground turmeric
- ½ tsp cumin seeds, ground
- ½ tsp coriander seeds, ground
- ½ tsp chilli powder
- ½ tsp Garam Masala (see page 12)
- 1 tsp red wine vinegar
- 1 small red pepper, deseeded and chopped
- 125 g/4½ oz frozen broad beans
- 500 g/1 lb 2 oz cooked chicken breasts, cut into bite-sized pieces
- salt
- fresh coriander sprigs, to garnish
- freshly cooked rice, to serve

variation

If time is limited, use ready-ground spices instead of grinding the cumin and coriander seeds yourself.

1. Heat the mustard oil in a large, heavy-based frying pan over a high heat for 1 minute, or until it begins to smoke. Add the vegetable oil, reduce the heat, then add the onion and garlic and fry until golden.

2. Add the tomato purée, chopped tomatoes, ground turmeric, cumin and coriander seeds, chilli powder, Garam Masala and vinegar to the frying pan. Stir the mixture until fragrant.

3. Add the red pepper and broad beans and stir for 2 minutes, or until the pepper is softened. Stir in the chicken, and season with salt to taste. Leave to simmer gently for 6–8 minutes, or until the chicken is heated through and the broad beans are tender. Transfer to warmed serving plates, garnish with coriander sprigs and serve with rice.

cook's tip

This dish is an ideal way of making use of leftover poultry. Any variety of beans works well, but vegetables are just as useful, especially root vegetables, courgettes, potatoes or broccoli.

chicken with whole spices

cook: 15 mins | **prep: 20 mins** | **serves 6**

NUTRITIONAL INFORMATION	
Calories	216
Protein	29g
Carbohydrate	5g
Sugars	4g
Fat	9g
Saturates	1g

variation

If you prefer, you can use 6 cherry tomatoes, halved, instead of 1 large one, and fresh red chillies instead of the green chillies.

This is a favourite northern Indian way of cooking, which gives the ingredients a very strong, rich flavour. Serve with Cucumber or Aubergine Raita (see page 228).

INGREDIENTS

- **3 fresh green chillies**
- **1 dried red chilli**
- **½ tsp pomegranate seeds**
- **½ tsp cumin seeds**
- **¼ tsp mustard seeds**
- **¼ tsp fenugreek seeds**
- **¼ tsp onion seeds**
- **¼ tsp fennel seeds**
- **salt**
- **2.5-cm/1-inch piece fresh root ginger, shredded**
- **2 garlic cloves, finely chopped**
- **2 curry leaves**
- **4 tbsp ghee or vegetable oil**
- **2 onions, sliced**
- **1 large tomato, sliced**
- **700 g/1 lb 9 oz, skinless, boneless chicken breasts or thighs, diced**
- **1 tbsp chopped fresh coriander, to garnish**

1

2

3

cook's tip

Fresh pomegranate seeds are extensively used in Indian and Pakistani cooking. Cut the fruit in half and scoop out the seeds with the point of a knife.

1 Slit the fresh chillies lengthways and reserve. Light crush the red chilli and pomegranate seeds in a mortar with a pestle, or with the end of a rolling pin, and place in a small bowl. Add the cumin, mustard, fenugreek, onion and fennel seeds and a pinch of salt and stir well. Add the ginger, garlic and curry leaves.

2 Heat the ghee in a large, heavy-based frying pan. Add the spice mixture, fresh chillies and onions and cook over a low heat, stirring constantly, for 5 minutes, or until the onion has softened.

3 Add the tomato and chicken, increase the heat to medium and cook, stirring occasionally, for 10 minutes, or until the chicken is tender and cooked through. Serve garnished with chopped coriander.

chicken dhansak

serves 6 **prep: 25 mins** **cook: 2 hrs 30 mins**

This is a classic dish of traditional Parsee cuisine from the west coast of India. This community originated in Persia and fled to India to escape religious persecution centuries ago, but has remained a distinctive cultural and culinary group.

NUTRITIONAL INFORMATION	
Calories	612
Protein	55g
Carbohydrate	51g
Sugars	10g
Fat	22g
Saturates	5g

variation

If you can find fresh fenugreek – methi – add the chopped leaves of 4 sprigs instead of the spinach.

INGREDIENTS

- 115 g/4 oz chana dal
- 115 g/4 oz moong dal
- 115 g/4 oz toor dal
- 115 g/4 oz masoor dal
- 100 ml/3½ fl oz vegetable oil
- 2 tsp Garlic Paste (see page 12)
- 2 tsp Ginger Paste (see page 12)
- 6 chicken portions
- 400 g/14 oz canned tomatoes, drained
- 225 g/8 oz peeled pumpkin, diced
- 3 onions, chopped
- 115 g/4 oz fresh spinach, chopped
- 1 aubergine, diced
- 1 tbsp chopped fresh mint
- salt
- 2 fresh green chillies, chopped
- 1½ tsp ground turmeric
- 1 tsp ground coriander
- ½ tsp ground cardamom
- ½ tsp ground cinnamon
- ½ tsp ground cloves
- ½ tsp chilli powder
- 2 tbsp chopped fresh coriander, to garnish

cook's tip

Cook books always used to say that you should pick over dal and lentils to remove stones. With today's reliable suppliers, this is usually unnecessary.

1. Place the dals in a large saucepan and add enough water to generously cover. Bring to the boil, reduce the heat, cover and simmer for 40 minutes. Meanwhile, heat 3 tablespoons of the vegetable oil in a frying pan. Add half the Garlic Paste and half the Ginger Paste and cook, stirring, for 1 minute. Add the chicken and cook until golden brown all over. Transfer the mixture to the saucepan containing the dals.

2. Stir in the tomatoes, pumpkin, two-thirds of the onions, the spinach, aubergine and mint and season with salt to taste. Bring to the boil, then cover and simmer for 45 minutes, or until the chicken is cooked through. Using a slotted spoon, transfer the chicken to a plate. Transfer the dal and vegetable mixture to a food processor or blender and process to a purée.

3. Heat the remaining vegetable oil in a clean saucepan. Add the remaining onion and cook over a low heat for 10 minutes, or until golden. Stir in the chillies and the remaining Garlic Paste and Ginger Paste and cook, stirring, for 2 minutes. Add the remaining spices and cook for 6 minutes, adding a little water if the mixture is very dry. Add to the dal mixture, stir, cover and simmer for 20 minutes. Add the chicken portions and simmer for a further 20 minutes. Serve sprinkled with chopped coriander.

chicken with spinach

cook: 1 hr **prep: 15 mins** **serves 4**

NUTRITIONAL INFORMATION	
Calories	233
Protein	21g
Carbohydrate	9g
Sugars	7g
Fat	13g
Saturates	2g

variation

Substitute 4 fresh tomatoes for the canned tomatoes. Peel and chop them before adding in Step 2.

This classic combination is a favourite in cuisines throughout the world. Here, it is given a southern Indian treatment to turn it into a mildly spiced and flavoursome curry.

INGREDIENTS

225 g/8 oz fresh spinach leaves, rinsed
1 fresh green chilli, deseeded and chopped
1 tbsp chopped fresh root ginger
2 garlic cloves, chopped
4 tbsp water
2 tbsp ghee or vegetable oil
8 black peppercorns
1 bay leaf
1 onion, finely chopped
200 g/7 oz canned tomatoes, drained
1 tsp chilli powder
1 tbsp Curry Paste (see page 12)
salt
150 ml/5 fl oz chicken Basic Meat Stock (see page 13) or water
4 tbsp natural yogurt, plus extra to garnish
8 skinless chicken thighs

1

2

3

cook's tip

Serve with Sheermal (see page 207), Naan Bread (see page 194) or Chapatis (see page 195), rather than rice, for a filling meal.

1 Place the spinach in a large saucepan with just the water clinging to the leaves after rinsing, cover and cook for 4–5 minutes, or until wilted. Transfer to a food processor or blender and add the green chilli, ginger, garlic and water. Process until smooth.

2 Heat the ghee in a karahi or saucepan. Add the peppercorns and bay leaf and cook over a low heat, stirring constantly, for 1–2 minutes, or until they give off their aroma. Add the onion and cook, stirring occasionally, for 10 minutes, or until golden. Add the tomatoes and cook for 2 minutes, breaking them up with a wooden spoon. Add the chilli powder and Curry Paste and season with salt to taste. Cook, stirring constantly, for 2 minutes.

3 Stir in the spinach and chilli purée with the Stock and simmer for 5 minutes. Add the yogurt, 1 tablespoon at a time, stirring well after each addition, then simmer for a further 5 minutes. Finally, add the chicken, stir well, cover and simmer for 30 minutes, or until tender and cooked through. Serve immediately, garnished with extra yogurt.

chicken breasts with coconut milk

serves 4 | **prep: 15 mins, plus 1–8 hrs marinating** | **cook: 15 mins**

This southern Indian dish is an absolutely perfect choice for entertaining, as not only does it look and taste delicious, but it is easy and straightforward to cook. Serve with Tomato Rice (see page 200) and Naan Bread (see page 194).

NUTRITIONAL INFORMATION	
Calories	199
Protein	31g
Carbohydrate	9g
Sugars	8g
Fat	5g
Saturates	1g

INGREDIENTS

- 1 small onion, chopped
- 1 fresh green chilli, deseeded and chopped
- 2.5-cm/1-inch piece fresh root ginger, chopped
- 2 tsp ground coriander
- 1 tsp ground cumin
- 1 tsp fennel seeds
- 1 tsp ground star anise
- 1 tsp cardamom seeds
- ½ tsp ground turmeric
- ½ tsp black peppercorns
- ½ tsp ground cloves
- 600 ml/1 pint canned coconut milk
- 4 skinless, boneless chicken breast portions
- vegetable oil, for brushing
- fresh coriander sprigs to garnish

variation

You can cook the chicken under a preheated grill or on a lit barbecue. Brush occasionally with the marinade to prevent it drying out.

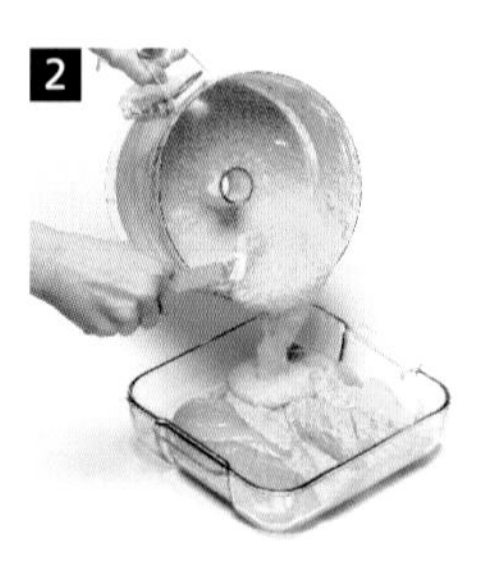

cook's tip

The longer you marinate the chicken, the better the flavour will be. When marinating, it is best to turn the meat occasionally to ensure that it is completely covered in the marinade.

1. Place the onion, chilli, ginger, ground coriander, cumin, fennel seeds, star anise, cardamom seeds, turmeric, peppercorns, cloves and 450 ml/16 fl oz of the coconut milk in a food processor and process to make a paste, adding more coconut milk if necessary.

2. Using a sharp knife, slash the chicken breasts several times and place in a large, shallow, non-metallic dish in a single layer. Pour over half the coconut milk mixture and turn to coat completely. Cover with clingfilm and leave to marinate in the refrigerator for at least 1 hour and up to 8 hours.

3. Heat a ridged griddle pan and brush lightly with vegetable oil. Add the chicken, in batches if necessary, and cook for 6–7 minutes on each side, or until tender.

4. Meanwhile, pour the remaining coconut milk mixture into a saucepan and bring to the boil, stirring occasionally. Arrange the chicken on a warmed serving dish, spoon over a little of the coconut sauce and garnish with coriander sprigs. Serve hot.

southern duck

serves 6 **prep: 20 mins** **cook: 1 hr 15 mins**

A coconut mollee or stew is a typical dish of southern India. Poultry is more expensive than in the West, so it is treated with care.

INGREDIENTS

2 tsp cumin seeds
2 tsp coriander seeds
1 tsp cardamom seeds
2 tsp Garam Masala (see page 12)
1 tsp chilli powder
½ tsp ground turmeric
salt
6 boneless duck breasts
2 garlic cloves, finely chopped
2 onions, sliced
850 ml/1½ pints canned coconut milk
125 ml/4 fl oz white wine vinegar
175 ml/6 fl oz water
2 tbsp chopped fresh coriander

NUTRITIONAL INFORMATION	
Calories	264
Protein	31g
Carbohydrate	12g
Sugars	9g
Fat	11g
Saturates	3g

2

3

4

1 Place the cumin, coriander and cardamom seeds, Garam Masala, chilli powder and turmeric into a mortar or spice grinder with a pinch of salt and grind finely. Reserve.

2 Place the duck breasts, skin-side down, in a large, heavy-based frying pan and cook over a medium heat, for 10 minutes, or until the skin is golden brown. Turn over and cook for a further 6–8 minutes, or until the second side is browned. Remove from the frying pan with a slotted spoon and drain on kitchen paper.

3 Drain off all but about 1 tablespoon of the fat from the frying pan and return to the heat. Add the garlic and onions and cook, stirring occasionally, for 8 minutes, or until golden brown. Stir in the ground spice mixture and cook, stirring constantly, for 2 minutes, or until the spices give off their aroma.

4 Return the duck breasts to the frying pan and stir in the coconut milk, vinegar and water. Bring to the boil, then reduce the heat, cover and simmer for 40–45 minutes, or until the duck is tender. Taste and add more salt, if necessary, stir in the chopped coriander and serve immediately.

cook's tip

Using a sharp knife, trim off any excess fat from the duck breasts before cooking them, but do not remove the skin.

duck curry

cook: 1 hr 20 mins | **prep: 20 mins, plus 10 mins soaking** | **serves 4**

Already a rich-tasting meat, duck breasts are cooked with cream, ground almonds and spices in this superb curry.

NUTRITIONAL INFORMATION	
Calories	683
Protein	41g
Carbohydrate	15g
Sugars	8g
Fat	52g
Saturates	15g

INGREDIENTS

- 3 onions
- 600 ml/1 pint chicken or duck Basic Meat Stock (see page 13)
- 5-cm/2-inch piece fresh root ginger
- 3 garlic cloves, finely chopped
- 4 whole cloves
- salt
- 4 tbsp ghee or vegetable oil
- 1 tsp cayenne pepper
- 2 tsp coriander seeds, lightly crushed
- 2.7 kg/6 lb duck, cut into portions
- large pinch of saffron threads
- 115 g/4 oz ground almonds
- 300 ml/10 fl oz single cream
- 1 tsp cardamom seeds, lightly crushed

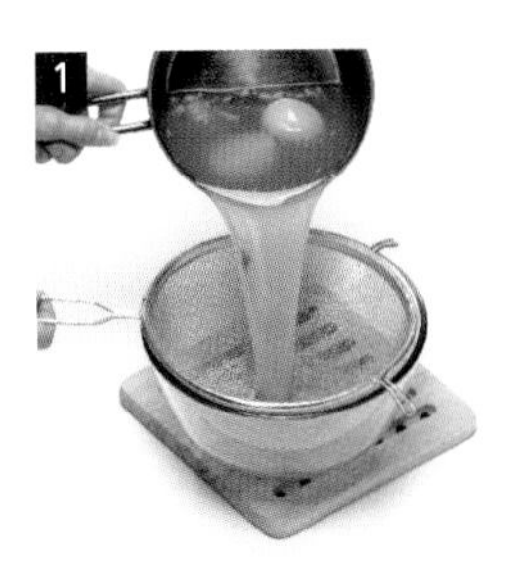

cook's tip

It is best to use home-made stock for this dish, if possible. If you have to use a stock cube, don't add any salt in Step 1, as stock cubes tend to be very salty.

1. Preheat the oven to 150°C/300°F/Gas Mark 2. Finely chop the ginger and reserve. Cut 1 onion in half and finely chop the others. Place the Stock in a large, heavy-based saucepan, add the onion halves, ginger, garlic, cloves and a pinch of salt and bring to the boil. Boil until reduced by half, then sieve into a bowl and reserve until required. Discard the contents of the sieve.

2. Heat the ghee or vegetable oil in a flameproof casserole. Add the chopped onions and cook over a low heat for 10 minutes, or until golden. Stir in the cayenne pepper and coriander seeds and cook for 1 minute, or until they give off their aroma. Add the duck portions and cook, turning frequently, until browned all over. Add the reserved Stock, season with salt to taste and bring to the boil. Reduce the heat, cover and cook for 20 minutes.

3. Place the saffron in a bowl and add enough boiling water to cover. Leave to soak for 10 minutes.

4. Mix the almonds, cream, cardamom seeds and saffron with its soaking liquid together. Pour the mixture into the casserole and stir well. Transfer to the preheated oven and cook for a further 20 minutes, or until the duck is tender. Serve immediately.

bengali-style fish

serves 4–8 **prep: 15 min** **cook: 25–35 mins**

Fresh fish is eaten a great deal in Bengal (Bangladesh), and this dish is made with mustard oil, which gives the fish a mouthwatering flavour. Serve with Naan Bread (see page 194).

NUTRITIONAL INFORMATION	
Calories	356
Protein	32g
Carbohydrate	5g
Sugars	4g
Fat	23g
Saturates	3g

INGREDIENTS

- 1 tsp ground turmeric
- 1 tsp salt
- 6 tbsp mustard oil
- 1 kg/2 lb 4 oz cod fillet, skinned and cut into pieces
- 4 fresh green chillies
- 1 tsp finely chopped fresh root ginger
- 1 tsp crushed garlic
- 2 onions, finely chopped
- 2 tomatoes, finely chopped
- 450 ml/16 fl oz water
- chopped fresh coriander leaves, to garnish
- Naan Bread, to serve (see page 194)

variation

Other white fish would be suitable for this recipe, such as monkfish, bass, plaice or halibut.

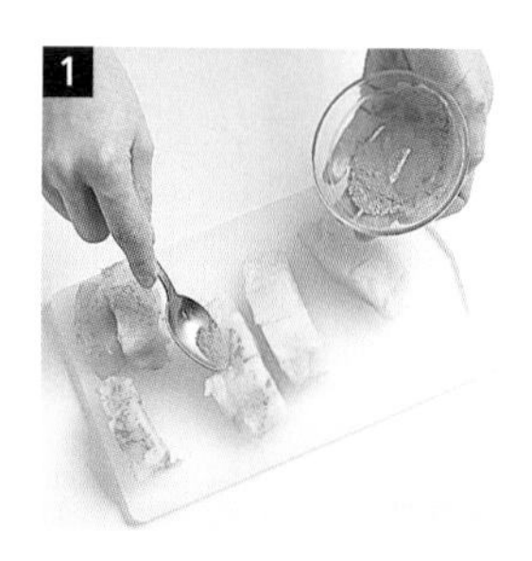

cook's tip

In the hot and humid eastern plains surrounding Bengal, the mustard plant flourishes, providing oil for cooking and seeds for flavouring. Fish appears in many meals, often flavoured with mustard oil.

1. Mix the turmeric and salt together in a small bowl, then spoon the mixture over the fish pieces.

2. Heat the mustard oil in a large, heavy-based frying-pan. Add the fish and fry until pale yellow. Remove the fish with a slotted spoon and reserve.

3. Place the green chillies, ginger, garlic, onions and tomatoes in a mortar and grind with a pestle to make a paste. Alternatively, place the ingredients in a food processor and process until ground.

4. Transfer the spice paste to a clean frying pan and dry-fry until golden brown.

5. Remove the frying pan from the heat and place the fish pieces in the paste without breaking up the fish. Return the frying pan to the heat, add the water and cook over a medium heat for 15–20 minutes. Transfer to a warmed serving dish, garnish with chopped coriander and serve with Naan Bread.

punjabi-style fish

serves 4 **prep: 15 mins** **cook: 30 mins**

Cod is not a typical Indian fish – it comes mainly from the North Atlantic – but it works well in this creamy, spiced sauce.

INGREDIENTS

2 tbsp ghee or vegetable oil
2 onions, sliced
1 tsp Garlic Paste (see page 12)
1 tsp Ginger Paste (see page 12)
1 tbsp ground cumin
2 tsp ground coriander
1 tsp Garam Masala (see page 12)
½ tsp ground cinnamon
½ tsp cayenne pepper
4 cardamom pods, lightly crushed
salt
800 g/1 lb 12 oz canned tomatoes
125 ml/4 fl oz single cream
1 tbsp lemon juice
800 g/1 lb 12 oz cod fillets, skinned and cut into 4-cm/1½-inch slices
chopped fresh coriander, to garnish

NUTRITIONAL INFORMATION	
Calories	345
Protein	41g
Carbohydrate	13g
Sugars	11g
Fat	5g
Saturates	2g

variation

Any firm-fleshed white fish fillet, such as monkfish or haddock, would work well in this dish.

cook's tip

It is important not to let the sauce boil in Step 2 because single cream has a tendency to curdle when heated, especially in the presence of an acidic ingredient such as lemon juice.

1. Heat the ghee in a large, heavy-based saucepan. Add the onions and cook over a low heat, stirring occasionally, for 10 minutes, or until golden. Add the Garlic Paste, Ginger Paste, cumin, ground coriander, Garam Masala, cinnamon, cayenne pepper, cardamoms and a pinch of salt and cook, stirring constantly, for 2 minutes, or until the spices give off their aroma.

2. Stir in the tomatoes and their can juices, cream and lemon juice and cook, stirring occasionally, for 5 minutes, or until slightly thickened. Do not allow the mixture to boil.

3. Add the pieces of fish, cover and simmer gently for 10 minutes, or until tender. Transfer to warmed serving dishes, sprinkle with chopped coriander and serve immediately.

baked fish with coconut & coriander

serves 6 | **prep: 15 mins, plus 30 mins marinating** | **cook: 25–30 mins**

This is a classic Parsee dish from the west coast. In India, the fish would be wrapped in banana leaves, which you can obtain from Indian and other specialist Asian food shops.

INGREDIENTS

2 large lemon sole, cleaned and scaled
salt
5 tbsp lemon juice
115 g/4 oz fresh coriander, chopped
40 g/1½ oz desiccated coconut
6 fresh green chillies, deseeded and chopped
4 garlic cloves, chopped
1 tsp cumin seeds
1 tbsp sugar
vegetable oil, for brushing

NUTRITIONAL INFORMATION	
Calories	119
Protein	18g
Carbohydrate	4g
Sugars	4g
Fat	4g
Saturates	0.5g

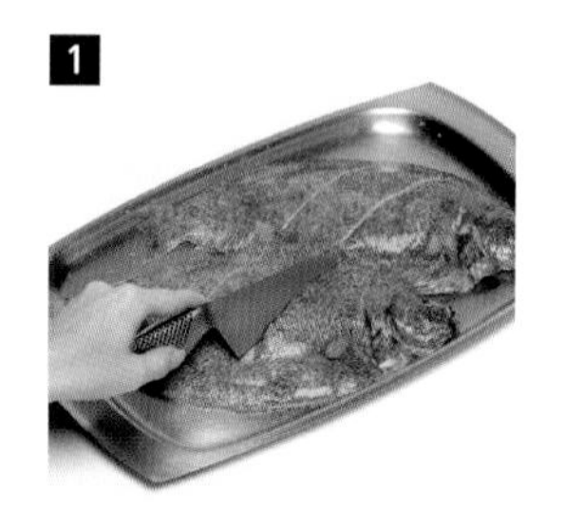

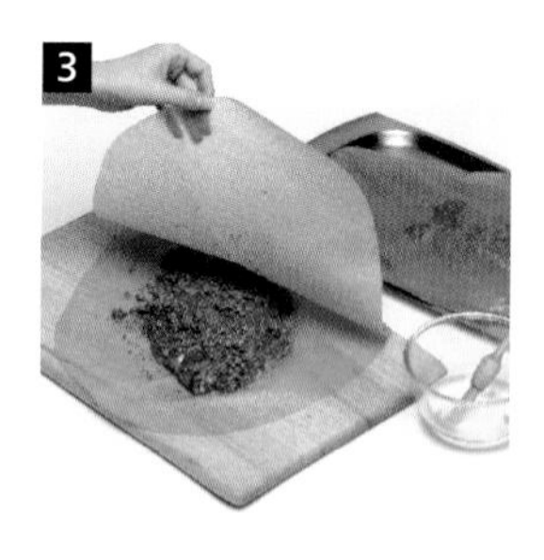

cook's tip

Do not marinate the fish in the lemon juice for longer than a maximum of 1 hour, otherwise the acid begins to denature the protein and 'cook' the fish.

1 Using a sharp knife, slash the fish diagonally twice on both sides. Rub all over the inside and outside of the fish with salt and 4 tablespoons of the lemon juice. Place on a large plate, cover with clingfilm and leave to marinate in a cool place for 30 minutes.

2 Preheat the oven to 200°C/400°F/Gas Mark 6. Place the remaining lemon juice, coriander, coconut, chillies, garlic, cumin seeds and sugar in a food processor and process until smooth. Alternatively, place the ingredients in a mortar and grind with a pestle.

3 Cut out 2 pieces of baking parchment or greaseproof paper large enough to enclose a fish completely, and brush with a little vegetable oil. Rub the fish all over with the coconut and coriander paste, then place each fish on a piece of baking parchment or greaseproof paper and fold in the sides to enclose. Place the parcels on a large baking sheet and bake in the preheated oven for 25–30 minutes, or until cooked through. Unwrap and serve immediately.

fried trout with ginger

cook: 15 mins **prep: 10 mins** **serves 4**

Farmed trout is inexpensive, but often rather bland in flavour. This simple, spicy way of cooking it gives it a bit of a kick. Serve with Onion Kachumbar (see page 224), if you like.

NUTRITIONAL INFORMATION	
Calories	235
Protein	32g
Carbohydrate	0.5g
Sugars	0.5g
Fat	12g
Saturates	2g

INGREDIENTS

- **1 tsp Ginger Paste (see page 12)**
- **1 tsp Garlic Paste (see page 12)**
- **2 fresh green chillies, deseeded and finely chopped**
- **1 tbsp chopped fresh coriander**
- **¼ tsp ground turmeric**
- **salt and pepper**
- **4 trout, cleaned**
- **vegetable oil, for brushing**

TO GARNISH

- **fresh coriander sprigs**
- **lime slices**

1 Preheat the grill to medium. Mix the Ginger Paste, Garlic Paste, fresh chillies, coriander, turmeric, 1 teaspoon of pepper and a pinch of salt together in a small bowl. Stir in a enough water to make a smooth paste.

2 Using a sharp knife, slash the trout diagonally on both sides 2–3 times. Rub the spice paste into the fish, especially the slashes.

3 Brush with vegetable oil and cook under the preheated grill for 15 minutes, turning once and brushing with more vegetable oil. Transfer to warmed serving plates, garnish with coriander sprigs and lime slices and serve immediately.

cook's tip

Fresh coriander is used extensively in Indian cooking and imparts a distinctive flavour to dishes. Finely chop the stems as well as the leaves of the herb.

deep-fried fish

serves 6

prep: 15 mins, plus 1 hr marinating/resting

cook: 15 mins

The Bay of Bengal is a marvellous source of all kinds of fish. In India, the most popular fish to prepare this way would be pomfret, which, if you can find, you can use instead of red mullet.

INGREDIENTS

8 red mullet fillets, halved
salt and pepper
125 ml/4 fl oz lemon juice
vegetable oil, for deep-frying
lime wedges, to garnish

BATTER

85 g/3 oz gram flour
25 g/1 oz rice flour
1 tsp chilli powder
1 tsp ground turmeric
125 ml/4 fl oz water

NUTRITIONAL INFORMATION	
Calories	304
Protein	28g
Carbohydrate	10g
Sugars	0.5g
Fat	17g
Saturates	1g

cook's tip

Make sure that the batter is well blended before resting. If you leave the batter to rest for more than 30 minutes, stir it well before using as it may have begun to separate.

1 Season the fish to taste with salt and pepper, place in a large, shallow, non-metallic dish and sprinkle with the lemon juice. Cover with clingfilm and leave to marinate in a cool place for 30 minutes.

2 Meanwhile, make the batter. Sift together the gram flour, rice flour, chilli powder and turmeric into a large bowl. Gradually stir in the water to make a smooth batter. Cover and leave to rest for 30 minutes.

3 Heat the vegetable oil in a deep-fat fryer or large, heavy-based saucepan to 180–190°C/350–375°F, or until a cube of bread browns in 30 seconds. Dip the fish pieces in the batter a few at a time, to coat, and drain off the excess. Add to the hot oil and deep-fry for 5 minutes, or until golden brown and crisp. Remove with a slotted spoon and drain on kitchen paper. Keep warm while you cook the remaining pieces of fish. Serve immediately, garnished with lime wedges.

fish in coconut sauce

cook: 45 mins | prep: 20 mins | serves 6

As it has no pin bones and a firm, meaty texture, monkfish is the perfect choice for this South Indian mollee. Serve with Naan Bread (see page 194) or Chapatis (see page 195).

NUTRITIONAL INFORMATION	
Calories	173
Protein	27g
Carbohydrate	10g
Sugars	9g
Fat	4g
Saturates	1g

INGREDIENTS

1 tbsp ghee or vegetable oil
2 onions, sliced
2 tsp ground cumin
1 tsp Garlic Paste (see page 12)
1 tsp ground coriander
1 tsp ground turmeric
4 whole cloves
4 cardamom pods, lightly crushed
6 curry leaves
700 ml/1¼ pints canned coconut milk
1 kg/2 lb 4 oz monkfish tail

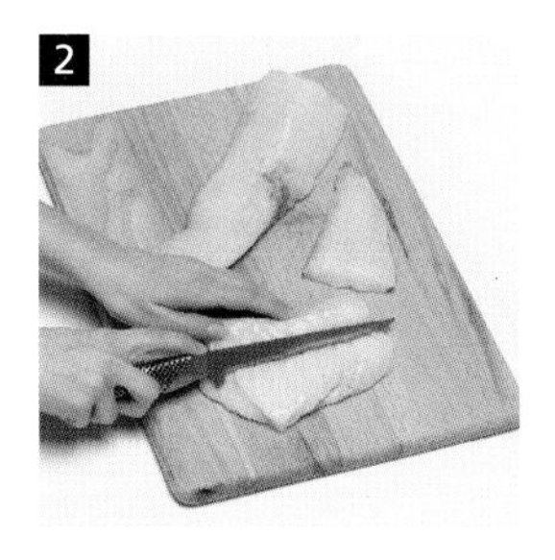

1 Heat the ghee in a large, heavy-based saucepan. Add the onions and cook over a low heat, stirring occasionally, for 10 minutes, or until golden. Stir in the cumin, Garlic Paste, ground coriander, turmeric, cloves and cardamoms and cook, stirring constantly, for 1–2 minutes, or until the spices give off their aroma. Add the curry leaves and coconut milk, stir well and simmer for 20 minutes.

2 Meanwhile, remove and discard any grey membrane from the monkfish. Using a sharp knife, cut down either side of the central bone and remove and discard it. Cut each fillet in half across the centre, then slice in half horizontally. Roll up each piece of fish as tightly as possible.

3 Gently add the fish rolls to the coconut sauce, cover and simmer for a further 10 minutes, or until the fish is tender and cooked through. Serve immediately, using the curry leaves as a garnish.

cook's tip

Try to ensure that all the pieces of fish are about the same size and thickness, so that they cook evenly. To test if the fish is cooked through, the flesh should be opaque and flake easily.

marinated fish

serves 4 | **prep: 15 mins, plus 8 hrs marinating** | **cook: 20 mins**

This delicious western Indian dish is the piscine equivalent of Tandoori-style Chicken (see page 107) – tandoori machee.

INGREDIENTS

1 fresh green chilli
4 red mullet or snapper, cleaned
125 ml/4 fl oz lime juice
4 tbsp natural yogurt
1 tsp Garlic Paste (see page 12)
1 tsp Ginger Paste (see page 12)
1 tbsp coriander seeds
1 tsp Garam Masala (see page 12)
few drops red food colouring (optional)
85 g/3 oz butter
2 tsp ground cumin

TO GARNISH
lime wedges
fresh coriander sprigs

NUTRITIONAL INFORMATION	
Calories	301
Protein	21g
Carbohydrate	4g
Sugars	4g
Fat	23g
Saturates	11g

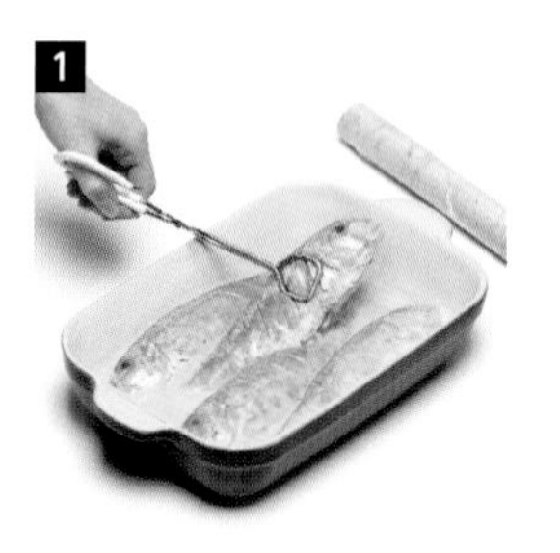

cook's tip

Do not let the butter turn brown when you are melting it over a low heat, otherwise it will taste bitter and may spoil the finished dish.

1 Deseed and chop the green chilli and reserve. Using a sharp knife, slash the fish diagonally several times on both sides and sprinkle with the lime juice. Place the yogurt, Garlic Paste, Ginger Paste, coriander seeds, chopped chilli and Garam Masala in a food processor and process to make a paste. Transfer to a shallow dish and stir in the red food colouring (if using). Add the fish, turning to coat. Cover with clingfilm and leave to marinate in the refrigerator for 8 hours, turning occasionally.

2 Preheat the oven to 190°C/375°F/Gas Mark 5. Remove the fish from the marinade and place on a rack in a roasting tin. Cook in the preheated oven for 10 minutes.

3 Meanwhile, melt the butter in a small saucepan over a low heat. Remove the saucepan from the heat and stir in the cumin. Brush the butter all over the fish and return to the oven for a further 6–7 minutes, or until cooked through. Transfer to warmed plates, garnish with lime wedges and coriander and serve immediately.

fish in tomato sauce

cook: 45 mins **prep: 20 mins** **serves 4–6**

Tomatoes are widely used in all kinds of Indian cooking. Choose firm, ripe specimens to achieve the best flavour in this dish.

NUTRITIONAL INFORMATION	
Calories	276
Protein	40g
Carbohydrate	6g
Sugars	5g
Fat	11g
Saturates	1g

INGREDIENTS

500 g/1 lb 2 oz tomatoes

4 fresh green chillies

1 kg/2 lb 4 oz haddock fillets, skinned

salt

2 tsp ground turmeric

4 tbsp ghee or vegetable oil

2 onions, sliced

1 tbsp ground coriander

2 tsp Garam Masala (see page 12)

1 tsp chilli powder

1 tsp sugar

2 tbsp natural yogurt

1 tbsp lemon juice

fresh coriander sprigs, to garnish

Pulao Rice (see page 197), to serve

cook's tip

To peel tomatoes, cut a cross in the stem end of each one and place in a bowl. Pour in boiling water to cover and leave for 1–2 minutes. Drain, then peel off the skins.

1 Peel, deseed and chop the tomatoes and reserve (see Cook's Tip). Using a sharp knife, slit the chillies lengthways along 1 side, deseed and reserve. Remove any pin bones from the fish and cut into large chunks. Mix 1 teaspoon of salt and 1½ teaspoons of the turmeric together in a bowl, then rub the mixture all over the fish.

2 Heat the ghee in a large frying pan. Add the fish, in batches if necessary, and cook over a medium heat, stirring frequently, until golden brown all over. Remove with a slotted spoon and reserve. Add the onions, reduce the heat and cook, stirring occasionally, for 10 minutes, or until golden.

3 Stir in the remaining turmeric, the coriander, Garam Masala, chilli powder and sugar and cook, stirring constantly for a further 2 minutes. Increase the heat to medium and add the tomatoes, yogurt, lemon juice and chillies. Bring to the boil, then reduce the heat and simmer for 15 minutes.

4 Return the fish to the frying pan and stir gently to coat well in the sauce. Simmer for a further 10 minutes, or until the fish is tender and cooked through. Taste and adjust the seasoning, garnish with coriander and serve with Pulao Rice.

monkfish kebabs

serves 4 | **prep: 20 mins, plus 30 mins marinating** | **cook: 10 mins**

The fish is marinated in a delicious mixture of herbs, spices and lime juice before being threaded on to skewers with a selection of colourful vegetables. Serve with Pulao Rice (see page 197).

NUTRITIONAL INFORMATION	
Calories	139
Protein	18g
Carbohydrate	7g
Sugars	7g
Fat	4g
Saturates	1g

INGREDIENTS

- 3 tbsp lime juice
- 1 tbsp finely chopped fresh mint
- 1 tbsp finely chopped fresh coriander
- 2 fresh green chillies, deseeded and finely chopped
- 1 tsp Ginger Paste (see page 12)
- ½ tsp Garlic Paste (see page 12)
- 1 tsp ground coriander
- salt
- 350 g/12 oz monkfish fillet, cubed
- 1 red pepper, deseeded and cut into chunks
- 1 green pepper, deseeded and cut into chunks
- 8 baby corn cobs, halved
- 8 button mushrooms
- 8 cherry tomatoes
- ½ small cauliflower, broken into florets
- 1 tbsp sunflower oil
- Pulao Rice (see page 197), to serve

TO GARNISH

- lime wedges
- fresh coriander sprigs

variation

Substitute large raw prawns, peeled but with their tails left intact, for the monkfish, if you like.

cook's tip

If using wooden or bamboo skewers, remember to soak them in a bowl of warm water while the fish is marinating to prevent them charring under the grill.

1. Mix the lime juice, mint, fresh coriander, chillies, Ginger Paste, Garlic Paste, ground coriander and a pinch of salt together in a large, shallow, non-metallic dish. Add the fish and stir to coat. Cover with clingfilm and leave to marinate in a cool place for 30 minutes.

2. Preheat the grill to medium. Drain the fish and reserve the marinade. Thread the monkfish, chunks of pepper, baby corn cobs, mushrooms, cherry tomatoes and cauliflower florets on to 4 long or 8 short skewers.

3. Brush the kebabs with any remaining marinade and the sunflower oil and cook under the preheated grill, turning and basting frequently, for 10 minutes, or until cooked. Serve immediately on a bed of Pulao Rice, garnished with lime wedges and coriander sprigs.

cod in spicy coconut sauce

cook: 30 mins

prep: 15 mins, plus 30 mins soaking

serves 4

With its combination of tamarind and coconut milk, this sweet and sour curry is very rich and creamy.

NUTRITIONAL INFORMATION	
Calories	340
Protein	35g
Carbohydrate	22g
Sugars	20g
Fat	14g
Saturates	2g

variation

For a more substantial dish, add 1 diced aubergine and 2 sliced courgettes with the onions in Step 2.

INGREDIENTS

25 g/1 oz dried tamarind, roughly chopped
150 ml/5 fl oz boiling water
4 tbsp ghee or vegetable oil
2 tsp mustard seeds
1 tsp fenugreek seeds
1 tsp Ginger Paste (see page 12)
2 fresh green chillies, deseeded and chopped
6 curry leaves
2 onions, chopped
1 tsp chilli powder
1 tsp ground turmeric
1 tsp ground cumin
400 g/14 oz canned tomatoes, drained
400 ml/14 fl oz canned coconut milk
salt
4 cod fillets, skinned
freshly cooked rice, to serve

TO GARNISH

3 tbsp chopped fresh coriander
lime slices

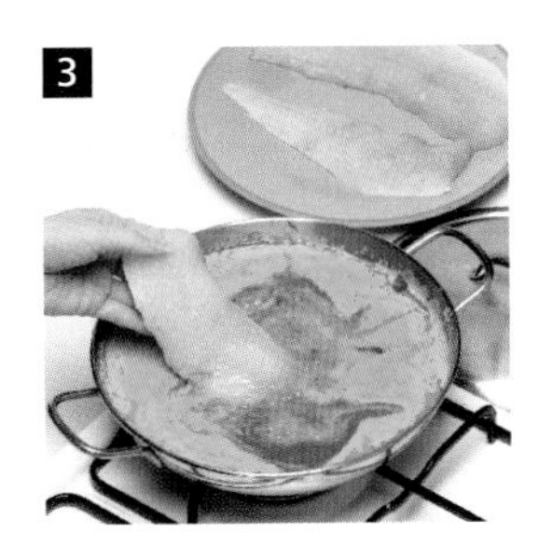

cook's tip

Reserve the can juices after draining the tomatoes and, if the mixture seems thick after you have added the coconut milk, add 1–2 tablespoons of the tomato juice.

1. Place the dried tamarind in a bowl and pour in the boiling water. Leave to soak for 30 minutes.

2. Heat the ghee in a karahi or large, heavy-based saucepan. Add the mustard seeds and cook over a low heat, stirring constantly, for 2 minutes, or until they give off their aroma. Add the fenugreek seeds, Ginger Paste, chillies and curry leaves and cook, stirring constantly, for 2 minutes, then add the onions. Cook, stirring occasionally, for 10 minutes, or until golden.

3. Stir in the chilli powder, turmeric, cumin and drained tomatoes and cook for 2–3 minutes, then add the coconut milk. Season with salt to taste and simmer, stirring occasionally, for 5 minutes. Sieve the tamarind into a clean bowl, pressing down on the pulp with the back of a wooden spoon. Discard the pulp and add the liquid to the karahi, or saucepan, with the fish.

4. Cover the karahi, or saucepan, and simmer gently for 6–10 minutes, or until the fish is tender and cooked through. The flesh should flake easily when tested with the point of a knife. Sprinkle with chopped coriander and serve with rice, garnished with lime slices.

tandoori-style prawns

serves 4 **prep: 15 mins** **cook: 20 mins**

These mouthwatering prawns can be served as a starter arranged on a bed of lettuce with a lemon wedge, or as an attractive side dish for almost any Eastern-style meal.

NUTRITIONAL INFORMATION	
Calories	214
Protein	5g
Carbohydrate	1g
Sugars	1g
Fat	22g
Saturates	13g

INGREDIENTS

- 12 king prawns
- 100 g/3½ oz unsalted butter
- 1 tsp finely chopped fresh root ginger
- 1 tsp crushed fresh garlic
- 1 tsp chilli powder
- ½ tsp salt
- 1 tsp ground coriander
- 1 tsp ground cumin
- fresh coriander leaves, finely chopped
- few drops of red food colouring
- 8 lettuce leaves, to serve

TO GARNISH

- 1–2 fresh green chillies, finely sliced
- 1 lemon, cut into wedges

variation

If you cannot find king prawns, then use 450 g/1 lb monkfish cut into 2.5-cm/1-inch cubes instead.

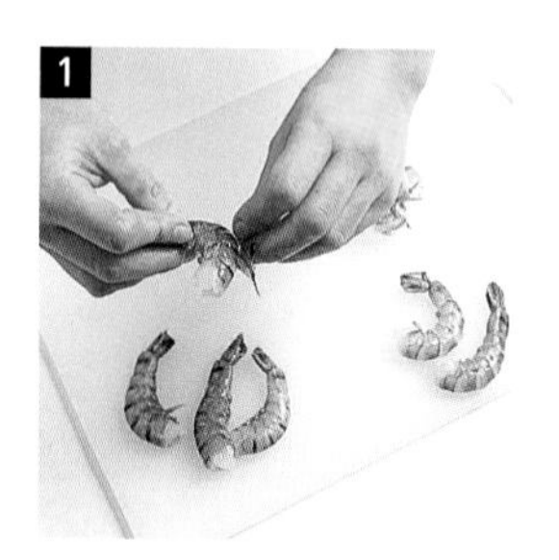

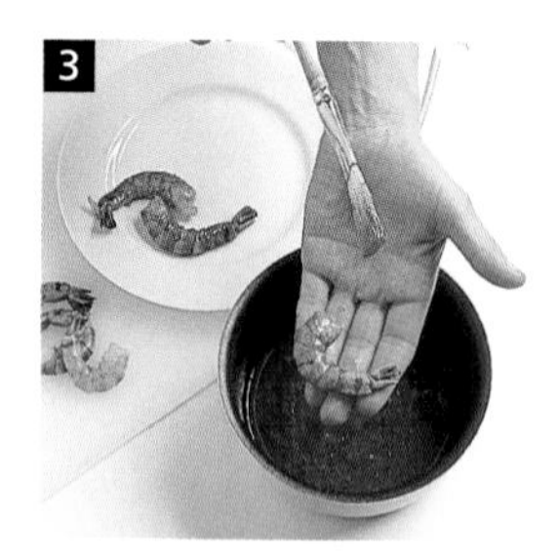

cook's tip

Though not essential, it is best to shell the prawns before cooking them as some people find it slightly awkward to shell them at the table.

1. Preheat the grill to high. Carefully remove the shells from the prawns and discard. Transfer the shelled prawns to a heatproof dish.

2. Melt the butter in a large, heavy-based saucepan. Add the ginger, garlic, chilli powder, salt, ground coriander, cumin, coriander leaves and red food colouring and mix together until the ingredients are well blended.

3. Brush the melted butter and spice mixture over the prawns and cook them under the preheated grill for 10–12 minutes, turning once.

4. Serve the prawns on a bed of lettuce, garnished with sliced green chillies and lemon wedges.

dried prawns

serves 6 **prep: 15 mins, plus 2 hrs soaking** **cook: 30 mins**

This is a more economical way of cooking prawns. You can buy the dried prawns in packets from most Asian food shops.

INGREDIENTS

- 200 g/7 oz dried prawns
- 300 ml/10 fl oz vegetable oil
- 2 onions, sliced
- 3 fresh green chillies, thinly sliced
- 2–3 tbsp finely chopped fresh coriander leaves
- 1½ tsp finely chopped fresh root ginger
- 1½ tsp crushed fresh garlic
- pinch of ground turmeric
- 1 tsp salt
- 1 tsp chilli powder, plus extra to garnish
- 2 tbsp lemon juice
- Chapatis (see page 195), to serve

NUTRITIONAL INFORMATION	
Calories	565
Protein	22g
Carbohydrate	4g
Sugars	3g
Fat	51g
Saturates	6g

variation

You could use 450 g/1 lb fresh prawns instead of the dried prawns and substitute lime juice for the lemon juice, if you prefer.

1. Soak the dried prawns in a bowl of cold water for 2 hours. Drain the prawns well and rinse twice. Drain the prawns again thoroughly.
2. Heat half the vegetable oil in a large frying pan. Add the onions, 2 chillies and half the coriander and stir-fry for 8–10 minutes, until the onions are golden.
3. Add the ginger, garlic, turmeric, salt and chilli powder and stir-fry for a further 2 minutes over a low heat. Reserve until required.
4. Heat the remaining vegetable oil in a separate saucepan. Add the prawns and fry, stirring occasionally, until crisp.
5. Add the fried prawns to the onions and blend together, then return to the heat and stir-fry for a further 3–5 minutes. Transfer the prawns to a serving dish, sprinkle over the lemon juice and garnish with a pinch of chilli powder. Serve immediately with Chapatis.

cook's tip

Fresh chillies will store well if they are taken out of any polythene bags and kept in a paper bag in the salad drawer of your refrigerator.

prawns in coconut milk

serves 4 **prep: 20 mins** **cook: 25 mins**

Lightly spiced coconut is the perfect foil to tender cooked prawns. Serve with spiced rice to bring out the flavour.

INGREDIENTS

500 g/1 lb 2 oz raw tiger prawns
4 onions
4 tbsp ghee or vegetable oil
1 tsp Garam Masala (see page 12)
1 tsp ground turmeric
1 cinnamon stick
2 cardamom pods, lightly crushed
½ tsp chilli powder
2 whole cloves
2 bay leaves
400 ml/14 fl oz canned coconut milk
1 tsp sugar
salt
fresh coriander leaves, to garnish
Pulao Rice (see page 197), to serve

NUTRITIONAL INFORMATION	
Calories	277
Protein	24g
Carbohydrate	18g
Sugars	14g
Fat	13g
Saturates	2g

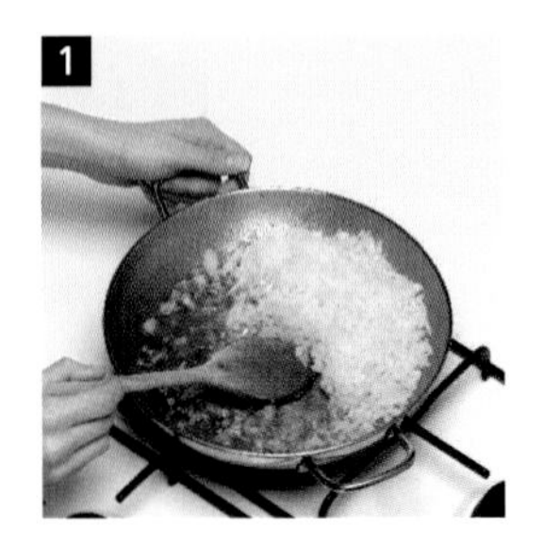

cook's tip

To prepare prawns, pull off the head and peel off the body shell. Pull off the shell covering the tail. Make a slit along the back of each prawn and, with the point of the knife, remove the dark vein.

1 Peel and devein the tiger prawns, then reserve until required. Finely chop 2 of the onions and grate the other 2. Heat the ghee in a large, heavy-based frying pan. Add the Garam Masala and cook over a low heat, stirring constantly, for 1 minute, or until it gives off its aroma. Add the chopped onions and cook, stirring occasionally, for 10 minutes, or until golden.

2 Stir in the grated onions, turmeric, cinnamon, cardamoms, chilli powder, cloves and bay leaves and cook, stirring constantly, for 5 minutes. Stir in half the coconut milk and the sugar and season with salt to taste. Add the prawns and cook, stirring frequently for 8 minutes, or until they have changed colour.

3 Stir in the remaining coconut milk and bring to the boil. Taste and adjust the seasoning, if necessary, and serve immediately with Pulao Rice, garnished with coriander.

bengali coriander prawns

cook: 15 mins **prep: 15 mins** **serves 4**

Mustard oil is characteristic of Bengali cuisine, as too is seafood. It is very pungent and has a unique flavour and aroma.

NUTRITIONAL INFORMATION	
Calories	232
Protein	24g
Carbohydrate	4g
Sugars	3g
Fat	14g
Saturates	2g

INGREDIENTS

500 g/1 lb 2 oz raw tiger prawns
4 fresh green chillies, deseeded
4 spring onions, chopped
3 garlic cloves
2.5-cm/1-inch piece fresh root ginger, chopped
2 tsp sunflower oil
4 tbsp mustard oil or vegetable oil
1 tbsp ground coriander
1 tsp mustard seeds, crushed
175 ml/6 fl oz canned coconut milk
salt
115 g/4 oz fresh coriander, chopped, plus a few leaves, to garnish
lemon halves, to garnish

1 Peel and devein the tiger prawns, then reserve until required. Place the chillies, spring onions, garlic, ginger and sunflower oil in a food processor and process to make a paste. Heat the mustard oil in a large, heavy-based frying pan. Add the spice paste and cook over a low heat, stirring constantly, for 2 minutes.

2 Add the ground coriander, mustard seeds and coconut milk and bring to the boil, stirring constantly. Reduce the heat and simmer for 5 minutes.

3 Stir in the prawns and simmer for a further 6–8 minutes, or until they have changed colour. Season with salt to taste, stir in the chopped coriander and serve immediately, garnished with lemon halves and a few coriander leaves.

cook's tip

Mustard oil is available from most Asian food shops and needs careful handling. Do not overheat, otherwise the smoke will sting your eyes.

prawns with vegetables

serves 6 **prep: 20 mins** **cook: 55 mins**

Almost a one-pot meal, this colourful combination of seafood, aubergines, peppers and courgettes would go well with a dal.

NUTRITIONAL INFORMATION	
Calories	190
Protein	22g
Carbohydrate	11g
Sugars	9g
Fat	8g
Saturates	1g

INGREDIENTS

- 3 tbsp ghee or vegetable oil
- 2 onions, chopped
- 1 tsp Garlic Paste (see page 12)
- 1 tsp Ginger Paste (see page 12)
- 2 fresh green chillies, deseeded and chopped
- 2 tbsp ground coriander
- 2 tsp paprika
- 1 tsp ground fennel
- 1 tsp ground turmeric
- 2 aubergines, diced
- 2 courgettes, diced
- 2 green peppers, deseeded and diced
- 400 g/14 oz canned tomatoes
- 2 tbsp lemon juice
- 300 ml/10 fl oz canned coconut milk
- salt
- 600 g/1 lb 5 oz raw tiger prawns, peeled and deveined
- fresh coriander sprigs, to garnish
- freshly cooked rice, to serve

variation

Add 225 g/8 oz okra in Step 3 instead of the courgettes. Trim the ends and cut them into 2.5-cm/1-inch lengths.

2

3

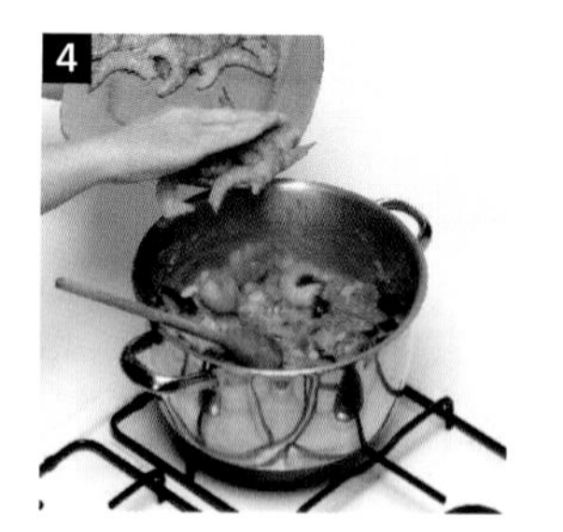
4

cook's tip

When frying whole or ground spices, turn the heat down as low as possible and stir constantly. If you have one, use a heat diffuser.

1. Heat the ghee in a large, heavy-based saucepan or flameproof casserole. Add the onions and cook over a low heat, stirring occasionally, for 10 minutes, or until golden.

2. Add the Garlic Paste, Ginger Paste and chopped chillies and cook, stirring constantly, for 2 minutes. Stir in the coriander, paprika, ground fennel and turmeric and cook, stirring constantly, for a further 5 minutes.

3. Add the aubergines, courgettes and green peppers and cook, stirring frequently, for 3 minutes, then stir in the tomatoes and their can juices, lemon juice and coconut milk. Season with salt to taste. Bring to the boil, stirring constantly, then cover and simmer gently for 25 minutes.

4. Add the prawns, stir, re-cover the saucepan or casserole and simmer for a further 10 minutes, or until the prawns have changed colour. Serve immediately with freshly cooked rice, garnished with coriander.

prawn korma

cook: 30 mins

prep: 15 mins, plus 30 mins marinating

serves 4

NUTRITIONAL INFORMATION	
Calories	248
Protein	27g
Carbohydrate	15g
Sugars	14g
Fat	10g
Saturates	1g

variation

This is delicious made with salmon steaks. Add them once the sauce has thickened and cook for 15 minutes, or until the flesh flakes easily.

Simplicity itself, this creamy seafood curry is quick to cook, but tastes absolutely wonderful – perfect for midweek entertaining.

INGREDIENTS

- 1–2 tsp ground turmeric
- 500 g/1 lb 2 oz raw tiger prawns, peeled and deveined
- 1 tbsp ground coriander
- 2 tsp chilli powder
- 1 tsp ground cumin
- 2 cardamom pods, lightly crushed
- 2 tbsp ghee or vegetable oil
- 1 onion, chopped
- 1 tsp Ginger Paste (see page 12)
- 1 tbsp ground almonds
- 1 tbsp raisins
- 1 tsp sugar
- 300 ml/10 fl oz natural yogurt
- salt
- fresh coriander sprigs, to garnish
- Pulao Rice (see page 197), to serve

cook's tip

Serve the korma with poppadums, Naan Bread (see page 194), Mint Raita (see page 228) and Golden Rice with Mustard Seeds (see page 202).

1. Spread out the turmeric on a small plate and roll the prawns in it, rubbing it well in. Cover and leave to marinate in the refrigerator for 30 minutes.

2. Mix the ground coriander, chilli powder, cumin and cardamoms with enough water to make a smooth paste.

3. Heat the ghee in a large, heavy-based frying pan. Add the onion and cook over a low heat, stirring occasionally, for 10 minutes, or until golden. Stir in the Ginger Paste and spice paste and cook, stirring constantly, for 2 minutes.

4. Add the almonds, raisins, sugar and yogurt and season with salt to taste. Simmer gently for 10 minutes, or until thickened. Stir in the prawns and cook for a further 6–8 minutes, or until they have changed colour. Serve immediately with Pulao Rice, garnished with coriander.

bombay prawns

serves 4 **prep: 20 mins** **cook: 30 mins**

The important west coast city port of Bombay, now more properly known as Mumbai, is famous for its seafood cuisine.

INGREDIENTS

- 2 fresh green chillies, deseeded and chopped
- 400 g/14 oz canned tomatoes
- 4 tbsp tomato purée
- 55 g/2 oz raw or dark brown sugar
- 1 tbsp lemon juice
- 5 tbsp fresh coriander leaves, plus extra to garnish
- 2 tbsp ghee or vegetable oil
- 2 onions, chopped
- 1 tsp Garlic Paste (see page 12)
- 2 tsp ground cumin
- 2 tsp Garam Masala (see page 12)
- 2 tsp ground coriander
- 1 tsp chilli powder
- 1 tsp ground turmeric
- 6 curry leaves
- salt
- 1 kg/2 lb 4 oz raw tiger prawns, peeled and deveined
- Pulao Rice (see page 197), to serve

NUTRITIONAL INFORMATION	
Calories	337
Protein	47g
Carbohydrate	21g
Sugars	20g
Fat	8g
Saturates	1g

variation

For a special occasion, use chopped cooked lobster tail and add to the thickened sauce, but cook only for 3–4 minutes to warm through.

2

3

4

cook's tip

If using frozen prawns, thaw thoroughly in the refrigerator before cooking. They must be used on the same day.

1. Place the chillies, tomatoes, tomato purée, sugar, lemon juice and coriander leaves in a food processor and process to make a paste.

2. Heat the ghee in a large, heavy-based saucepan. Add the onions and cook over a low heat, stirring occasionally, for 10 minutes, or until golden. Stir in the Garlic Paste, cumin, Garam Masala, ground coriander, chilli powder and turmeric and cook for 2 minutes, or until the spices give off their aroma.

3. Increase the heat, stir in the tomato mixture and curry leaves, add salt to taste and bring to the boil. Reduce the heat and simmer for 10 minutes, or until the mixture is slightly thickened.

4. Add the prawns and stir to coat well in the sauce. Simmer for a further 6–8 minutes, or until they have changed colour. Serve immediately with Pulao Rice, garnished with coriander.

mussels in coconut sauce

cook: 20 mins | prep: 20 mins | serves 4

NUTRITIONAL INFORMATION	
Calories	182
Protein	10g
Carbohydrate	13g
Sugars	10g
Fat	11g
Saturates	2g

variation

Substitute 2 cooked crabs for the mussels. Add the crabmeat with the claws in Step 3 and cook until just heated through.

This quick and easy dish from the west coast of India is wonderfully aromatic and would be a good choice for a dinner party.

INGREDIENTS

- 3 tbsp ghee or vegetable oil
- 1 onion, finely chopped
- 1 tsp Garlic Paste (see page 12)
- 1 tsp Ginger Paste (see page 12)
- 1 tsp ground cumin
- 1 tsp ground coriander
- ½ tsp ground turmeric
- salt
- 600 ml/1 pint canned coconut milk
- 1 kg/2 lb 4 oz live mussels, scrubbed and debearded
- chopped fresh coriander, to garnish

1. Heat the ghee in a large, heavy-based frying pan. Add the onion and cook over a low heat, stirring occasionally, for 10 minutes, or until golden.

2. Add the Garlic Paste and Ginger Paste and cook, stirring constantly, for 2 minutes. Add the cumin, ground coriander, turmeric and a pinch of salt and cook, stirring constantly, for a further 2 minutes. Stir in the coconut milk and bring to the boil.

3. Add the mussels, cover and cook for 5 minutes, or until the mussels have opened. Discard any mussels that remain shut. Transfer the mussels, with the coconut sauce, to a large, warmed serving dish. Sprinkle with chopped coriander and serve immediately.

cook's tip

To prepare mussels, scrub them well under cold running water and pull off any beards that are still attached to them. Discard any with broken shells or that do not shut when sharply tapped.

vegetarian

As many Indians, perhaps even the majority, do not eat meat, it is hardly surprising that the country can claim to have one of the world's richest, most varied vegetarian cuisines. Humble day-to-day vegetables, such as potatoes, spinach and cauliflower, are given a complete make-over in the hands of Indian cooks in wonderful medleys, creamy combinations and both mild and fiery curries. Sometimes a single vegetable plays a starring role, as in Okra with Spices & Coconut Milk (see page 157) and Stuffed Peppers (see page 186), at other times several are combined in a lively mixture of colours, textures and flavours. Try Kashmiri Vegetables (see page 182), for example.

Beans and other pulses play an important role in the vegetarian diet, providing plenty of protein, and they make delicious and substantial curries, such as Red & White Bean Curry (see page 154). Alternatively, you can serve a dal (see pages 208–14) with vegetable dishes to ensure a balanced diet. They were, after all, made for each other.

For those who are not so strictly vegetarian that they avoid dairy products, there are some tasty recipes made with paneer, a mild, fresh-tasting Indian cheese. You can buy it from Asian food shops or make it yourself (see pages 12–13) and combine it with vegetables and flavourings for a perfectly balanced meal.

green bean & potato curry

serves 6 **prep: 15 mins** **cook: 30 mins**

You can use fresh or canned, ready-sliced green beans for this curry. An Oil-dressed Dal (see page 212) would make an excellent accompaniment, for a good contrast of flavours and colours.

INGREDIENTS

- 300 ml/10 fl oz vegetable oil
- 1 tsp white cumin seeds
- 1 tsp mixed mustard and onion seeds
- 4 dried red chillies
- 3 fresh tomatoes, sliced
- 1 tsp salt
- 1 tsp finely chopped fresh root ginger
- 1 tsp crushed fresh garlic
- 1 tsp chilli powder
- 200 g/7 oz green beans, sliced diagonally into 2.5 cm/1 inch pieces
- 2 potatoes, peeled and diced
- 300 ml/10 fl oz water

TO GARNISH

- chopped fresh coriander
- 2 finely sliced fresh green chillies

NUTRITIONAL INFORMATION	
Calories	690
Protein	3g
Carbohydrate	16g
Sugars	4g
Fat	69g
Saturates	7g

variation

If you like, substitute half of the green beans with fresh or frozen peas. Add with the potato in Step 4.

cook's tip

Mustard seeds are small brown seeds, which are often fried in ghee or vegetable oil to bring out their flavour before being combined with other ingredients.

1. Heat the vegetable oil in a large, heavy-based saucepan. Add the white cumin seeds, mustard and onion seeds and dried red chillies, stirring well.

2. Add the tomatoes to the pan and stir-fry the mixture for 3–5 minutes.

3. Mix the salt, ginger, garlic and chilli powder together in a bowl and spoon into the saucepan. Blend the whole mixture together.

4. Add the green beans and potatoes to the saucepan and stir-fry for 5 minutes.

5. Add the water to the saucepan, reduce the heat and simmer for 10–15 minutes, stirring occasionally. Transfer to a warmed serving dish, garnish with chopped coriander leaves and green chillies and serve.

mixed vegetable curry

cook: 35 mins **prep: 20 mins** **serves 4**

NUTRITIONAL INFORMATION	
Calories	273
Protein	14g
Carbohydrate	37g
Sugars	21g
Fat	10g
Saturates	2g

variation

If you like, add 1 teaspoon of lemon or lime juice to the raita, then chill in the refrigerator until ready to serve.

A vegetable curry is often served as part of a selection of dishes that may also contain meat or fish, but it also makes an excellent vegetarian meal. Here, it is served with a cooling raita.

INGREDIENTS

- 175 g/6 oz okra
- 2 tbsp ghee or vegetable oil
- 1 onion, sliced
- 1 tsp Garlic Paste (see page 12)
- 1 tsp Ginger Paste (see page 12)
- 2 tsp ground cumin
- 2 tsp ground coriander
- 400 g/14 oz canned tomatoes
- 150 ml/5 fl oz Basic Vegetable Stock (see page 13) or water
- 1 small cauliflower, broken into florets
- 2 potatoes, diced
- 2 carrots, sliced
- 2 courgettes, sliced
- 1 fresh green chilli, chopped
- salt
- fresh curry leaves, to garnish

TOMATO & CUCUMBER RAITA

- 300 ml/10 fl oz natural yogurt
- 1 cucumber, peeled and diced
- 2 tomatoes, diced
- 1 small onion, finely chopped
- 1 tsp ground cumin
- salt
- 1 tbsp ghee or vegetable oil
- 1 tsp black mustard seeds

cook's tip

Raitas are versatile side dishes because they can be served with any Indian meal to cool down the hotness of the chillies. The natural yogurt is also very good for calming upset stomachs.

1. To make the raita, mix the yogurt, cucumber, tomatoes, onion and cumin together in a serving bowl and season with salt to taste. Heat the ghee in a small frying pan. Add the mustard seeds and cook over a low heat, stirring constantly, for 1–2 minutes, or until they give off their aroma. Sprinkle the seeds over the raita and chill until ready to serve.

2. For the curry, cut the okra into 2.5-cm/1-inch lengths and reserve. Heat the ghee in a large, heavy-based saucepan. Add the onion and cook over a low heat, stirring occasionally, for 5 minutes, or until softened. Stir in the Garlic Paste, Ginger Paste, cumin and ground coriander and cook, stirring constantly, for 2 minutes, or until the spices give off their aroma.

3. Add the tomatoes, Stock, cauliflower, potatoes, carrots, courgettes, chilli and okra and season with salt to taste. Stir well, breaking up the tomatoes with a wooden spoon, then cover and simmer for 25 minutes, or until the vegetables are tender. Transfer to a warmed dish, garnish with curry leaves and serve with the raita.

red & white bean curry

serves 4 | **prep: 20 mins, plus 4 hrs soaking** | **cook: 2 hrs 30 mins**

Because of their high protein content and the fact that they are filling, beans form an important part of a vegetarian diet in India.

NUTRITIONAL INFORMATION

Calories	274
Protein	15g
Carbohydrate	35g
Sugars	8g
Fat	9g
Saturates	1g

INGREDIENTS

- 85 g/3 oz red kidney beans
- 85 g/3 oz haricot beans
- 55 g/2 oz black-eyed beans
- 2 tbsp ghee or vegetable oil
- 1 tsp black mustard seeds
- 1 tsp cumin seeds
- 1 onion, finely chopped
- 1 tsp Garlic Paste (see page 12)
- 1 tsp Ginger Paste (see page 12)
- 2 tbsp Curry Paste (see page 12)
- 2 fresh green chillies, deseeded and chopped
- 400 g/14 oz canned tomatoes
- 2 tbsp tomato purée
- 125–150 ml/4–5 fl oz water (optional)
- salt
- 2 tbsp chopped fresh coriander, plus extra to garnish

variation

You can make this curry with most types of dried bean, such as aduki, cannellini and flageolet. A mixture of different colours looks attractive.

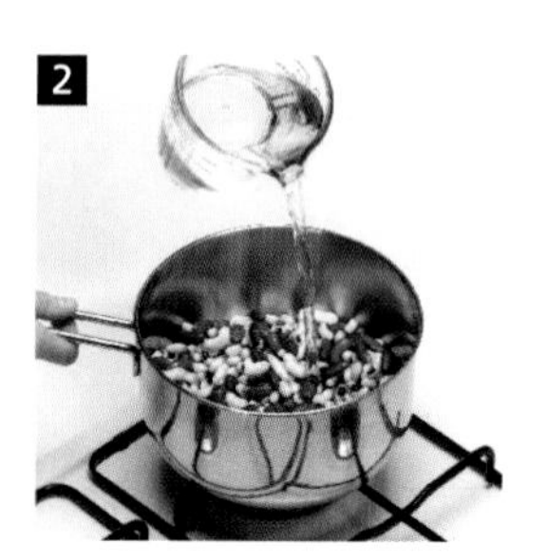

cook's tip

Red kidney beans and black-eyed beans contain a toxin that is destroyed by cooking. This is why it is important that the beans are boiled vigorously for 15 minutes to begin with.

1. Place all the beans in a large bowl, add enough cold water to cover and leave to soak for at least 4 hours or overnight.

2. Drain the beans and place in a large, heavy-based saucepan. Add enough cold water to cover and bring to the boil over a high heat. Boil vigorously for 15 minutes, then reduce the heat, cover and simmer for 1½ hours, or until the beans are tender.

3. Heat the ghee in a separate large saucepan. Add the mustard seeds and cumin seeds and cook over a low heat, stirring, for 2 minutes, or until they give off their aroma. Add the onion and cook, stirring frequently, for 5 minutes, or until softened. Add the Garlic Paste, Ginger Paste, Curry Paste and chillies and cook, stirring, for 2 minutes. Stir in the tomatoes and their can juices and the tomato purée. If the sauce seems thick, add the water. Break up the tomatoes with a wooden spoon. Season with salt to taste and simmer for 5 minutes.

4. Drain the beans and add them to the sauce, then stir in the chopped coriander. Cover and simmer for a further 30 minutes, or until the beans are tender and the sauce has thickened. Garnish with extra chopped coriander and serve immediately.

lobia curry

serves 4

prep: 20 mins, plus 4 hrs soaking

cook: 2 hrs

This fragrant curry is made with black-eyed beans, which originated in Asia and became one of the most popular pulses in Indian cuisine. It can be served hot or cold

INGREDIENTS

225 g/8 oz black-eyed beans
4 tbsp ghee or vegetable oil
1 onion, chopped
1 tsp Garlic Paste (see page 12)
1 tsp Ginger Paste (see page 12)
1 tsp ground coriander
1 tsp chilli powder
¼ tsp ground turmeric
1 cinnamon stick
1 bay leaf
200 g/7 oz canned tomatoes
2 fresh green chillies, chopped
salt
2 tbsp chopped fresh coriander

NUTRITIONAL INFORMATION	
Calories	302
Protein	15g
Carbohydrate	35g
Sugars	5g
Fat	13g
Saturates	2g

cook's tip

The sauce should be quite thick, but if it looks as if it might dry out, add 125–150 ml/4–5 fl oz water to keep it moist.

1. Place the beans in a large bowl, add enough cold water to cover and leave to soak for at least 4 hours or overnight.

2. Drain the beans and place them in a large, heavy-based saucepan. Add enough cold water to cover, then bring to the boil and boil vigorously for 15 minutes. Reduce the heat, cover and simmer for 1 hour.

3. Heat the ghee in a separate large saucepan. Add the onion and cook over a low heat, stirring occasionally, for 5 minutes, or until softened. Add the Garlic Paste and Ginger Paste, ground coriander, chilli powder, turmeric, cinnamon stick and bay leaf and cook, stirring constantly, for 2 minutes. Stir in the tomatoes and their can juices, and break up with a wooden spoon. Stir in the chillies and add salt to taste.

4. Drain the beans and add to the saucepan with the chopped coriander. Cover and simmer for a further 25–30 minutes, or until the beans are tender. Serve immediately.

okra with spices & coconut milk

cook: 45–50 mins | prep: 15 mins | serves 4

Okra, known as bhindi in India, is a very popular vegetable throughout the subcontinent. The pods contain edible seeds and a sticky juice, which gives okra dishes a delectable texture.

NUTRITIONAL INFORMATION	
Calories	195
Protein	6g
Carbohydrate	19g
Sugars	16g
Fat	11g
Saturates	2g

INGREDIENTS

600 g/1 lb 5 oz okra
3 tbsp ghee or vegetable oil
2 onions, finely chopped
1 tsp Garlic Paste (see page 12)
1 tsp Ginger Paste (see page 12)
1 tsp ground coriander
1 tsp ground cumin
1 tsp paprika
½ tsp ground turmeric
½ tsp chilli powder
5 tomatoes, coarsely chopped
400 ml/14 fl oz canned coconut milk
salt

1 Cut the okra into 2.5-cm/1-inch lengths and reserve. Heat the ghee in a large, heavy-based frying pan. Add the onions and cook over a low heat, stirring occasionally, for 10 minutes, or until golden. Add the Garlic Paste and Ginger Paste and cook, stirring constantly, for 2 minutes.

2 Add the ground coriander, cumin, paprika, turmeric and chilli powder and cook, stirring constantly, for 2 minutes, or until the spices give off their aroma. Add the okra and cook, stirring, for 3 minutes.

3 Increase the heat to medium, add the tomatoes and stir in the coconut milk. Season with salt to taste and bring to the boil. reduce the heat, cover and simmer for 25–30 minutes, or until the okra is tender. Serve immediately.

cook's tip

To prepare your own coconut milk, mix together 175 g/6 oz desiccated coconut with 1 litre/1¾ pints boiling water. Leave for 1 hour. Process until nearly smooth, then sieve, squeezing out all the liquid.

okra curry

serves 4 **prep: 10 mins** **cook: 30 mins**

This is a delicious dry vegetarian curry, which should be served hot with Chapatis (see page 195). As okra is such a tasty vegetable, it does not need many spices to boost its flavour.

INGREDIENTS

450 g/1 lb okra
150 ml/5 fl oz vegetable oil
2 onions, sliced
3 fresh green chillies, finely chopped
2 curry leaves
1 tsp salt
1 tomato, sliced
2 tbsp lemon juice
2 tbsp chopped fresh coriander

NUTRITIONAL INFORMATION	
Calories	371
Protein	4g
Carbohydrate	10g
Sugars	8g
Fat	35g
Saturates	4g

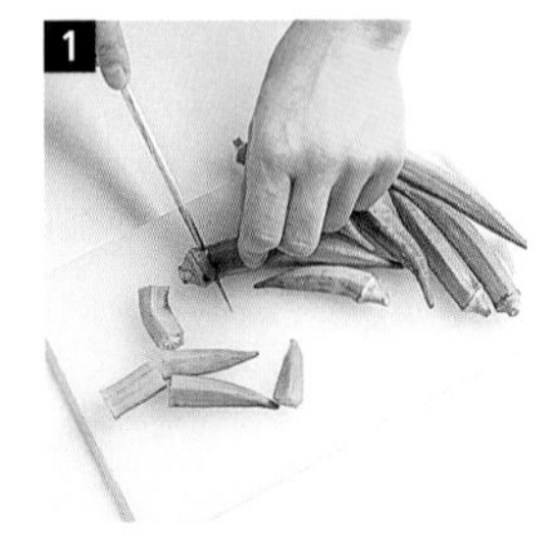

cook's tip

When topped and tailed and cut, okra have a remarkable glutinous quality which naturally thickens spicy curries and casseroles.

1 Rinse the okra and drain thoroughly. Using a sharp knife, chop and discard the ends of the okra. Cut the okra into 2.5-cm/1-inch long pieces.

2 Heat the vegetable oil in a large, heavy-based frying-pan. Add the onions, green chillies, curry leaves and salt and stir-fry for 5 minutes.

3 Gradually add the okra, mixing in gently with a slotted spoon, then stir-fry over a medium heat for 12–15 minutes.

4 Add the sliced tomato to the frying pan and sprinkle over the lemon juice sparingly.

5 Sprinkle with chopped fresh coriander, cover and leave to simmer for 3–5 minutes. Transfer to serving plates and serve hot.

dry split okra

cook: 20 mins **prep: 10 mins** **serves 4**

This is an unusual way of cooking a delicious vegetable. The dish is dry when cooked, and should be served hot with Chapatis (see page 195) and a dal, such as Oil-dressed Dal (see page 212).

NUTRITIONAL INFORMATION	
Calories	190
Protein	3g
Carbohydrate	5g
Sugars	4g
Fat	18g
Saturates	2g

INGREDIENTS

450 g/1 lb okra

150 ml/5 fl oz vegetable oil

100 g/3½ oz dried onions

2 tsp aamchoor (dried mango powder)

1 tsp ground cumin

1 tsp chilli powder

1 tsp salt

1 Prepare the okra by cutting the ends off and discarding them. Carefully split the okra down the centre without cutting through completely.

2 Heat the vegetable oil in a large, heavy-based saucepan. Add the dried onions and fry until crisp. Remove the onions with a slotted spoon and leave to drain thoroughly on kitchen paper.

3 When cool enough to handle, roughly tear the dried onions and place in a large bowl. Add the aamchoor, ground cumin, chilli powder and salt and blend well. Spoon the onion and spice mixture into the split okra.

4 Reheat the vegetable oil in the saucepan. Gently add the okra to the hot oil and cook over a low heat for 10–12 minutes. Transfer the cooked okra to a serving dish and serve immediately.

cook's tip

Ground cumin has a warm, pungent, aromatic flavour and is used extensively in Indian cooking. It is an excellent storecupboard standby.

cauliflower & sweet potato curry

serves 4 **prep: 25 mins** **cook: 40 mins**

This is a delicious variation of a popular, traditional dish known as aloo gobi, full of fragrance and subtly sweet flavours.

INGREDIENTS

- 4 tbsp ghee or vegetable oil
- 2 onions, finely chopped
- 1 tsp Panch Phoran (see page 12)
- 1 cauliflower, broken into florets
- 350 g/12 oz sweet potatoes, diced
- 2 fresh green chillies, deseeded and finely chopped
- 1 tsp Ginger Paste (see page 12)
- 2 tsp paprika
- 1½ tsp ground cumin
- 1 tsp ground turmeric
- ½ tsp chilli powder
- 3 tomatoes, quartered
- 225 g/8 oz fresh or frozen peas
- 3 tbsp natural yogurt
- 225 ml/8 fl oz Basic Vegetable Stock (see page 13) or water
- salt
- 1 tsp Garam Masala (see page 12)

NUTRITIONAL INFORMATION	
Calories	307
Protein	11g
Carbohydrate	38g
Sugars	17g
Fat	14g
Saturates	2g

variation

Substitute ordinary potatoes for the sweet potatoes and omit the peas for a classic aloo gobi.

cook's tip

If you don't want to make your own Panch Phoran, you can buy it from many Asian food shops, where it may be labelled Indian five-spice mixture.

1. Heat the ghee in a large, heavy-based frying pan. Add the onions and Panch Phoran and cook over a low heat, stirring frequently, for 10 minutes, or until the onions are golden. Add the cauliflower, sweet potatoes and chillies and cook, stirring frequently, for 3 minutes.

2. Stir in the Ginger Paste, paprika, cumin, turmeric and chilli powder and cook, stirring constantly, for 3 minutes. Add the tomatoes and peas and stir in the yogurt and Stock. Season with salt to taste, cover and simmer for 20 minutes, or until the vegetables are tender.

3. Sprinkle the Garam Masala over the curry, transfer to a warmed serving dish and serve immediately.

aubergine & sweetcorn pulao

cook: 40 mins

prep: 15 mins, plus 10 mins soaking

serves 4

NUTRITIONAL INFORMATION	
Calories	669
Protein	13g
Carbohydrate	111g
Sugars	14g
Fat	20g
Saturates	2g

variation

Substitute fresh or frozen peas or broad beans for the French beans, if you prefer.

This is a complete vegetarian one-pot meal and all it requires as an accompaniment is a raita, such as Aubergine Raita (see page 228) or Tomato & Cucumber Raita (see page 153).

INGREDIENTS

- 450 g/1 lb basmati rice
- 6 tbsp ghee or vegetable oil
- 1 onion, chopped
- 2 bay leaves
- 6 cardamom pods
- 6 whole cloves
- 1 cinnamon stick
- 3 aubergines, diced
- 175 g/6 oz sweetcorn kernels, thawed if frozen and drained if canned
- 4 carrots, diced
- 55 g/2 oz French beans, cut into 5-cm/2-inch lengths
- 1 tsp Garam Masala (see page 12)
- 1 tsp chilli powder
- 1 tsp ground coriander
- ¼ tsp ground turmeric
- 1.2 litres/2 pints water
- salt

TO SERVE

- Cucumber Raita (see page 228)
- poppadums

1

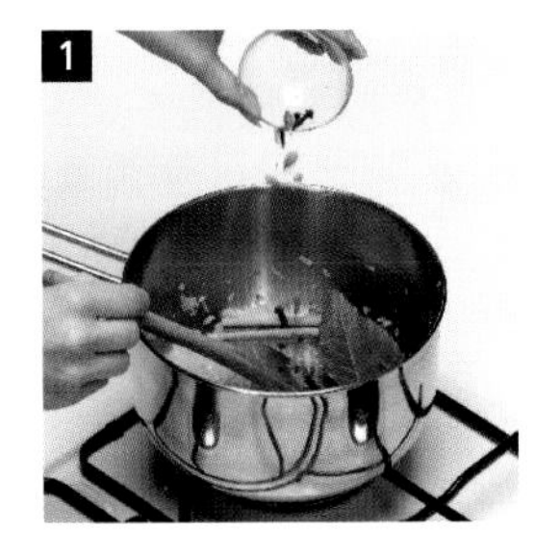

2

2

1 Rinse the rice in several changes of water and leave to soak for 10 minutes. Drain well. Meanwhile, heat the ghee in a large, heavy-based saucepan. Add the onion and cook over a low heat, stirring occasionally, for 10 minutes, or until golden. Add the bay leaves, cardamoms, cloves and cinnamon and cook, stirring constantly, for 1–2 minutes, or until the spices give off their aroma.

2 Add the aubergines, sweetcorn, carrots and beans and cook for 5 minutes. Stir in the rice, Garam Masala, chilli powder, ground coriander and turmeric and pour in the water. Add salt to taste and bring to the boil.

3 Reduce the heat, cover and cook, without stirring, for 15 minutes, or until the rice is tender. Serve immediately.

cook's tip

It is not essential to soak the rice if your time is limited, but it does help to lighten the grain. However, it is essential to rinse the rice as this helps to remove the starch.

aubergine curry

serves 4 **prep: 20 mins, plus 30 mins soaking/standing** **cook: 35 mins**

Three favourite ingredients of southern Indian cuisine feature in this rich vegetable curry – aubergines, coconut and yellow mustard seeds. Red chillies are also more popular in dishes from this region than they are in dishes from the north.

NUTRITIONAL INFORMATION	
Calories	214
Protein	5g
Carbohydrate	34g
Sugars	31g
Fat	8g
Saturates	5g

INGREDIENTS

- 40 g/1½ oz dried tamarind, roughly chopped
- 125 ml/4 fl oz boiling water
- 2 large aubergines, sliced
- salt
- 2 tbsp ghee or vegetable oil
- 3 onions, sliced
- 1 tsp Garlic Paste (see page 12)
- 1 tsp Ginger Paste (see page 12)
- 4 curry leaves
- 1 fresh green chilli, deseeded and finely chopped
- 2 fresh red chillies, deseeded and finely chopped
- 1 tbsp ground coriander
- 2 tsp cumin seeds
- 2 tsp yellow mustard seeds
- 2 tbsp tomato purée
- 500 ml/18 fl oz canned coconut milk
- 3 tbsp chopped fresh coriander, plus extra to garnish

variation

Complete Step 3 in a casserole, add the tamarind liquid, coconut milk and aubergines and cook at 200°/400°F/Gas Mark 6 for 30 minutes.

1

3

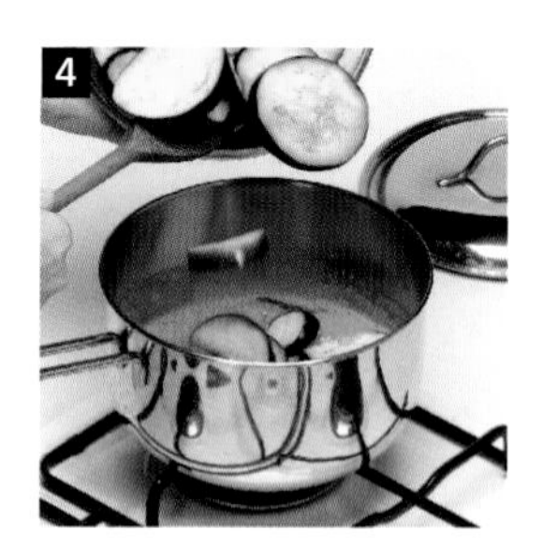
4

cook's tip

Most contemporary varieties of aubergine no longer need salting to remove the bitter juices. However, doing so stops the vegetable from becoming too soggy.

1. Place the dried tamarind in a bowl, add the boiling water and stir. Leave to soak for 30 minutes. Meanwhile, place the aubergine slices in a colander, sprinkling each layer with salt. Leave to drain for 30 minutes.

2. Sieve the tamarind into bowl, pressing down on the pulp with the back of a wooden spoon. Discard the contents of the sieve. Rinse the aubergine slices under cold running water and pat dry with kitchen paper.

3. Heat the ghee in a large saucepan. Add the onions and cook over a low heat, stirring occasionally, for 10 minutes, or until golden. Stir in the Garlic Paste and Ginger Paste and cook, stirring constantly, for 2 minutes. Add the curry leaves, green and red chillies, ground coriander, cumin and mustard seeds and tomato purée and cook, stirring constantly, for 2 minutes, or until the spices give off their aroma.

4. Add the tamarind liquid and coconut milk and bring to the boil. Add the aubergine slices, cover and simmer for 12–15 minutes, or until the aubergine is tender. Uncover the pan and simmer for a further 5 minutes, or until the sauce has thickened. Stir in the chopped coriander, sprinkle the extra chopped herb on top and serve immediately.

aubergines & yogurt

serves 4

prep: 10 mins, plus 30 mins cooling

cook: 55 mins

This is an unusual dish, in that the aubergine is first baked in the oven, then cooked in a saucepan. Serve the aubergines with plain boiled rice or Pulao Rice (see page 197) for a filling supper.

INGREDIENTS

2 aubergines
4 tbsp vegetable oil
1 onion, sliced
1 tsp white cumin seeds
1 tsp chilli powder
1 tsp salt
3 tbsp natural yogurt
½ tsp mint sauce
fresh mint leaves, chopped, to garnish

NUTRITIONAL INFORMATION	
Calories	140
Protein	3g
Carbohydrate	6g
Sugars	5g
Fat	12g
Saturates	1g

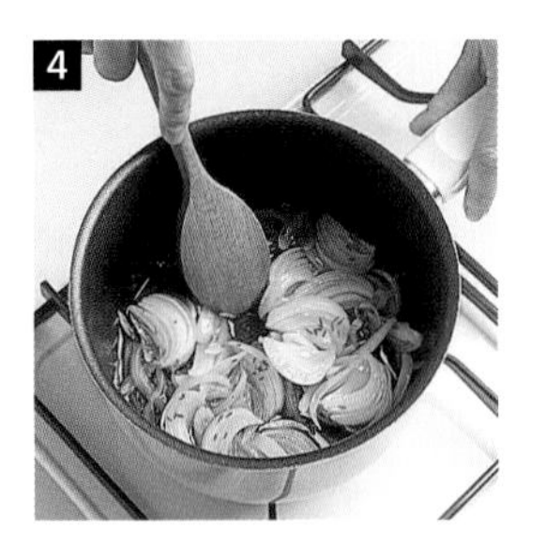

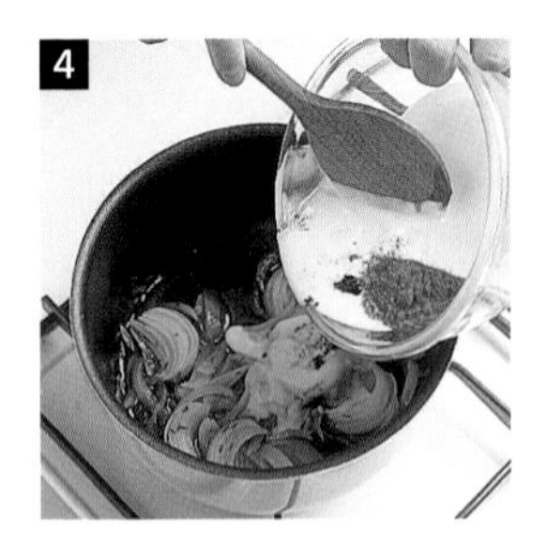

cook's tip

Rich in protein and calcium, yogurt plays an important part in Indian cooking. Thick natural yogurt most closely resembles the yogurt made in many Indian homes.

1. Preheat the oven to 160°C/325°F/Gas Mark 3. Rinse the aubergines under cold running water and pat dry with kitchen paper.

2. Place the aubergines in an ovenproof dish. Bake in the preheated oven for 45 minutes. Remove the baked aubergines from the oven and leave to cool.

3. Using a spoon, scoop out the aubergine flesh and reserve.

4. Heat the vegetable oil in a large, heavy-based saucepan. Add the onions and cumin seeds and fry, stirring, for 1–2 minutes. Add the chilli powder, salt, yogurt and the mint sauce to the saucepan and stir well to mix.

5. Add the aubergines to the onion and yogurt mixture and stir-fry for 5–7 minutes, or until all of the liquid has been absorbed and the mixture is quite dry.

6. Transfer the aubergine and yogurt mixture to a serving dish and garnish with chopped fresh mint leaves.

chickpea curry

cook: 20 mins **prep: 10 mins** **serves 4**

This curry is very popular among the many vegetarian people in India. There are many different ways of cooking chickpeas, but this version is probably one of the most delicious.

NUTRITIONAL INFORMATION	
Calories	313
Protein	8g
Carbohydrate	29g
Sugars	5g
Fat	19g
Saturates	2g

INGREDIENTS

6 tbsp vegetable oil
2 onions, sliced
1 tsp finely chopped fresh root ginger
1 tsp ground cumin
1 tsp ground coriander
1 tsp fresh garlic, crushed
1 tsp chilli powder
2 fresh green chillies
2–3 tbsp fresh coriander leaves
150 ml/5 fl oz water
1 large potato
400 g/14 oz canned chickpeas, drained
1 tbsp lemon juice

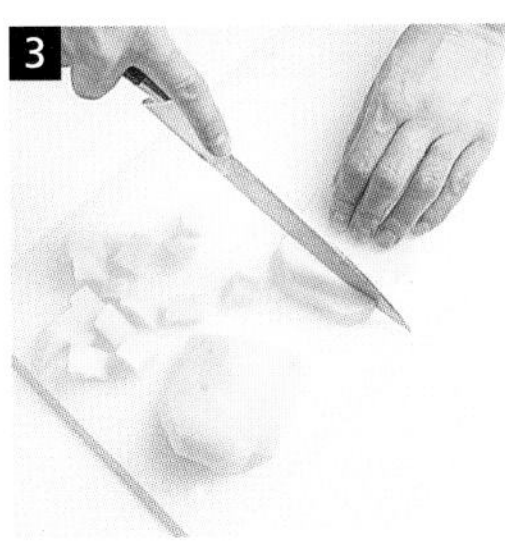

1 Heat the vegetable oil in a large, heavy-based saucepan. Add the onions and fry, stirring occasionally, until golden. Reduce the heat, add the ginger, ground cumin, ground coriander, garlic, chilli powder, fresh green chillies and fresh coriander leaves and stir-fry for 2 minutes.

2 Add the water to the mixture in the saucepan and stir to mix.

3 Using a sharp knife, cut the potato into dice, then add with the chickpeas to the saucepan. Cover and leave to simmer, stirring occasionally, for 5–7 minutes.

4 Sprinkle the lemon juice over the curry. Transfer the chickpea curry to serving dishes and serve hot.

cook's tip

Using canned chickpeas saves time, but drain and rinse before using. However, you can use dried chickpeas, if you prefer. First, soak them overnight, then boil them for 15–20 minutes, or until soft.

dumplings in yogurt sauce

serves 4 **prep: 35 mins** **cook: 35 mins**

Gram flour is used to flavour and thicken the sauce in this recipe, and a baghaar (seasoned oil dressing) is added just before serving.

NUTRITIONAL INFORMATION	
Calories	719
Protein	9g
Carbohydrate	38g
Sugars	9g
Fat	60g
Saturates	7g

INGREDIENTS

DUMPLINGS

100 g/3½ oz gram flour
1 tsp chilli powder
salt
½ tsp bicarbonate of soda
1 onion, finely chopped
2 fresh green chillies, deseeded and chopped
2–3 tbsp fresh coriander leaves
150 ml/5 fl oz water
300 ml/10 fl oz vegetable oil

YOGURT SAUCE

300 ml/10 fl oz natural yogurt
3 tbsp gram flour
150 ml/5 fl oz water
1 tsp chopped fresh root ginger
1 tsp crushed fresh garlic
1½ tsp chilli powder
½ tsp ground turmeric
1 tsp ground coriander
1 tsp ground cumin
1½ tsp salt

SEASONED DRESSING

150 ml/5 fl oz vegetable oil
1 tsp white cumin seeds
6 dried red chillies, deseeded and chopped

variation

If you prefer, remove the seeds from the green chillies before chopping and adding to the dumpling mix.

1

1

2

cook's tip

Take care when adding the dumplings to hot oil in the frying pan as it may splutter. Do not leave the frying pan unattended.

1 To make the dumplings, sieve the gram flour into a large bowl. Add the chilli powder, salt, bicarbonate of soda, onion, green chillies and coriander and mix together. Add the water and mix to form a thick paste. Heat the vegetable oil in a heavy-based frying pan. Place teaspoonfuls of the paste in the hot oil and fry, turning once, over a medium heat, until a crisp golden brown. reserve until required.

2 To make the sauce, place the yogurt in a bowl and whisk with the gram flour and the water. Add the ginger, garlic, chilli powder, turmeric, ground coriander, cumin and salt and mix well.

3 Push this mixture through a large sieve into a saucepan. Bring to the boil over a low heat, stirring constantly. If the yogurt sauce becomes too thick, add a little extra water.

4 Pour the sauce into a deep serving dish and arrange all of the dumplings on top. Keep warm.

5 To make the dressing, heat the vegetable oil in a frying pan. Add the white cumin seeds and the dried red chillies and fry until darker in colour. Pour the dressing over the dumplings and serve hot.

courgettes & fenugreek seeds

serves 4 **prep: 20 mins** **cook: 15 mins**

This delicious vegetable curry contains fenugreek seeds, which have a beautiful aroma and a very distinctive taste.

INGREDIENTS

- 6 tbsp vegetable oil
- 1 onion, finely chopped
- 3 fresh green chillies, finely chopped
- 1 tsp finely chopped fresh root, ginger
- 1 tsp crushed fresh garlic
- 1 tsp chilli powder
- 450 g/1 lb courgettes, sliced
- 2 tomatoes, sliced
- 2 tsp fenugreek seeds
- fresh coriander leaves, to garnish

NUTRITIONAL INFORMATION	
Calories	188
Protein	3g
Carbohydrate	6g
Sugars	5g
Fat	17g
Saturates	2g

1

2

2

1 Heat the oil in a large frying pan. Add the onion, green chillies, ginger, garlic and chilli powder to the frying pan, stirring well.

2 Add the courgettes and tomatoes to the frying pan and stir-fry for 5–7 minutes.

3 Add the fenugreek seeds to the courgette mixture in the frying pan and stir-fry for a further 5 minutes.

4 Remove the frying pan from the heat and transfer the courgette and fenugreek seed mixture to warmed serving dishes. Garnish with coriander leaves and serve hot.

cook's tip

Both the leaves and seeds of fenugreek are used, but the stalks and root should be discarded, as they taste bitter. Fresh fenugreek is sold in bunches. Fenugreek seeds are flat and yellowish brown.

green pumpkin curry

cook: 30 mins **prep: 10 mins** **serves 4**

The Indian pumpkin used in this curry is long and green and sold by weight. It can easily be bought from any Asian food shop.

NUTRITIONAL INFORMATION	
Calories	347
Protein	2g
Carbohydrate	8g
Sugars	6g
Fat	34g
Saturates	4g

INGREDIENTS

150 ml/5 fl oz vegetable oil
2 onions, sliced
½ tsp white cumin seeds
450 g/1 lb green pumpkin, cubed
1 tsp aamchoor (dried mango powder)
1 tsp finely chopped fresh root ginger
1 tsp crushed fresh garlic
1 tsp crushed red chilli
½ tsp salt
300 ml/10 fl oz water
Chapatis (see page 195), to serve

1

2

3

1 Heat the vegetable oil in a large, heavy-based frying pan. Add the onions and cumin seeds and fry, stirring occasionally, for 5–6 minutes, until a light golden brown colour.

2 Add the pumpkin to the frying pan and stir-fry for 3–5 minutes over a low heat.

3 Mix the aamchoor, ginger, garlic, chilli and salt together in a bowl. Add the spice mixture to the onion mixture and stir well.

4 Add the water, cover and cook over a low heat for 10–15 minutes, stirring occasionally. Transfer the curry to serving plates and serve hot with Chapatis.

cook's tip

Cumin seeds are popular with Indian cooks because of their warm, pungent flavour and aroma. The seeds are sold whole or ground, and are usually included as one of the flavourings in Garam Masala.

potato & pepper curry

serves 4 **prep: 15 mins** **cook: 20 mins**

This is a very quick vegetarian dish that makes an excellent light meal served with a helping of Naan Bread (see page 194).

INGREDIENTS

- 3 tbsp ghee or vegetable oil
- 1 onion, chopped
- 2 potatoes, cut into large chunks
- 1 tsp chilli powder
- 1 tsp ground coriander
- ¼ tsp ground turmeric
- 2 green peppers, deseeded and cubed
- 225 g/8 oz fresh or frozen broad beans
- 200 g/7 oz canned tomatoes
- 2 fresh green chillies, roughly chopped
- 1 tbsp chopped fresh coriander
- 125 ml/4 fl oz Basic Vegetable Stock (see page 13) or water
- salt
- Naan Bread (see page 194), to serve

NUTRITIONAL INFORMATION	
Calories	199
Protein	7g
Carbohydrate	24g
Sugars	7g
Fat	10g
Saturates	1g

cook's tip

Indian Vegetable Stock (see page 13) works particularly well with this dish – substitute it for the Basic Vegetable Stock for a more spicy taste.

1. Heat the ghee in a large, heavy-based saucepan. Add the onion and cook over a low heat, stirring occasionally, for 5 minutes, or until softened. Add the potatoes and cook, stirring occasionally, for 5 minutes.

2. Add the chilli powder, ground coriander and turmeric and stir well, then add the green peppers, broad beans and the tomatoes and their can juices, breaking up the tomatoes slightly with a wooden spoon.

3. Stir in the chillies and chopped coriander, pour in the Stock and season with salt to taste. Cover and simmer for 8–10 minutes, or until the potatoes are tender. Serve immediately.

spiced potatoes & spinach

cook: 40 mins | **prep: 15 mins** | **serves 4**

Known as aloo saag, this is a favourite dish in many Indian restaurants in the West – rightly so, as it is absolutely delicious.

NUTRITIONAL INFORMATION	
Calories	258
Protein	8g
Carbohydrate	42g
Sugars	7g
Fat	8g
Saturates	1g

INGREDIENTS

- **500 g/1 lb 2 oz fresh spinach leaves**
- **2 tbsp ghee or vegetable oil**
- **1 tsp black mustard seeds**
- **1 onion, halved and sliced**
- **1 tsp Ginger Paste (see page 12)**
- **1 tsp Garlic Paste (see page 12)**
- **900 g/2 lb waxy potatoes, cut into small chunks**
- **1 tsp chilli powder**
- **125 ml/4 fl oz Basic Vegetable Stock (see page 13) or water**
- **salt**

1

2

3

1 Bring a large saucepan of water to the boil. Add the spinach leaves and blanch for 4 minutes. Drain well, then tip into a clean tea towel, roll up and squeeze out the excess liquid.

2 Heat the ghee in a separate saucepan. Add the mustard seeds and cook over a low heat, stirring constantly, for 2 minutes, or until they give off their aroma. Add the onion, Ginger Paste and Garlic Paste and cook, stirring frequently, for 5 minutes, or until softened.

3 Add the potatoes, chilli powder and Vegetable Stock and season with salt to taste. Bring to the boil, cover and cook for 10 minutes. Add the spinach and stir it in, then cover and simmer for a further 10 minutes, or until the potatoes are tender. Serve immediately.

cook's tip

Mustard seeds are most commonly used for flavouring vegetable dishes and dals. They have a slightly nutty taste that is released on being cooked in hot oil.

paneer with spinach

cook: 25 mins **prep: 15 mins** **serves 4**

NUTRITIONAL INFORMATION	
Calories	191
Protein	12g
Carbohydrate	9g
Sugars	7g
Fat	12g
Saturates	3g

variation

If paneer is not available, use halloumi cheese instead. While not authentic, it is a good cheese for frying, but do not let it cool or it will become rubbery.

Spinach and cheese is a classic combination in many countries of the world, each partnering the vegetable with a local or home-produced cheese. India is no exception.

INGREDIENTS

- **500 g/1 lb 2 oz fresh spinach leaves**
- **3 tbsp ghee or vegetable oil**
- **225 g/8 oz Paneer (see pages 12–13), diced**
- **1 onion, finely chopped**
- **1 tsp Ginger Paste (see page 12)**
- **200 g/7 oz canned tomatoes, drained**
- **1 tsp ground coriander**
- **1 tsp chilli powder**
- **¼ tsp ground turmeric**
- **1 tbsp lemon juice**
- **salt**
- **butter, to serve**

cook's tip

If using home-made Paneer (see pages 12–13), make it the day before, so it has time to firm up slightly. Otherwise, buy it from Asian food shops, which sell a vacuum-packed, long-life version.

1. Bring a large saucepan of water to the boil. Add the spinach leaves and blanch for 4–5 minutes. Drain well, reserving the cooking water. Chop the spinach finely or process until smooth in a food processor.

2. Heat the ghee in a heavy-based frying pan. Add the Paneer and cook, turning frequently, for 3 minutes, or until lightly browned. Remove with a slotted spoon and drain on kitchen paper.

3. Add the onion to the frying pan and cook over a low heat, stirring occasionally, for 5 minutes, or until softened. Stir in the Ginger Paste and cook, stirring constantly, for a further 2 minutes.

4. Add the tomatoes and break up with a wooden spoon, then stir in the ground coriander, chilli powder and turmeric. Cook, stirring constantly, for 2–3 minutes. Return the Paneer to the frying pan and add the spinach and lemon juice. Season with salt to taste. Cover and cook for a further 3–4 minutes. If the mixture is too dry, add 1–2 tablespoons of the reserved spinach cooking liquid. Serve immediately dotted with a little butter.

paneer with mushrooms & yogurt

serves 4 **prep: 15 mins** **cook: 15 mins** 

Served with Parathas (see page 215) or Sheermal (see page 207), this is a filling one-pot dish that smells lovely and tastes delicious.

NUTRITIONAL INFORMATION	
Calories	261
Protein	13g
Carbohydrate	13g
Sugars	9g
Fat	18g
Saturates	2g

INGREDIENTS

- 5 tbsp ghee or vegetable oil
- 225 g/8 oz Paneer (see pages 12–13), diced
- 1 onion, roughly chopped
- 2 bunches of fresh coriander, roughly chopped
- leaves of 1 fresh mint sprig, roughly chopped
- 2 garlic cloves, halved
- 2.5-cm/1-inch piece fresh root ginger, roughly chopped
- 2 fresh green chillies, deseeded and halved
- 1 tsp chilli powder
- 1 tsp Garam Masala (see page 12)
- ½ tsp ground turmeric
- 225 g/8 oz button mushrooms, halved
- 225 g/8 oz French beans, cut into 5-cm/2-inch lengths
- 1 tsp cornflour
- 175 ml/6 fl oz natural yogurt
- salt

variation

You can use other vegetables instead of the French beans. Try fresh or frozen broad beans or peas. If using frozen, thaw and drain first.

cook's tip

If the Paneer is too fresh to dice neatly, break it into small lumps with your fingers, then add to the frying pan in Step 1 and cook for 1–2 minutes, or until brown.

1. Heat the ghee in a frying pan. Add the Paneer and cook, turning frequently, for 3 minutes, or until browned on all sides. Remove with a slotted spoon and drain on kitchen paper. Drain off all but about 1 tablespoon of the ghee from the frying pan, removing the frying pan from the heat.

2. Place the onion, fresh coriander, mint, garlic, ginger and chillies in a food processor and process until smooth. Alternatively, place in a mortar and grind with a pestle. Return the frying pan to the heat and stir in the coriander paste, chilli powder, Garam Masala and turmeric. Cook over a low heat, stirring constantly, for 2 minutes.

3. Add the mushrooms and beans and return the Paneer to the frying pan. Stir the cornflour into the yogurt and gradually add to the pan. Season with salt to taste. Simmer, stirring occasionally, for 10 minutes. Serve immediately.

paneer koftas

serves 4 **prep: 10 mins, plus 1 hr 20 mins cooling/chilling** **cook: 35 mins**

In this recipe, freshly made paneer is used because it crumbles easily and can be mixed in easily with the other ingredients.

NUTRITIONAL INFORMATION	
Calories	656
Protein	29g
Carbohydrate	45g
Sugars	12g
Fat	41g
Saturates	19g

INGREDIENTS

- 500 g/1 lb 2 oz floury potatoes, cut into chunks
- salt
- 500 g/1 lb 2 oz freshly made Paneer (see pages 12–13), crumbled
- 4 tbsp chopped fresh coriander
- 1 tsp ground cumin
- 2 eggs, beaten
- 55 g/2 oz plain flour, plus extra for dusting
- 6 tbsp vegetable oil

MINT & COCONUT CHUTNEY

- 2 bunches of fresh mint
- 6 tbsp desiccated coconut
- 175 ml/6 fl oz natural yogurt
- 1 tsp sesame seeds
- salt

variation

You can substitute ricotta cheese for the paneer. It is not authentic, but will have the right consistency for the dish.

cook's tip

Leftover koftas (should there be any) can be chopped and used to fill pitta breads, mixed with salad leaves and topped with the mint and coconut chutney.

1. Boil the potatoes in a large saucepan of lightly salted water for 20 minutes, or until tender. Drain well, tip into a large bowl and mash, then cool.

2. Meanwhile, make the mint and coconut chutney. Place the mint in a food processor, reserving a sprig to garnish, then add the coconut, yogurt, sesame seeds and a pinch of salt and process until smooth. Transfer to a bowl, cover with clingfilm and leave to chill in the refrigerator until cold.

3. Mix the cooled potatoes, Paneer, chopped coriander, cumin, eggs and flour together in a bowl until thoroughly combined. Season with salt to taste. Cover the bowl with clingfilm and leave to chill in the refrigerator for 30 minutes.

4. Shape heaped tablespoonfuls of potato and cheese mixture into sausages and dust lightly with flour. Heat the vegetable oil in a large, heavy-based frying pan. Add the koftas, in batches if necessary, and cook over a low heat for 10–15 minutes, turning frequently, until lightly browned all over. Remove with a slotted spoon and drain on kitchen paper. Serve immediately with the mint and coconut chutney.

mixed vegetables

cook: 45 mins | prep: 5 mins | serves 4

NUTRITIONAL INFORMATION	
Calories	669
Protein	7g
Carbohydrate	36g
Sugars	17g
Fat	57g
Saturates	8g

variation

Replace the cauliflower with broccoli, cut into florets, potatoes with sweet potatoes and green chillies with red chillies, if you like.

You can make this dish with any vegetables you have to hand. Serve with plain boiled rice, Naan Bread (see page 194) and Aubergine Raita (see page 228), if you like.

INGREDIENTS

300 ml/10 fl oz vegetable oil
1 tsp mustard seeds
1 tsp onion seeds
½ tsp white cumin seeds
3–4 curry leaves, chopped
450 g/1 lb onions, finely chopped
3 tomatoes, chopped
½ red pepper, deseeded and sliced
½ green pepper, deseeded and sliced
1 tsp finely chopped fresh root ginger
1 tsp crushed fresh garlic
1 tsp chilli powder
¼ tsp ground turmeric
1 tsp salt
425 ml/15 fl oz water
2 potatoes, peeled and cut into pieces
½ cauliflower, cut into small florets
4 carrots, sliced
3 fresh green chillies, finely chopped
2–3 tbsp fresh coriander leaves
1 tbsp lemon juice
freshly cooked rice, to serve

1

2

3

cook's tip

Curry leaves are similar in appearance to bay leaves, but have a very different flavour. They are available dried or sometimes fresh from Asian food shops.

1 Heat the vegetable oil in a large, heavy-based saucepan. Add the mustard seeds, onion seeds and white cumin seeds with the curry leaves and fry until they turn a darker colour.

2 Add the onions to the saucepan and fry over a medium heat for 8 minutes, until golden.

3 Add the tomatoes and peppers and stir-fry for 5 minutes. Add the ginger, garlic, chilli powder, turmeric and salt and mix well.

4 Add 300 ml/10 fl oz of the water, cover and simmer for 10–12 minutes, stirring occasionally.

5 Add the potatoes, cauliflower, carrots, green chillies and coriander leaves and stir-fry for 5 minutes. Add the remaining water and lemon juice, and stir well. Cover and leave to simmer for 15 minutes, stirring occasionally. Transfer the mixed vegetables to serving plates and serve with rice.

kashmiri vegetables

serves 4 **prep: 20 mins** **cook: 30 mins**

This is a richly flavoured, mixed vegetable curry from northern India, and would be a great choice for a vegetarian dinner party. Serve with boiled rice or Indian bread and a mixed salad.

INGREDIENTS

3 tbsp ghee or vegetable oil
2 tbsp flaked almonds
8 cardamom seeds
8 black peppercorns
2 tsp cumin seeds
1 cinnamon stick
2 fresh green chillies, deseeded and chopped
1 tsp Ginger Paste (see page 12)
1 tsp chilli powder
3 potatoes, cut into chunks
salt
225 g/8 oz okra cut into 2.5-cm/1-inch pieces
½ cauliflower, broken into florets
150 ml/5 fl oz natural yogurt
150 ml/5 fl oz Basic Vegetable Stock (see page 13) or water
freshly cooked rice, to serve

NUTRITIONAL INFORMATION	
Calories	232
Protein	9g
Carbohydrate	26g
Sugars	6g
Fat	12g
Saturates	2g

variation

Use sweet potatoes instead of ordinary potatoes to give the dish a delicately sweet flavour.

2

3

4

cook's tip

When cooking the flaked almonds, keep a sharp eye open, as they can burn very easily. Make sure the heat is very low and stir constantly.

1 Heat 1 tablespoon of the ghee in a heavy-based saucepan. Add the almonds and cook over a low heat, stirring constantly, for 2 minutes, or until golden. Remove from the saucepan with a slotted spoon, drain on kitchen paper and reserve.

2 Place the cardamom seeds, peppercorns, cumin seeds and cinnamon stick in a spice grinder or mortar and grind finely.

3 Add the remaining vegetable oil to the saucepan and heat. Add the chillies and cook, stirring frequently, for 2 minutes. Stir in the Ginger Paste, chilli powder and ground spices and cook, stirring constantly, for 2 minutes, or until they give off their aroma.

4 Add the potatoes, season with salt to taste, cover and cook, stirring occasionally, for 8 minutes. Add the okra and cauliflower and cook for a further 5 minutes. Gradually stir in the yogurt and Stock and bring to the boil. Cover and simmer for a further 10 minutes, until all the vegetables are tender. Serve with rice, garnished with the flaked almonds.

balti vegetables

cook: 30 mins | **prep: 20 mins** | **serves 4**

NUTRITIONAL INFORMATION	
Calories	252
Protein	8g
Carbohydrate	33g
Sugars	15g
Fat	11g
Saturates	1g

variation

This is a very mildly spiced dish. If you like a hotter flavour, add 2 chopped fresh green chillies with the Garlic and Ginger Pastes in Step 1.

The great thing about this dish is that you can use whatever vegetables you happen to have at hand, providing that you have a fairly colourful and attractive mix.

INGREDIENTS

3 tbsp ghee or vegetable oil
1 onion, chopped
1 tsp Garlic Paste (see page 12)
1 tsp Ginger Paste (see page 12)
2 tsp ground coriander
1 tsp chilli powder
½ tsp ground turmeric
½ cauliflower, broken into florets
2 potatoes, diced
2 carrots, diced
115 g/4 oz frozen peas, thawed
1 small swede, diced
115 g/4 oz French beans, cut into 5-cm/2-inch pieces
55 g/2 oz sweetcorn kernels, thawed if frozen
4 tomatoes, peeled and chopped
salt
4–8 tbsp Basic Vegetable Stock (see page 13) or water
fresh coriander sprigs, to garnish

1

2

3

cook's tip

Sun-ripened tomatoes are sweeter and much more flavoursome than those grown under glass or in polytunnels. Look for labels in supermarkets or buy tomatoes still on the vine.

1 Heat the ghee in a large saucepan. Add the onion and cook over a low heat, stirring occasionally, for 10 minutes, or until golden. Stir in the Garlic Paste and Ginger Paste and cook for 1 minute. Add the ground coriander, chilli powder and turmeric and cook, stirring, for 2 minutes, or until the spices give off their aroma.

2 Add the cauliflower, potatoes, carrots, peas, swede, French beans and sweetcorn and cook, stirring, for a further 3 minutes. Add the tomatoes, add salt to taste and pour in 4 tablespoons of the Vegetable Stock.

3 Cover and simmer for 10 minutes, or until all the vegetables are tender. Check the mixture while it is cooking and if the vegetables look as if they might catch on the base of the pan, add more Stock. Serve immediately, garnished with coriander sprigs.

stuffed peppers

serves 4 **prep: 20 mins, plus 15 mins cooling** **cook: 50 mins**

Stuffed vegetables, especially peppers and tomatoes, not only taste terrific, but they also look wonderful too. Serve with Tomato Rice (see page 200) and Parathas (see page 215).

NUTRITIONAL INFORMATION	
Calories	290
Protein	6g
Carbohydrate	22g
Sugars	10g
Fat	21g
Saturates	3g

variation

Substitute other vegetables in the filling, such as broccoli, chopped mushrooms, diced courgettes and aubergine.

INGREDIENTS

- 100 ml/3½ fl oz vegetable oil
- 1 onion, finely chopped
- 1 potato, diced
- 55 g/2 oz peas, thawed if frozen
- 55 g/2 oz broad beans
- 55 g/2 oz small cauliflower florets
- 55 g/2 oz carrot, diced
- 55 g/2 oz sweetcorn kernels
- 2 tsp aamchoor (dried mango powder)
- 1 tsp Garam Masala (see page 12)
- ½ tsp chilli powder
- salt
- 4 large or 8 small green peppers

cook's tip

Chilli powder is made from dried red chillies and is usually very hot, so use with caution. It is available from most large supermarkets.

1. Preheat the oven to 160°C/325°F/Gas Mark 3. Heat 4 tablespoons of the vegetable oil in a heavy-based saucepan. Add the onion and cook over a low heat, stirring occasionally, for 5 minutes, or until softened. Add the potato and cook, stirring occasionally, for a further 5 minutes.

2. Add the peas, beans, cauliflower, carrot, sweetcorn, aamchoor, Garam Masala and chilli powder, season with salt to taste, stir well, then cover and cook for 15 minutes, or until all the vegetables are tender. Remove the saucepan from the heat and leave to cool.

3. Cut the tops off the peppers to make 'lids', then deseed. Heat the remaining vegetable oil in a frying pan and cook the peppers, turning frequently, for 3 minutes. Remove with a slotted spoon and drain on kitchen paper. Spoon the vegetable mixture into the peppers and arrange them in a single layer in an ovenproof dish. Bake in the preheated oven for 20 minutes, then serve immediately.

stuffed aubergines

serves 4 **prep: 25 mins, plus 10 mins cooling** **cook: 55 mins**

Warm, rather than extra-hot spices provide the keynote flavour to these wonderfully tender vegetable-stuffed aubergines.

NUTRITIONAL INFORMATION	
Calories	107
Protein	5g
Carbohydrate	21g
Sugars	8g
Fat	2g
Saturates	0.5g

INGREDIENTS

- 2 large aubergines
- 2 carrots, diced
- 2 potatoes, diced
- 2 courgettes, diced
- 150 ml/5 fl oz Basic Vegetable Stock (see page 13) or ½ vegetable stock cube dissolved in 150 ml/5 fl oz hot water
- ½ tsp ground coriander
- ½ tsp ground cumin, plus extra for sprinkling
- ½ tsp ground cardamom
- ½ tsp ground turmeric
- ¼ tsp ground cinnamon
- ¼ tsp cayenne pepper
- ¼ tsp ground cloves
- ¼ tsp ground mace
- 1 onion, thinly sliced
- salt
- 1 tbsp chopped fresh mint
- fresh mint sprigs to garnish

variation

Substitute large courgettes for the aubergines and prepare in the same way. Substitute 1 diced aubergine for the courgettes in the filling.

1

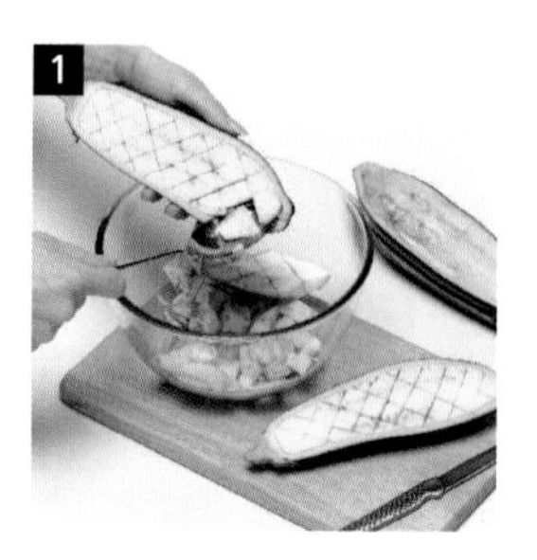

2

3

cook's tip

This is a terrific recipe for anyone following a low-fat eating plan, as steaming and simmering the vegetables is a healthy way of cooking.

1 Preheat the oven to 190°C/375°F/Gas Mark 5. Halve the aubergines lengthways and, using a sharp knife, cut all around the edges without piercing the skins. Cut a criss-cross pattern in the flesh and carefully scoop out with a spoon, leaving the shells intact. Steam the shells over a saucepan of boiling water for 5 minutes, or until tender, but not disintegrating. Remove and leave to cool. Place the carrots and potatoes in the steamer and cook for 3 minutes, then add the courgettes and cook for a further 3 minutes. Transfer the vegetables to a bowl.

2 Chop the aubergine flesh. Bring the Stock to the boil in a saucepan. Stir in the coriander, cumin, cardamom, turmeric, cinnamon, cayenne, cloves and mace and add the onion. Simmer, stirring occasionally, for 5 minutes. Add the aubergine flesh and simmer for a further 5 minutes. Stir in the carrots, potatoes and courgettes, add salt to taste and remove the saucepan from the heat. Add the mint.

3 Arrange the aubergine shells in a single layer in an ovenproof dish. Divide the vegetable mixture between them and sprinkle very lightly with a little extra ground cumin. Cover with foil and bake in the preheated oven for 30 minutes, or until tender. Serve immediately, garnished with fresh mint sprigs.

kitchiri

serves 4 **prep: 20 mins** **cook: 50 mins**

It is no coincidence that this rich and substantial rice and lentil dish has a similar sounding name to kedgeree. It is the original on which Indian cooks based the delicious smoked fish breakfast dish they prepared for British colonials in the nineteenth century.

NUTRITIONAL INFORMATION	
Calories	428
Protein	13g
Carbohydrate	66g
Sugars	4g
Fat	13g
Saturates	2g

INGREDIENTS

225 g/8 oz basmati rice
115 g/4 oz masoor dal
4 tbsp ghee or vegetable oil
1 onion, chopped
1 tsp Garlic Paste (see page 12)
4 cardamom pods
2 tsp ground coriander
2 tsp cumin seeds
2 bay leaves
2 whole cloves
1 cinnamon stick
1 litre/1¾ pints Basic Vegetable Stock (see page 13) or 1½ vegetable stock cubes dissolved in 1 litre/1¾ pints hot water
2 tbsp tomato purée
salt
2 tbsp chopped fresh mint

variation

If you like, you can stir in some diced vegetables, such as carrots and peas or beans with the dal in Step 3.

cook's tip

It is a matter of personal choice whether you remove and discard whole spices from a dish before serving. It is often better to remove bay leaves before serving, as they are easily eaten.

1. Rinse the rice in several changes of water and leave to soak for 10 minutes. Drain well. Meanwhile, place the dal in a heavy-based saucepan, add enough water to cover and bring to the boil. Reduce the heat and simmer for 20 minutes, then drain thoroughly.

2. Heat the ghee in a large, heavy-based saucepan. Add the onion and cook over a low heat, stirring occasionally, for 5 minutes, or until softened. Add the Garlic Paste and cook, stirring constantly, for 1 minute. Add the rice and stir to coat all the grains in the ghee. Stir in the cardamoms, coriander, cumin seeds, bay leaves, cloves and cinnamon stick and cook, stirring constantly, for 2 minutes, or until the spices give off their aroma.

3. Pour in the Stock, add the dal and tomato purée and season with salt to taste. Bring to the boil, then reduce the heat, cover and simmer for 20–25 minutes, or until the liquid has been absorbed and the rice and dal are tender. Stir in the mint and serve.

breads, rice & accompaniments

Bread is to the north of India what rice is to the south, although both are eaten all over the country. While most supermarkets stock a range of plain and filled Indian breads, they are both fun and satisfying to make at home. Once you get the knack, most of them are surprisingly easy, too. As rice is a staple, Indian cooks have invented a wide range of interesting ways to prepare it, both as a separate accompaniment, as in the classic Pulao Rice (see page 197), or as an integral part of the dish, as in Chicken Biryani (see page 205).

The distinction between accompanying dishes and main dishes is not a clear-cut one, as an Indian meal always consists of several dishes. Dals form an important part of vegetarian cooking because pulses are protein packed, but they are also great served with meat and fish dishes too. Salads are popular accompaniments, providing a cooling contrast to spicy curries.

No Indian table is complete without a mass of little dishes containing sauces, chutneys and pickles, all providing extra flavour or piquancy. In some ways, these are just as important as the main dishes. Recipes here include cooling and delicately flavoured Raitas (see page 228), tangy Tamarind Chutney (see page 231) and fiery Prawn Sambal (see page 227).

naan bread

serves 6–8 **prep: 35 mins, plus 1 hr 40 mins standing/rising** **cook: 10 mins**

There are many ways of making naan bread, but this particular recipe is very easy to follow. Naan bread should be served warm, preferably immediately after it has been cooked.

INGREDIENTS

1 tsp sugar
1 tsp fresh yeast
150 ml/5 fl oz warm water
200 g/7 oz plain flour, plus extra for dusting
1 tbsp ghee
1 tsp salt
50 g/1¾ oz unsalted butter, plus extra for greasing
1 tsp poppy seeds

NUTRITIONAL INFORMATION	
Calories	152
Protein	3g
Carbohydrate	20g
Sugars	1g
Fat	7g
Saturates	4g

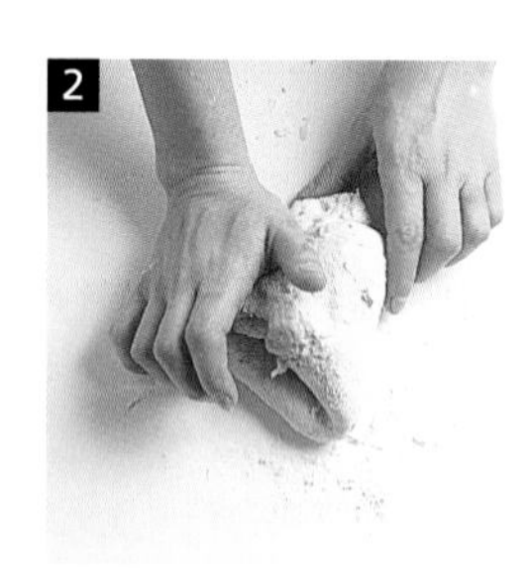

cook's tip

A tandoor oven throws out a ferocious heat; this bread is cooked on the side wall of the oven where the heat is slightly less. For an authentic effect, leave your grill on for a long time before cooking.

1. Place the sugar and yeast in a small bowl or jug, add the warm water and mix well until the yeast has dissolved. Leave to stand for 10 minutes, or until the mixture is frothy.

2. Place the flour in a large bowl. Make a well in the centre, add the ghee and salt and pour in the yeast mixture. Mix with your hands to form a dough, adding more water, if necessary. Turn out on to a lightly floured work surface and knead for 5 minutes, or until smooth.

3. Return the dough to the bowl, cover and leave to rise in a warm place for 1½ hours, or until doubled in size.

4. Preheat the grill to high, and grease a sheet of foil. Turn the dough out on to a floured work surface and knead for 2 minutes. Break off small balls with your hand and pat them into rounds 12 cm/4½ inches in diameter and 1 cm/½ inch thick.

5. Place the dough rounds on to the greased foil and cook under the very hot grill for 7–10 minutes, turning twice, brushing with the butter and sprinkling with the poppy seeds. Serve warm, or keep wrapped in foil until required.

chapati

cook: 25 mins | **prep: 20 mins, plus 20 mins resting (optional)** | **serves 8**

This is one of the less fattening Indian breads, because it contains only salt, flour and water, but some people like to brush chapatis with a little melted butter before serving.

NUTRITIONAL INFORMATION	
Calories	61
Protein	2g
Carbohydrate	13g
Sugars	0.5g
Fat	0.3g
Saturates	0g

INGREDIENTS

225 g/8 oz wholemeal flour (ata or chapati flour), plus extra for dusting

½ tsp salt

200 ml/7 fl oz water

1

1

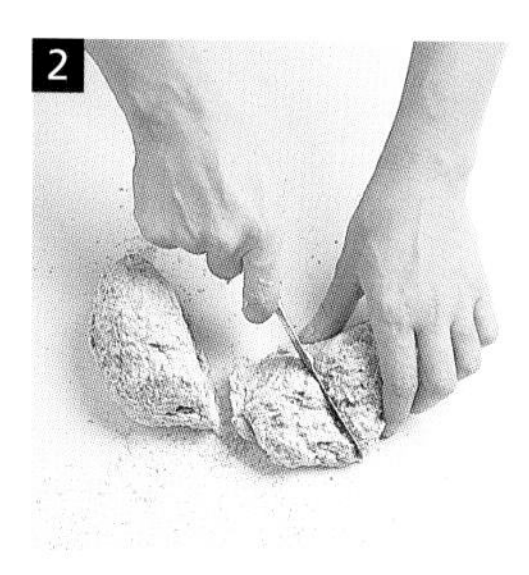

2

cook's tip

Ideally, chapatis should be eaten as they come out of the frying pan, but if that is not practical, keep them warm after cooking by wrapping them up in foil. Allow about 2 chapatis per person.

1. Place the flour in a large bowl. Add the salt and mix well. Make a well in the centre of the flour and gradually pour in the water, mixing well with your fingers to form a supple dough.

2. Knead the dough for 7–10 minutes, then cover and leave to stand for 15–20 minutes. If time is limited, roll out the dough immediately. Divide the dough into 16 equal-sized portions. Roll out each piece of dough on a well floured work surface.

3. Place a heavy-based frying pan on a high heat. When steam begins to rise from the frying pan, reduce the heat to medium.

4. Place a chapati in the frying pan and when the chapati begins to bubble turn it over. Carefully press down on the chapati with a clean tea towel or a flat spoon and turn the chapati over once again. Remove the chapati from the pan and keep warm while you make the others. Repeat the process until all of the chapatis are cooked. Serve immediately.

pooris

makes 10 **prep: 20 mins, plus 15 mins standing** **cook: 15–20 mins**

This bread is served mostly with vegetarian meals and particularly with a potato curry, such as Green Bean & Potato Curry (see page 150). Although pooris are deep-fried, they are very light.

INGREDIENTS

225 g/8 oz wholemeal flour (ata or chapati flour)
½ tsp salt
150 ml/5 fl oz water
600 ml/1 pint vegetable oil, plus extra for oiling

NUTRITIONAL INFORMATION	
Calories	165
Protein	3g
Carbohydrate	17g
Sugars	0.7g
Fat	10g
Saturates	1g

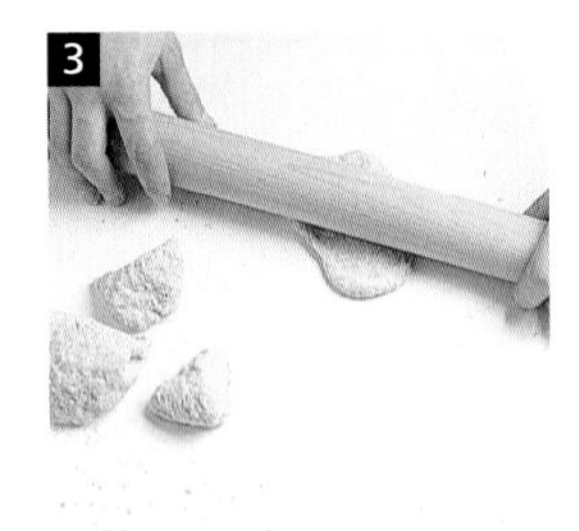

cook's tip

You can serve pooris either piled one on top of the other or spread out in a layer on a large serving platter so that they remain puffed up.

1. Place the flour and salt in a large bowl and stir well. Make a well in the centre and gradually pour in the water, mixing well with a wooden spoon to form a dough, adding more water if necessary.

2. Turn the dough out on to a floured work surface and knead until it is smooth and elastic. Leave to stand in a warm place for 15 minutes.

3. Divide the dough into 10 equal-sized portions and with lightly oiled hands pat each into a smooth ball. On a lightly oiled work surface, roll out each ball to form a thin round.

4. Heat the vegetable oil in a deep frying-pan. Deep-fry the rounds in batches for 5–8 minutes, turning once, until golden in colour. Remove the pooris from the frying pan and drain. Serve hot.

pulao rice

cook: 25 mins | prep: 5 mins | Serves 2–4

Plain boiled rice is eaten by most people in India every day, but for entertaining, a more interesting rice dish is often served, such as this one, which contains different-coloured grains and spices.

NUTRITIONAL INFORMATION	
Calories	265
Protein	4g
Carbohydrate	43g
Sugars	0g
Fat	10g
Saturates	6g

INGREDIENTS

200 g/7 oz basmati rice
2 tbsp ghee
3 green cardamoms
2 whole cloves
3 black peppercorns
½ tsp salt
½ tsp saffron threads
400 ml/14 fl oz water

1 Rinse the rice twice under cold running water and reserve.

2 Heat the ghee in a large, heavy-based saucepan. Add the cardamoms, cloves and peppercorns and fry, stirring, for 1 minute. Add the rice and stir-fry for a further 2 minutes.

3 Add the salt, saffron and water to the rice mixture and reduce the heat. Cover the saucepan and leave to simmer over a low heat for 20 minutes, until all the water has evaporated.

4 Transfer the rice to a large, warmed serving dish and serve hot.

cook's tip

Cloves should be used with caution because the flavour can be overwhelming if too many are used, and this may spoil the finished dish.

chana dal cooked with rice

cook: 1 hr

prep: 15 mins, plus 3 hrs soaking

serves 6

Saffron is used in this dish, which makes it rather special. It is delicious served with any Raita (see page 228) and a meat curry such as Lamb Vindaloo (see page 64).

NUTRITIONAL INFORMATION	
Calories	479
Protein	12g
Carbohydrate	80g
Sugars	7g
Fat	14g
Saturates	8g

variation

If you do not have ghee, then use the same amount of vegetable oil or butter instead.

INGREDIENTS

- **100 g/3½ oz chana dal**
- **450 g/1 lb basmati rice**
- **4 tbsp ghee**
- **2 onions, sliced**
- **1 tsp finely chopped fresh root ginger**
- **1 tsp crushed fresh garlic**
- **½ tsp ground turmeric**
- **2 tsp salt**
- **½ tsp chilli powder**
- **1 tsp Garam Masala (see page 12)**
- **5 tbsp natural yogurt**
- **1.3 litres/2¼ pints water**
- **150 ml/5 fl oz milk**
- **1 tsp saffron threads**
- **3 black cardamoms**
- **3 black cumin seeds**
- **3 tbsp lemon juice**
- **2 fresh green chillies, sliced**
- **2–3 tbsp fresh coriander leaves**
- **chopped fresh coriander, to garnish**

cook's tip

Saffron is the most expensive spice in the world because it is the dried stigmas of the saffron crocus, which are hand-picked. Only a very small amount is needed to flavour and colour dishes.

1. Rinse and soak the chana dal for 3 hours. Rinse the rice, removing any stones and reserve.

2. Heat the ghee in a heavy-based frying pan. Add the onions and fry until golden brown. Using a slotted spoon, transfer half of the onion with a little of the ghee to a bowl and reserve.

3. Add the ginger, garlic, turmeric, half the salt, the chilli powder and the Garam Masala to the frying pan and stir-fry for 5 minutes. Stir in the yogurt and add the chana dal and 150 ml/5 fl oz of the water. Cover and cook for 15 minutes. Remove the frying pan from the heat and reserve. Boil the milk with the saffron and reserve.

4. Meanwhile, in a separate saucepan, boil the remaining water and add the remaining salt and the cardamoms, cumin seeds and rice. Cook, stirring, until the rice is half-cooked, then drain. Transfer half of the rice to a bowl and reserve, and return the rest to the saucepan. Pour the dal mixture over the rice in the saucepan. Scatter over half of the reserved fried onion and half of the saffron milk, lemon juice, chillies and coriander. Place the reserved rice on top of this and the rest of the fried onion, saffron milk, lemon juice, chillies and coriander on top. Cover tightly with a lid and cook for 20 minutes over a very low heat. Mix well, garnish with chopped coriander and serve.

tomato rice

serves 4

prep: 15 mins, plus 5 mins standing

cook: 30 mins

This colourful dish makes a fabulous accompaniment and could also be served as a vegetarian meal, perhaps with a salad.

NUTRITIONAL INFORMATION	
Calories	488
Protein	11g
Carbohydrate	95g
Sugars	7g
Fat	7g
Saturates	1g

INGREDIENTS

- 400 g/14 oz basmati rice
- 2 tbsp ghee or vegetable oil
- ¼ tsp onion seeds
- ¼ tsp kalonji seeds
- 1 onion, thinly sliced
- 1 yellow pepper, deseeded and sliced
- 4 tomatoes, sliced
- 1 potato, diced
- 1 tsp Garlic Paste (see page 12)
- 1 tsp Ginger Paste (see page 12)
- 1 tsp chilli powder
- 55 g/2 oz frozen broad beans or peas
- 1 tbsp chopped fresh coriander
- salt
- 700 ml/1¼ pints water
- fresh coriander sprigs, to garnish

variation

For a change, add 55 g/2 oz button mushrooms and substitute 1 tablespoon of chopped fresh mint for the coriander.

cook's tip

The word basmati means fragrant in Hindi, and this type of rice is very aromatic. However, you can use other varieties of long-grain rice for this dish, if you prefer.

1. Rinse the rice in several changes of water and leave to soak for 10 minutes.

2. Meanwhile, heat the ghee in a large, heavy-based saucepan. Add the onion and kalonji seeds and cook over a low heat, stirring, for 1–2 minutes, or until they give off their aroma. Add the onion and cook, stirring occasionally, for 5 minutes, or until softened. Drain the rice.

3. Add the yellow pepper, tomatoes, potato, Garlic Paste, Ginger Paste and chilli powder and cook, stirring constantly, for 3 minutes. Add the beans or peas and coriander, add salt to taste and cook, stirring, for 2 minutes.

4. Add the rice and stir until the grains glisten and the ingredients are thoroughly blended. Pour in the water and bring to the boil over a high heat. Cover tightly, reduce the heat and simmer for 15 minutes.

5. Remove the saucepan from the heat and leave to stand, still covered, for 5 minutes. Serve garnished with fresh coriander sprigs.

golden rice with mustard seeds

serves 4 | **prep: 10 mins, plus 5 mins standing** | **cook: 20 mins**

The rice in this dish owes its lovely colour to ground turmeric, which also gives it a warm, spicy aroma and flavour.

INGREDIENTS

225 g/8 oz basmati rice
1 dried red chilli
2 tbsp ghee or vegetable oil
½ tsp black mustard seeds
½ tsp ground turmeric
finely grated rind of 1 lemon
2 tbsp chopped fresh coriander
salt
475 ml/17 fl oz boiling water

NUTRITIONAL INFORMATION	
Calories	252
Protein	4g
Carbohydrate	45g
Sugars	0g
Fat	6g
Saturates	1g

cook's tip

Before serving the golden rice, lightly fluff up the grains with a fork. Remove and discard the dried red chilli, if you like. Leave the rice to stand before serving.

1. Rinse the rice in several changes of water and leave to soak for 10 minutes.

2. Meanwhile, slit the chilli lengthways and deseed. Heat the ghee in a heavy-based saucepan. Add the mustard seeds and cook over a low heat, stirring constantly, for 1–2 minutes, or until they give off their aroma. Add the chilli and cook, stirring, for 1 minute, then remove from the heat while you drain the rice.

3. Return the pan to the heat, add the turmeric and rice and cook, stirring constantly, for 2 minutes, or until all the grains are coated. Stir in the lemon rind and coriander and add salt to taste.

4. Pour in the boiling water and return to the boil. Reduce the heat, cover tightly and simmer for 10–15 minutes. Remove the saucepan from the heat and leave to stand, still covered, for 5 minutes before serving.

rice with warm spices

cook: 20 mins

prep: 10 mins, plus 15 mins soaking/standing

serves 4

This dish is the perfect accompaniment to the southern Indian poultry and vegetable dishes known as mollees.

NUTRITIONAL INFORMATION	
Calories	324
Protein	7g
Carbohydrate	56g
Sugars	11g
Fat	8g
Saturates	1g

INGREDIENTS

225 g/8 oz basmati rice

600 ml/1 pint water

2 whole cloves

4 cardamom pods, lightly crushed

1 cinnamon stick

pinch of saffron threads, lightly crushed

salt

2 tbsp lime juice

1 tbsp finely grated lime rind

55 g/2 oz sultanas

55 g/2 oz pistachio nuts, roughly chopped

1 Rinse the rice in several changes of water and leave to soak for 10 minutes. Drain well.

2 Pour the water into a large, heavy-based saucepan, add the cloves, cardamoms, cinnamon stick, saffron and a pinch of salt and bring to the boil over a medium heat. Add the rice and return to the boil. Reduce the heat, cover tightly and simmer for 10–15 minutes. Remove the saucepan from the heat and leave to stand, still covered, for 5 minutes.

3 Uncover the rice and fluff up the grains with a fork, then gently stir in the lime juice, rind, sultanas and pistachio nuts. Taste and adjust the seasoning, if necessary, and serve immediately.

cook's tip

Although saffron and ground turmeric both give Indian rice dishes a vibrant yellow colour, they are not interchangeable as they taste very different.

chicken biryani

cook: 1 hr 30 mins –1 hr 45 mins

prep: 15 mins, plus 3 hrs marinating

serves 8

NUTRITIONAL INFORMATION	
Calories	382
Protein	42g
Carbohydrate	10g
Sugars	8g
Fat	20g
Saturates	11g

variation

Use the same amount of vegetable oil or butter instead of the ghee and replace the basmati rice with long-grain rice, if you prefer.

This biryani recipe may look rather complicated, but is not difficult to follow. You can substitute lamb for chicken, if you prefer, but you would have to marinate it overnight.

INGREDIENTS

- 1½ tsp finely chopped fresh root ginger
- 1½ tsp crushed fresh garlic
- 1 tbsp Garam Masala (see page 12)
- 1 tsp chilli powder
- ½ tsp ground turmeric
- 2 tsp salt
- 5 green/white cardamom pods, crushed
- 300 ml/10 fl oz natural yogurt
- 1.5 kg/3 lb 5 oz chicken, skinned and cut into 8 pieces
- 150 ml/5 fl oz milk
- 1 tsp saffron strands
- 6 tbsp ghee
- 2 onions, sliced
- 450 g/1 lb basmati rice
- 2 cinnamon sticks
- 4 black peppercorns
- 1 tsp black cumin seeds
- 4 fresh green chillies
- 2–3 tbsp finely chopped fresh coriander leaves
- 4 tbsp lemon juice

cook's tip

Cardamoms are native to India and are available in green, white and black varieties. The green and white pods are traditionally used to flavour rice dishes.

1 Blend the ginger, garlic, Garam Masala, chilli powder, turmeric, half the salt and the cardamoms together in a bowl. Add the yogurt and chicken pieces and mix well. Cover and leave to marinate in the refrigerator for 3 hours.

2 Boil the milk in a small saucepan, pour over the saffron and reserve.

3 Heat the ghee in a saucepan, add the onions and fry until golden. Transfer half of the onions and ghee into a bowl and reserve.

4 Place the rice, cinnamon sticks, peppercorns and black cumin seeds in a saucepan of water. Bring the rice to the boil and remove from the heat when half-cooked. Drain and place in a bowl. Mix with the remaining salt.

5 Chop the chillies and reserve. Add the chicken mixture to the saucepan containing the onions and ghee. Add half each of the chopped green chillies, coriander, lemon juice and saffron milk. Add the rice, then the rest of the ingredients, including the reserved fried onions and ghee. Cover tightly so no steam escapes. Cook on a low heat for 1 hour. Check that the meat is cooked through before serving. If the meat is not cooked, return to the heat and cook for a further 15 minutes. Mix well before serving.

biryani with mint masala

serves 6 **prep: 10 mins, plus 15 mins soaking/standing** **cook: 30 mins**

Biryanis were originally meat dishes from Persia, but this delicious vegetarian version was created in central India. It would go well with lamb dishes, such as Saffron & Almond Lamb (see page 50).

INGREDIENTS

- 400 g/14 oz basmati rice
- 55 g/2 oz fresh mint leaves
- 1 fresh green chilli, deseeded and roughly chopped
- ½ tsp Garam Masala (see page 12)
- 125 ml/4 fl oz canned coconut milk
- 4 tbsp vegetable oil
- salt
- 2 onions, sliced
- 2 potatoes, diced
- 1 tsp cumin seeds
- 1 litre/1¾ pints water
- 115 g/4 oz frozen peas
- fresh coriander sprigs, to garnish

NUTRITIONAL INFORMATION	
Calories	575
Protein	12g
Carbohydrate	104g
Sugars	7g
Fat	12g
Saturates	1g

2

4

4

1 Rinse the rice in several changes of water and leave to soak for 10 minutes.

2 Meanwhile, place the mint, chilli, Garam Masala, coconut milk, half the vegetable oil and a pinch of salt in a food processor and process until smooth, scraping down the sides of the goblet, if necessary.

3 Heat the remaining vegetable oil in a large, heavy-based saucepan. Add the onions and potatoes and cook over a low heat, stirring occasionally, for 10 minutes, or until golden. Meanwhile, drain the rice.

4 Stir the mint purée and cumin seeds into the onion and potato mixture and cook, stirring constantly, for 2 minutes. Add the rice and stir to coat the grains. Pour in the water and add the peas. Bring to the boil, cover and simmer for 10–15 minutes. Leave to stand, covered, for 5 minutes, garnish with coriander sprigs and serve.

cook's tip

The heat in chillies is in the membrane around the seeds. The seeds do not contain capsaicin, the substance that makes chillies hot, but it is easiest to remove the seeds with the membrane.

sheermal

cook: 30 mins

prep: 15 mins, plus 1 hr 30 mins rising

makes 10

Like Naan Bread (see page 194), these breads include yeast as a raising agent. They are amazingly easy to make and look extremely attractive and appetizing.

NUTRITIONAL INFORMATION	
Calories	214
Protein	4g
Carbohydrate	35g
Sugars	1g
Fat	8g
Saturates	5g

INGREDIENTS

225 ml/8 fl oz hand-hot water

1 tbsp easy-blend dried yeast

75 g/2¾ oz caster sugar

450 g/1 lb self-raising flour, plus extra for dusting

salt

85 g/3 oz butter, melted and cooled

milk, for brushing

white sesame seeds, for sprinkling

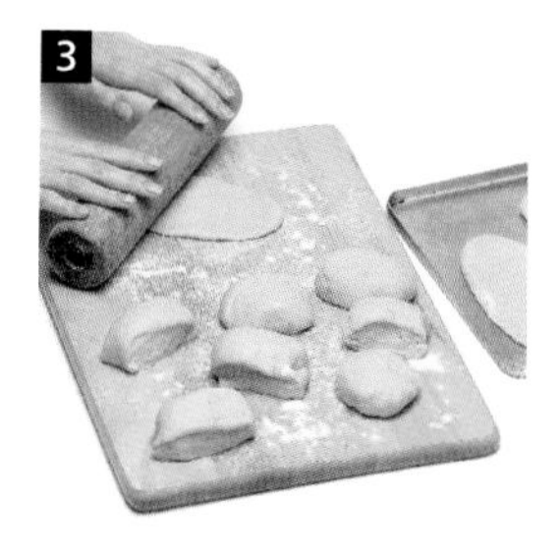

1 Pour the water into a small bowl or jug and mix well with the yeast and 1 teaspoon of the sugar. Leave to stand for 10 minutes, or until frothy.

2 Sift the flour with a pinch of salt into a bowl. Stir in the remaining sugar. Make a well in the centre of the flour and add the yeast mixture and butter and knead together to form a soft dough. Cover with clingfilm and leave to stand in a warm place for 1–1½ hours, or until doubled in size.

3 Preheat the oven to 190°C/375°F/Gas Mark 5. Turn the dough out on to a lightly floured work surface and knead for 5 minutes. Divide into 10 equal-sized portions and roll out each into a round or oval about 5 mm/¼ inch thick. Brush with milk and sprinkle with sesame seeds. Place on baking sheets and bake, in batches, in the preheated oven for 5 minutes, then turn the breads over and bake for a further 5 minutes, or until golden brown.

cook's tip

The water must be just tepid. If it's too cold, it won't activate the yeast, but if it's too hot, it will kill the yeast and the bread will not rise. Test the water with your finger before adding.

lemon dal

serves 4 **prep: 10 mins** **cook: 30 mins**

This dal is eaten almost every day in most households in Hyderabad in India. Traditionally, it is cooked with tamarind, but you can use lemon juice instead, which is easier and adds extra flavour.

INGREDIENTS

- 100 g/3½ oz masoor dal
- 1 tsp finely chopped fresh root ginger
- 1 tsp crushed fresh garlic
- 1 tsp chilli powder
- ½ tsp ground turmeric
- 425 ml/15 fl oz water
- 1 tsp salt
- 3 tbsp lemon juice
- 2 fresh green chillies, deseeded and chopped
- 2–3 tbsp chopped fresh coriander leaves

BAGHAAR

- 150 ml/5 fl oz vegetable oil
- 4 whole garlic cloves
- 6 dried red chillies
- 1 tsp white cumin seeds
- lemon slices, quartered, to garnish

NUTRITIONAL INFORMATION	
Calories	386
Protein	5g
Carbohydrate	12g
Sugars	0.7g
Fat	35g
Saturates	4g

variation

For a slightly different baghaar, replace the vegetable oil with sunflower oil and the cumin seeds with onion seeds.

cook's tip

This dish is an excellent accompaniment to Lamb Koftas (see page 60) or Beef Korma with Almonds (see page 83).

1. Rinse the masoor dal under cold running water and place in a large, heavy-based saucepan. Add the ginger, garlic, chilli powder and turmeric to the dal. Stir in 300 ml/10 fl oz of the water and bring to the boil over a medium heat with the lid left slightly ajar. Cook for 15–20 minutes, until the dal is soft enough to be mashed.

2. Mash the dal with a potato masher. Add the salt, lemon juice and remaining water, and stir to mix well. It should be of a fairly smooth consistency.

3. Add the green chillies and fresh coriander leaves to the dal and reserve.

4. To make the baghaar, heat the vegetable oil in a saucepan. Add the garlic, red chillies and cumin seeds and fry for 1 minute. Turn off the heat, allow to cool slightly, then pour the baghaar over the dal. If the dal is too runny, cook, uncovered, over medium heat for 3–5 minutes. Transfer to a serving dish and serve hot, garnished with lemon slices.

onion dal

cook: 35–40 mins **prep: 10 mins** **serves 4**

NUTRITIONAL INFORMATION	
Calories	187
Protein	4g
Carbohydrate	31g
Sugars	2g
Fat	3g
Saturates	2g

variation

If you prefer, deseed the fresh green chillies before adding to the dish. Alternatively, use red chillies.

This dal is semi-dry when cooked, so it is best to serve it with a curry which has a sauce. Ordinary onions can be used as a substitute if spring onions are not available.

INGREDIENTS

100 g/3½ oz masoor dal
6 tbsp vegetable oil
1 small bunch of spring onions, trimmed and chopped, including the green part
1 tsp finely chopped fresh root ginger
1 tsp crushed fresh garlic
½ tsp chilli powder
½ tsp ground turmeric
300 ml/10 fl oz water
1 tsp salt

TO GARNISH

1 finely chopped fresh green chilli
chopped fresh coriander leaves

2

2

2

cook's tip

Masoor dal are small, round, pale orange split lentils. They turn a pale yellow colour when cooked. They are available from specialist Asian food shops.

1 Rinse the dal under cold running water and reserve until required.

2 Heat the vegetable oil in a large, heavy-based saucepan. Add the spring onions and fry until lightly browned. Reduce the heat and add the ginger, garlic, chilli powder and turmeric and stir-fry for a few minutes. Add the dal and mix together until blended. Add the water to the saucepan, reduce the heat further and cook for 20–25 minutes.

3 When the dal is cooked thoroughly, add the salt and stir with a wooden spoon to gently mix.

4 Transfer the onion dal to a large, warmed serving dish, garnish with the chopped green chillies and coriander and serve.

oil-dressed dal

serves: 4 **prep: 5 mins** **cook: 30 mins**

This dal is given a baghaar (seasoned oil dressing) of ghee, onion and a combination of seeds, just before serving. Try serving it with Pork with Cinnamon & Fenugreek (see page 95).

INGREDIENTS

- 75 g/2¾ oz masoor dal
- 50 g/1¾ oz moong dal
- 450 ml/16 fl oz water
- 1 tsp finely chopped fresh root ginger
- 1 tsp crushed fresh garlic
- 2 fresh red chillies, chopped
- 1 tsp salt

BAGHAAR

- 2 tbsp ghee
- 1 onion, sliced
- 1 tsp mixed mustard and onion seeds

NUTRITIONAL INFORMATION	
Calories	173
Protein	8g
Carbohydrate	20g
Sugars	3g
Fat	8g
Saturates	5g

variation

Replace the ghee with vegetable or sunflower oil and the red chilli with a fresh green chilli, deseeded and chopped, if you prefer.

cook's tip

This dish makes a a very good accompaniment, especially for a dry vegetarian or meat curry. It also freezes well – simply re-heat it in a saucepan or covered in the oven.

1. Rinse the dals under cold running water, removing any stones, then place in a large, heavy-based saucepan and pour over the water, stirring. Add the ginger, garlic and red chillies and bring to the boil over a medium heat, half covered with a lid, for 15–20 minutes, or until they are soft enough to be mashed.

2. Mash the dals with a potato masher and add more water if necessary to make a thick sauce. Add the salt to the dal mixture and stir well. Transfer the dal to a heatproof serving dish.

3. Just before serving, make the baghaar. Melt the ghee in a small saucepan, add the onion and fry for 8 minutes, until golden. Add the mustard and onion seeds and stir to mix. Pour the onion mixture over the lentils while still hot. Transfer to a serving dish and serve immediately.

dry urid dal

serves 4 **prep: 5 mins** **cook: 15 mins**

Urid dal are available with their dark husks stripped off, in which case they are creamy white. This dish makes a wonderful accompaniment to vegetable curries served in sauce.

INGREDIENTS

225 g/8 oz de-husked urid dal
4 tbsp ghee or vegetable oil
1 onion, sliced
2.5-cm/1-inch piece fresh root ginger, thinly sliced
1 fresh green chilli, deseeded and sliced
salt
chopped fresh coriander, to garnish

NUTRITIONAL INFORMATION	
Calories	271
Protein	15g
Carbohydrate	27g
Sugars	3g
Fat	12g
Saturates	1g

1 Place the dal in a large, heavy-based saucepan and pour in enough water to just cover the dal. Bring to the boil, then simmer over a low heat for 10–15 minutes, or until all the water has evaporated.

2 Meanwhile, heat the ghee in a heavy-based frying pan. Add the onion and cook over a low heat, stirring occasionally, for 10 minutes, or until golden. Add the ginger and chilli and cook, stirring occasionally, for 3 minutes.

3 As soon as the dal is cooked and dry, remove the saucepan from the heat. Season with salt to taste and transfer to a serving dish. Top with the onion mixture, garnish with chopped coriander and serve hot.

cook's tip

Always wash dal in several changes of cold water before cooking to remove any stones and impurities. Urid dal is available from Asian food shops.

parathas

cook: 1 hr

prep: 20 mins, plus 30 mins resting

makes 12

These thin fried breads are similar to Chapatis (see page 195), but are softer and richer, and more time-consuming to make and cook. They are delicious served with curries and vegetable dishes.

NUTRITIONAL INFORMATION	
Calories	123
Protein	4g
Carbohydrate	22g
Sugars	1g
Fat	3g
Saturates	1g

INGREDIENTS

350 g/12 oz wholemeal flour (ata or chapati flour), plus extra for dusting

55 g/2 oz plain flour

salt

2 tbsp ghee, melted

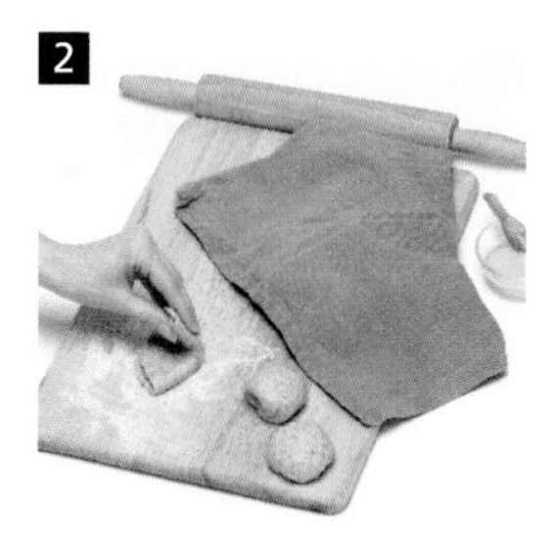

1 Sift the wholemeal flour, plain flour and a pinch of salt into a large bowl. Make a well in the centre of the flours and add 2 teaspoons of the ghee. Rub it into the flour with your fingertips, then gradually knead in enough cold water to make a soft dough. Cover with clingfilm and leave to rest for 30 minutes.

2 Divide the dough into 12 equal-sized pieces and roll into balls. Keep the balls that you are not working on covered to prevent them drying out. Roll out a ball of dough on a lightly floured work surface to a 10-cm/4-inch round and brush with ghee. Fold in half, brush with ghee again and fold in half once more. Either shape into a ball and roll out to an 18-cm/7-inch round or roll into a 15-cm/6-inch triangle. Repeat with the remaining balls, stacking the parathas interleaved with clingfilm.

3 Heat a heavy-based frying pan or griddle pan. Add 1–2 parathas at a time and cook for 1 minute, then flip over with a spatula and cook for a further 2 minutes. Brush with ghee and flip back to the first side and cook until golden. Brush with ghee, flip over again and cook until golden. Keep warm while you cook the remaining parathas in the same way.

cook's tip

Press each paratha down gently with a spatula or flat spoon while you are frying it to make sure that it cooks evenly on both sides.

parathas stuffed with vegetables

cook: 30–35 mins **prep: 25 mins** **makes 6–8**

NUTRITIONAL INFORMATION	
Calories	391
Protein	6g
Carbohydrate	40g
Sugars	2g
Fat	24g
Saturates	2.5g

variation

If you like, serve these parathas on their own with a bowl of Mango Chutney (see page 230).

Stuffed parathas can be quite rich and are usually made for special occasions. They can be eaten either on their own or as an accompaniment to any meat or vegetable curry.

INGREDIENTS

DOUGH

- **225 g/8 oz wholemeal flour (ata or chapati flour), plus extra for dusting**
- **½ tsp salt**
- **200 ml/7 fl oz water**
- **100 g/3½ oz pure or vegetable ghee, plus extra for frying**

FILLING

- **3 potatoes**
- **½ tsp ground turmeric**
- **1 tsp Garam Masala (see page 12)**
- **1 tsp finely chopped fresh root ginger**
- **2–3 tbsp fresh coriander leaves**
- **3 fresh green chillies, finely chopped**
- **1 tsp salt**

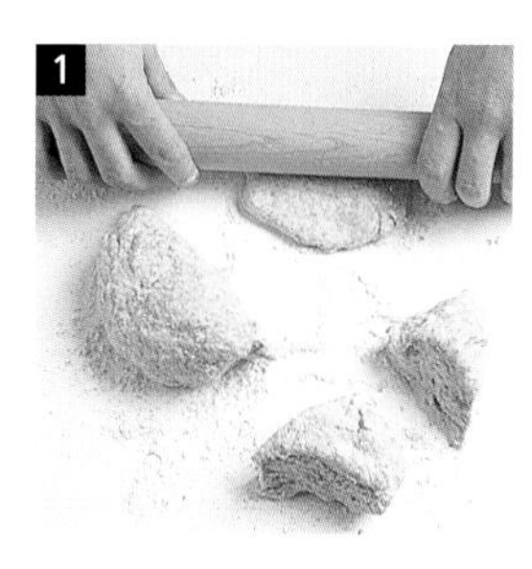

1. To make the dough, mix the flour, salt, water and ghee together in a bowl. Divide the dough into 6–8 equal-sized portions. Roll each portion out on a lightly floured work surface. Brush the centre of the dough portions with ½ teaspoon of ghee. Fold the dough portions in half, roll into a pipe-like shape, flatten with the palms of your hand, then roll around your finger to form a coil. Roll each portion out again to form a round 18 cm/7 inches in diameter.

2. To make the filling, cook the potatoes in a saucepan of boiling water for 20 minutes, or until soft enough to be mashed.

3. Blend the turmeric, Garam Masala, ginger, coriander, chillies and salt together in a bowl. Add the spice mixture to the mashed potato and mix well. Spread 1 tablespoon of the spicy potato mixture on each dough portion and cover with another portion of dough. Seal the edges well.

cook's tip

When frying the parathas you don't need very much ghee – about 2 tablespoons will be enough. If ghee is unavailable, then use butter instead.

4. Heat 2 teaspoons of ghee in a heavy-based frying pan. Place the parathas gently in the frying pan, in batches, and fry, turning and moving them about gently with a flat spoon, until golden. Remove the parathas from the frying pan and serve hot.

vegetable sambar

serves 6 **prep: 25 mins** **cook: 55 mins**

Sambars, a mixture of dal and vegetables, come from southern India, where they are often served with pancakes for breakfast. However, they're just as good as accompaniments to meat, poultry and fish served at an evening meal.

NUTRITIONAL INFORMATION	
Calories	408
Protein	17g
Carbohydrate	76g
Sugars	23g
Fat	7g
Saturates	2g

INGREDIENTS

- 800 g/1 lb 12 oz canned tomatoes
- 2 tbsp desiccated coconut
- 2 tbsp lemon juice
- 1 tbsp yellow mustard seeds
- 40 g/1½ oz raw or muscovado sugar
- 2 tbsp ghee or vegetable oil
- 2 onions, sliced
- 4 cardamom pods, lightly crushed
- 6 curry leaves, plus extra to garnish
- 2 tsp ground coriander
- 2 tsp ground cumin
- 1 tsp ground turmeric
- 1 tsp Ginger Paste (see page 12)
- 200 g/7 oz toor dal
- 450 g/1 lb sweet potatoes, cut into chunks
- 900 g/2 lb potatoes, cut into chunks
- 2 carrots, sliced
- 2 courgettes, cut into chunks
- 1 aubergine, cut into chunks
- salt

variation

You can use any vegetables that you have to hand to make this dish. Add fibrous ones with the sweet potatoes and softer ones with the courgettes.

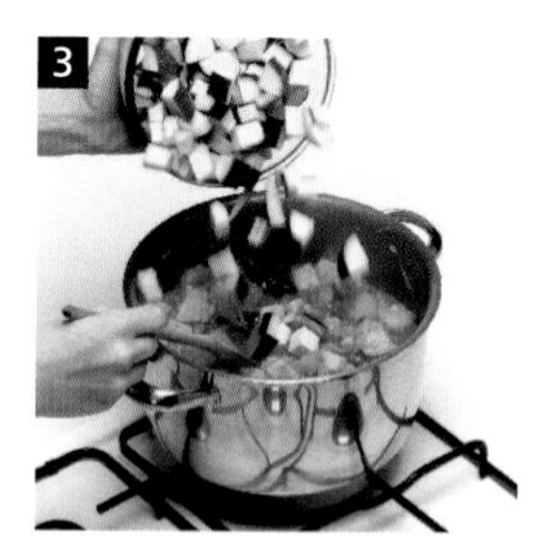

cook's tip

Yellow mustard seeds are not as pungent as black or brown mustard seeds, but they do have a bitter taste. They are available from Asian food shops.

1. Place the tomatoes and their can juices, coconut, 1 tablespoon of the lemon juice, the mustard seeds and sugar in a food processor or blender and process until smooth.

2. Heat the ghee in a large, heavy-based saucepan. Add the onion and cook over a low heat, stirring occasionally, for 10 minutes, or until golden. Add the cardamoms, curry leaves, coriander, cumin, turmeric and Ginger Paste and cook, stirring constantly, for 1–2 minutes, or until the spices give off their aroma. Stir in the tomato mixture and dal and bring to the boil. Reduce the heat, cover and simmer for 10 minutes.

3. Add the sweet potatoes, potatoes and carrots, re-cover the saucepan and simmer for a further 15 minutes. Add the courgettes, aubergine and remaining lemon juice, add salt to taste, re-cover and simmer for a further 10–15 minutes, or until the vegetables are tender. Serve garnished with curry leaves.

bombay potatoes

serves 6 **prep: 10 mins** **cook: 30 mins**

Typical of the vegetarian cuisine of Gujarat in north-west India, these spicy potatoes are delicious with meat dishes.

INGREDIENTS

- 500 g/1 lb 2 oz new potatoes, diced
- 1 tsp ground turmeric
- salt
- 4 tbsp ghee or vegetable oil
- 6 curry leaves
- 1 dried red chilli
- 2 fresh green chillies, chopped
- ½ tsp kalonji seeds
- 1 tsp mixed mustard and onion seeds
- ½ tsp cumin seeds
- ½ tsp fennel seeds
- ¼ tsp asafoetida
- 2 onions, chopped
- 5 tbsp chopped fresh coriander
- juice of ½ lime

NUTRITIONAL INFORMATION	
Calories	143
Protein	2g
Carbohydrate	17g
Sugars	4g
Fat	8g
Saturates	1g

1 Place the potatoes in a large, heavy-based saucepan and pour in just enough cold water to cover. Add ½ teaspoon of the turmeric and a pinch of salt and bring to the boil. Simmer for 10 minutes, or until tender, then drain and reserve until required.

2 Heat the ghee in a large, heavy-based frying pan. Add the curry leaves and dried red chilli and cook, stirring frequently, for a few minutes, or until the chilli is blackened. Add the remaining turmeric, the fresh chillies, the kalonji, mustard, onion, cumin and fennel seeds and the asafoetida, onions and fresh coriander and cook, stirring constantly, for 5 minutes, or until the onions have softened.

3 Stir in the potatoes and cook over a low heat, stirring frequently, for 10 minutes, or until heated through. Squeeze over the lime juice and serve.

cook's tip

Asafoetida is thought to aid digestion and combat flatulence. It is best bought as a powder rather than as a resin, although the powder quickly loses its flavour and must be stored in a sealed jar.

jumping potatoes

cook: 22 mins

prep: 10 mins, plus 30 mins cooling

serves 6

India has a small community of Middle Eastern Jews, and this unusual dish is a traditional part of their festive meals.

NUTRITIONAL INFORMATION	
Calories	273
Protein	4g
Carbohydrate	29g
Sugars	1g
Fat	17g
Saturates	2g

INGREDIENTS

1 kg/2 lb 4 oz small potatoes

½ tsp ground turmeric

salt

vegetable oil, for deep-frying

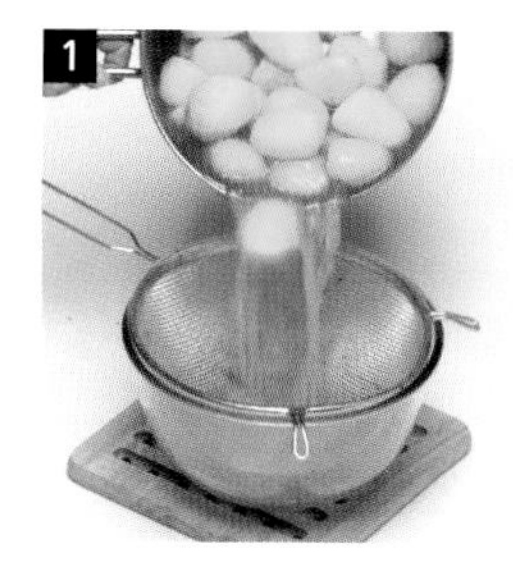

1 Place the potatoes in a large, heavy-based saucepan and pour in just enough cold water to cover. Add the turmeric and a pinch of salt and bring to the boil. Boil for 30 seconds, then remove the saucepan from the heat and drain.

2 Heat the vegetable oil in a large, heavy-based frying pan over a low heat until it is hot but not sizzling – it should not be hot enough to fry the potatoes. Add the potatoes in a single layer and cook over a very low heat for 15 minutes, or until they are beginning to soften. Remove the frying pan from the heat and leave to cool, leaving the potatoes in the oil.

3 Fill the sink or a deep roasting tray with cold water to a depth of about 5 cm/2 inches. Place the frying pan over a high heat. Time the cooking from the moment the potatoes begin to float to the top of the hot oil and cook, stirring constantly, for 5 minutes, or until crisp and golden brown. Remove the frying pan from the heat and stand in the cold water. Stir gently for 2 minutes. Using a slotted spoon, transfer the potatoes to a warmed serving dish and serve immediately.

cook's tip

Make sure that the water in the roasting tray or sink is not so deep that it will come up over the sides of the frying pan, because it will flood the potatoes.

lime pickle

makes 225 g/8 oz

prep: 10 minutes, plus 19 days standing

cook: 5 mins

If you are planning to serve this hot pickle on a particular occasion, it is best to begin preparing it a month in advance. Unlike most Indian chutneys, it cannot be eaten immediately after making.

INGREDIENTS

12 limes, halved and deseeded
115 g/4 oz salt
70 g/2½ oz chilli powder
25 g/1 oz mustard powder
25 g/1 oz ground fenugreek
1 tbsp ground turmeric
300 ml/10 fl oz mustard oil
15 g/½ oz yellow mustard seeds, crushed
½ tsp asafoetida

NUTRITIONAL INFORMATION	
Calories	142
Protein	1g
Carbohydrate	0.5g
Sugars	0g
Fat	16g
Saturates	2g

1

2

3

1 Cut each lime half into 4 pieces and pack them into a large sterilized jar (see Cook's Tip, page 232), sprinkling over the salt at the same time. Cover and leave to stand in a warm place for 10–14 days, or until the limes have turned brown and softened.

2 Mix the chilli powder, mustard powder, fenugreek and turmeric together in a small bowl and add to the jar of limes. Stir to mix, then re-cover and leave to stand for 2 days.

3 Transfer the lime mixture to a heatproof bowl. Heat the mustard oil in a heavy-based frying pan. Add the mustard seeds and asafoetida and cook, stirring constantly, until the oil is very hot and just beginning to smoke. Pour the oil and spices over the limes and mix well. Cover and leave to cool. When cool, pack into a sterilized jar, seal and store in a sunny place for 1 week before serving.

cook's tip

If you are absolutely certain that the jar won't crack when you add the hot oil in Step 3, then there is no need to transfer the lime mixture to a bowl to cool.

tomato kachumbar

cook: 0 mins **prep: 10 mins, plus 30 mins chilling** **serves 6**

Drinking water with a hot curry is never recommended. A far better idea is to serve a cooling salad that will counterbalance the 'fire' generated by any strong spices.

NUTRITIONAL INFORMATION	
Calories	25
Protein	1g
Carbohydrate	4g
Sugars	4g
Fat	0.5g
Saturates	0g

INGREDIENTS

125 ml/4 fl oz lime juice

½ tsp sugar

salt

6 tomatoes, chopped

½ cucumber, chopped

8 spring onions, chopped

1 fresh green chilli, deseeded and chopped

1 tbsp chopped fresh coriander

1 tbsp chopped fresh mint

1 Mix the lime juice, sugar and a pinch of salt together in a large bowl and stir until the sugar has completely dissolved.

2 Add the tomatoes, cucumber, spring onions, chilli, coriander and mint and toss well to mix.

3 Cover with clingfilm and leave to chill in the refrigerator for at least 30 minutes. Toss the vegetables before serving.

cook's tip

Chop all the vegetables into fairly small, even-sized pieces for the best texture and presentation. You can use whatever vegetables you have in the refrigerator, as long as they can be eaten raw.

onion kachumbar

serves 4 | **prep: 10 minutes, plus 30 mins standing** | **cook: 0 mins**

No Indian meal is complete without an appetizing collection of small side dishes, which invariably include a simple salad. This one is the perfect foil for tandoori dishes and kebabs.

INGREDIENTS

2 red onions or 1 Spanish onion, thinly sliced
1 fresh green chilli, deseeded and chopped
1 tbsp lime juice
¼ tsp chilli powder
1 tbsp chopped fresh coriander
salt

NUTRITIONAL INFORMATION	
Calories	41
Protein	2g
Carbohydrate	9g
Sugars	6g
Fat	0.5g
Saturates	0g

1 Place the onion slices in a large serving bowl. Sprinkle with the chopped chilli, lime juice, chilli powder, coriander and salt to taste.

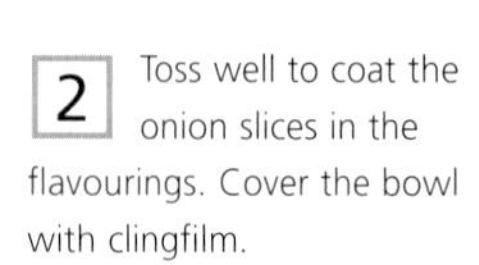

2 Toss well to coat the onion slices in the flavourings. Cover the bowl with clingfilm.

3 Set aside in a cool place, but not the refrigerator, for 30 minutes, to allow the onion to release its juices. Toss the mixture again and taste and adjust the seasoning, if necessary, before serving.

cook's tip

Red and Spanish onions are much sweeter than brown onions and are, therefore, a better choice for serving raw in this salad.

aubergine purée

cook: 1 hr 15 mins

prep: 20 mins, plus 30 mins cooling

serves 6

Spiced vegetable purées, or bharthas, are popular side dishes throughout northern India. Aubergines are particularly well suited to this type of culinary treatment.

NUTRITIONAL INFORMATION	
Calories	107
Protein	2g
Carbohydrate	7g
Sugars	6g
Fat	8g
Saturates	1g

INGREDIENTS

2 large aubergines, halved lengthways
3 tbsp chopped fresh coriander
2 tsp ground coriander
1 tsp ground cumin
1 tsp ground turmeric
4 tomatoes, finely chopped
4 tbsp ghee or vegetable oil
1 onion, finely chopped
1 tsp Ginger Paste (see page 12)
1 tsp Garlic Paste (see page 12)
1 fresh green chilli, finely chopped
salt
2 tbsp lemon juice
fresh mint sprig, to garnish

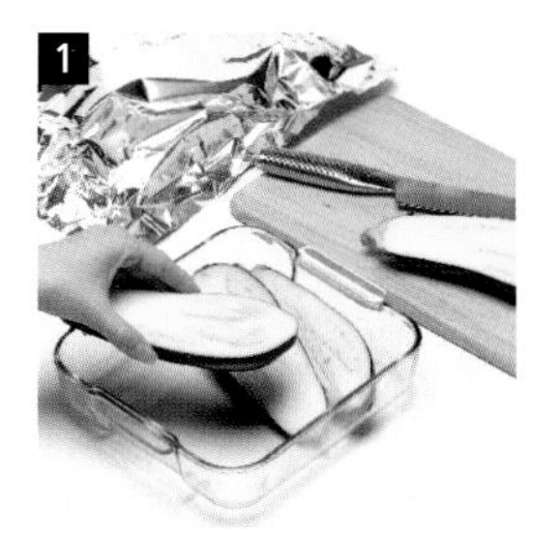

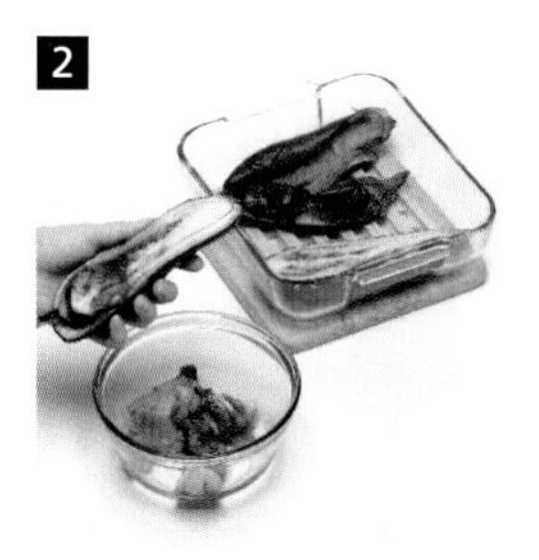

cook's tip

Before baking the aubergines in the oven, use a sharp knife to slash the flesh of each half 2 or 3 times.

1 Preheat the oven to 180°C/350°F/Gas Mark 4. Place the aubergines, cut-sides up, in a shallow, ovenproof dish, cover with foil and bake for 1 hour, or until the flesh is very soft. Leave to cool.

2 Scoop the aubergine flesh into a bowl and mash well. Beat in the fresh coriander, ground coriander, cumin, turmeric and tomatoes with a wooden spoon.

3 Heat the ghee in a heavy-based frying pan. Add the onion and cook over a low heat, stirring occasionally, for 5 minutes, or until softened. Stir in the Ginger Paste, Garlic Paste and chilli and cook, stirring constantly, for 2 minutes. Add the aubergine mixture, season with salt to taste and cook, stirring frequently, until the liquid has evaporated and the purée is thickened and fairly smooth. Sprinkle with the lemon juice, spoon into a warmed bowl and serve immediately, garnished with a mint sprig.

spicy potato salad

serves 4 **prep: 15 mins, plus 40 mins cooling** **cook: 30 mins**

A tasty accompaniment from north-west India, this requires a little advance planning, but is worth it because it's so delicious.

INGREDIENTS

450 g/1 lb potatoes, halved if large, left unpeeled
salt and pepper
4 tbsp ghee or vegetable oil
1 tsp cumin seeds
225 ml/8 fl oz natural yogurt
½ tsp chilli powder
1 tbsp chopped fresh coriander
baby spinach leaves, to serve

NUTRITIONAL INFORMATION	
Calories	215
Protein	5g
Carbohydrate	24g
Sugars	5g
Fat	12g
Saturates	2g

cook's tip

When you dice the potatoes, try to make sure that all the pieces are the same size so that they cook evenly. Keep tossing them over the heat to brown on all sides.

1 Cook the potatoes in a large saucepan of lightly salted boiling water for 20 minutes, or until tender. Drain and leave until cool enough to handle. Peel the cooled potatoes, if you like, and cut into small dice.

2 Heat the ghee in a large, heavy-based frying pan and add half the cumin seeds and all of the potatoes. Cook over a low heat for 10 minutes, stirring constantly, until the potatoes are golden brown all over. Remove with a slotted spoon and leave to cool completely.

3 Mix the yogurt, chilli powder, coriander, the remaining cumin seeds and salt and pepper to taste together in a bowl. Add the potatoes and toss well to mix. Taste and adjust the seasoning, then serve, surrounded by baby spinach leaves.

prawn sambal

cook: 0 mins

prep: 15 mins, plus 30 mins chilling

serves 6

This delicious spicy mix goes extremely well with both fish and vegetable curries and couldn't be easier to make.

NUTRITIONAL INFORMATION	
Calories	97
Protein	13g
Carbohydrate	4g
Sugars	3g
Fat	3g
Saturates	1g

INGREDIENTS

250 g/9 oz cooked, peeled prawns, chopped

3 hard-boiled eggs, shelled and sliced

1 large onion, finely chopped

3-cm/1¼-inch piece fresh root ginger, finely chopped

½ tsp chilli powder

3 tbsp canned coconut milk

salt

½ tsp cumin seeds

TO GARNISH

lime wedges

fresh coriander sprigs

1 Place the prawns, hard-boiled eggs, onion, ginger, chilli powder and coconut milk in a serving bowl and mix well. Season with salt to taste.

2 Place the cumin seeds in a mortar and lightly crush with a pestle.

3 Sprinkle the crushed cumin seeds over the sambal, cover with clingfilm and leave to chill in the refrigerator for at least 30 minutes. Serve garnished with lime wedges and coriander sprigs.

cook's tip

If you shell the eggs immediately after hard-boiling them, you can avoid any discolouration around the yolk. To cool the cooked eggs quickly, rinse them under cold running water.

raitas

serves 4 **prep: 15 mins** **cook: 45 mins**

Raitas are very easy to prepare, very versatile and have a cooling effect which will be appreciated if you are serving hot, spicy dishes.

NUTRITIONAL INFORMATION	
Calories	509
Protein	17g
Carbohydrate	36g
Sugars	10g
Fat	34g
Saturates	9g

INGREDIENTS

MINT RAITA

200 ml/7 fl oz natural yogurt
4 tbsp water
1 small onion, finely chopped
½ tsp mint sauce
½ tsp salt
fresh mint, to garnish

CUCUMBER RAITA

225 g/8 oz cucumber
1 onion
½ tsp salt
½ tsp mint sauce
300 ml/10 fl oz natural yogurt
150 ml/5 fl oz water
fresh mint leaves, to garnish

AUBERGINE RAITA

1 aubergine
1 tsp salt
1 small onion, finely chopped
2 fresh green chillies, finely chopped
200 ml/7 fl oz natural yogurt
3 tbsp water

variation

Add 2 teaspoons of dry-roasted and ground cumin seeds to the Aubergine Raita, if you like.

cook's tip

Raitas can be served with almost any spicy meal as they cool down the hotness of the chillies. Use unsweetened natural yogurt, if possible.

1. To make the Mint Raita, place the yogurt in a bowl and whisk with a fork. Gradually add the water, whisking well. Add the onion, mint sauce and salt and blend together. Garnish with mint.

2. To make the Cucumber Raita, peel and slice the cucumber. Using a sharp knife, chop the onion finely. Place the cucumber and onion in a bowl, then add the salt and mint sauce. Add the yogurt and water. Place the mixture in a blender and blend well. Transfer to a serving bowl and serve garnished with fresh mint.

3. To make the Aubergine Raita, rinse the aubergine. Remove and discard the top end and chop the rest into small pieces. Boil the aubergine in a saucepan of water until soft and mushy. Drain and transfer to a serving bowl, then add the salt, onion and green chillies, mixing well. Whisk the yogurt with the water in a separate bowl and pour over the aubergine mixture. Mix well and serve.

mango chutney

serves 4

prep: 10–15 mins, plus 8 hrs standing

cook: 1 hr 5 mins

Everyone's favourite chutney, this has a sweet and sour taste and is particularly good served with a Mint Raita (see page 228). It is best made well in advance and stored for at least 2 weeks before use.

INGREDIENTS

- **1 kg/2 lb 4 oz mangoes**
- **4 tbsp salt**
- **600 ml/1 pint water**
- **450 g/1 lb sugar**
- **450 ml/16 fl oz vinegar**
- **2 tsp finely chopped fresh root ginger**
- **2 tsp crushed fresh garlic**
- **2 tsp chilli powder**
- **2 cinnamon sticks**
- **75 g/2¾ oz raisins**
- **100 g/3½ oz dates, stoned**

NUTRITIONAL INFORMATION	
Calories	2819
Protein	12g
Carbohydrate	734g
Sugars	731g
Fat	2g
Saturates	1g

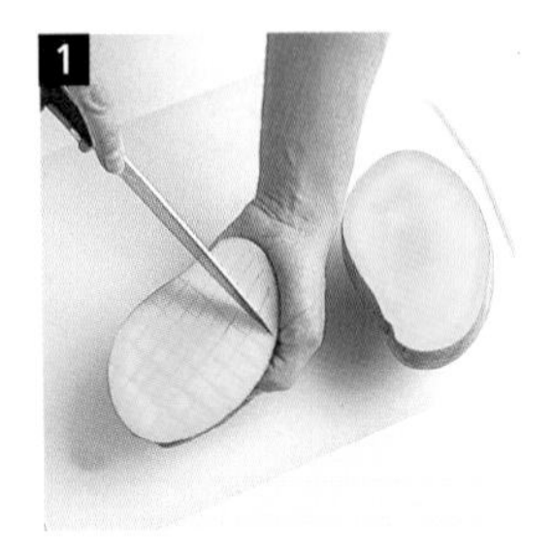

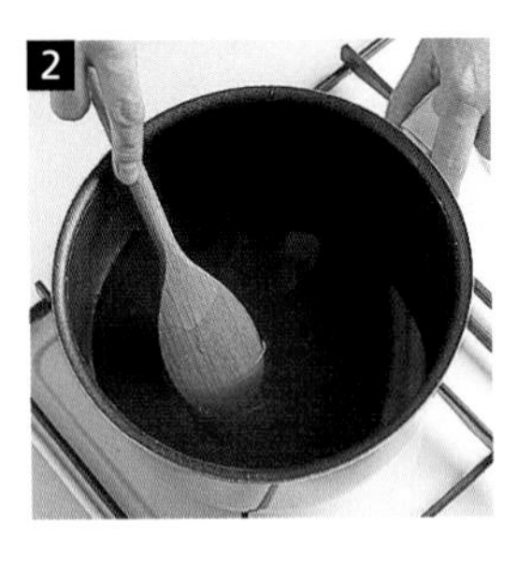

1. Using a sharp knife, peel, halve and stone the mangoes. Cut the flesh into cubes and place in a large bowl. Add the salt and water and leave to stand overnight. Drain the liquid from the mangoes.

2. Bring the sugar and vinegar to the boil in a large, heavy-based saucepan over a low heat, stirring. Gradually add the mango cubes to the sugar and vinegar mixture, stirring to coat the mango in the mixture.

3. Add the ginger, garlic, chilli powder, cinnamon sticks, raisins and dates, and return to the boil, stirring occasionally. Reduce the heat and cook for 1 hour, or until the mixture thickens. Remove from the heat and leave to cool.

4. Remove the cinnamon sticks and discard. Spoon the chutney into clean, dry jars and cover tightly with lids. Leave in a cool place to allow the flavours to develop.

cook's tip

When choosing mangoes, select ones that are shiny with unblemished skins. To test if they are ripe, cup the mango in your hand and squeeze it – it should give slightly to the touch if ready for eating.

tamarind chutney

cook: 0 mins | **prep: 10 mins** | **serves 4–6**

This mouthwatering chutney, which is extremely popular all over India, is served with various vegetarian snacks. It tastes particularly good served with Samosas (see page 26).

NUTRITIONAL INFORMATION	
Calories	8
Protein	0.3g
Carbohydrate	1g
Sugars	1g
Fat	0.3g
Saturates	0g

INGREDIENTS

2 tbsp tamarind paste

5 tbsp water

1 tsp chilli powder

½ tsp ground ginger

½ tsp salt

1 tsp sugar

finely chopped coriander leaves, to garnish

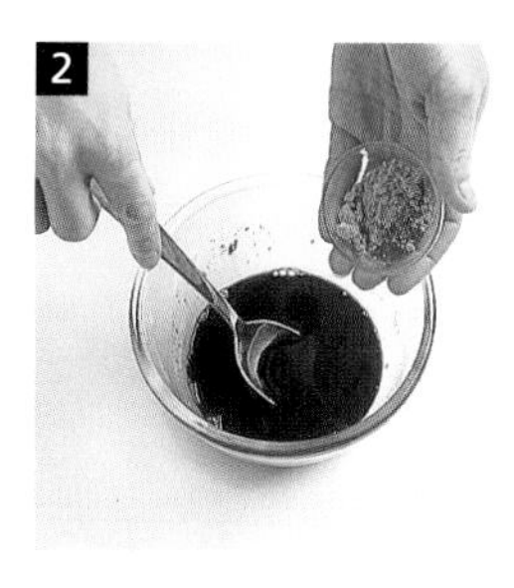

1. Place the tamarind paste in a large bowl. Gradually add the water, gently whisking with a fork to make a smooth, runny paste.

2. Add the chilli powder and ginger to the mixture and blend. Add the salt and sugar and mix well.

3. Transfer the chutney to a serving dish, garnish with chopped fresh coriander and serve.

cook's tip

Tamarind paste is sold in jars from Asian food shops. It is much easier and quicker to use than dried tamarind.

nine jewels chutney

serves 4–6 **prep: 25 mins, plus 1 hr cooling** **cook: 25 mins**

The 'jewels' in this quick and easy chutney are the fruit, chillies and ginger. It is quite sweet and wonderfully thick and sticky.

INGREDIENTS

- 1 tsp coriander seeds
- ½ tsp cumin seeds
- ½ tsp onion seeds
- ½ tsp aniseed
- 55 g/2 oz almonds, chopped
- 1 ripe mango, peeled, stoned and sliced
- 1 eating apple, cored and chopped
- 1 banana, peeled and sliced
- 4 fresh pineapple slices, chopped or 4 canned pineapple slices in juice, drained and chopped
- 225 g/8 oz canned peaches in fruit juice, drained and chopped
- 115 g/4 oz dried dates, stoned and sliced
- 55 g/2 oz raisins
- 2 dried red chillies
- 40 g/1½ oz fresh root ginger, chopped
- 200 g/7 oz raw or muscovado sugar
- 175 ml/6 fl oz white wine or malt vinegar
- salt

NUTRITIONAL INFORMATION	
Calories	424
Protein	5g
Carbohydrate	90g
Sugars	89g
Fat	7g
Saturates	1g

variation

This chutney is even better made with fresh peaches. Blanch them briefly in boiling water, then peel, halve and stone before chopping.

cook's tip

To sterilize jars, place clean jars in a saucepan of water, bring to the boil and boil for 10 minutes. Transfer to a preheated oven, 140°C/275°F/Gas Mark 1, place upside down and dry for 15 minutes.

1. Heat a heavy-based frying pan. Add the coriander seeds, cumin seeds, onion seeds, aniseed and almonds and cook over a low heat, stirring constantly, for 1–2 minutes, or until the spices give off their aroma. Remove the frying pan from the heat and reserve.

2. Place the mango, apple, banana, pineapple, peaches, dates, raisins, chillies, ginger and sugar in a heavy-based saucepan. Pour in the vinegar, add a pinch of salt and bring to the boil, stirring constantly. Reduce the heat and simmer gently, stirring frequently, for 15 minutes, or until thickened.

3. Stir in the spice mixture and cook, stirring frequently, for a further 5 minutes. Remove from the heat and leave to cool. Either serve immediately or ladle into a sterilized jar (see Cook's Tip) and seal.

desserts & drinks

While fresh fruit may simply be served at the end of everyday meals, Indians do love sweetmeats and have created some superb desserts. Those with a sweet tooth can indulge themselves with Sago & Coconut Pudding (see page 239) or Almond & Pistachio Dessert (see page 243), while the home-made ice creams are a treat for all the family (see pages 244–5). Try adding an Eastern twist to traditional desserts, such as Rice Pudding (see page 240) and fruit and custard (see page 238).

Naturally, tea features as the main drink in most Indian homes – several times a day – and this chapter includes recipes for both hot and cold teas flavoured with spices (see pages 246–7). Tropical fruit also makes delicious – and healthy – thirst quenchers that will be enjoyed by both adults and children. Lassi is a classic Indian drink made from buttermilk or yogurt, by a rather laborious process in the past, but very easily nowadays. It is almost as popular as tea and is served throughout the country. It is wonderfully refreshing and there are recipes to suit all tastes, from sweet to savoury and including tropical fruit (see pages 248–51). Recommended as an aid to digestion, lassi is the perfect accompaniment to a spicy meal.

sweet potato dessert

Serves 8–10 **prep: 15 mins** **cook: 20 mins**

This delicious, milky dessert can be eaten either hot or cold, and will make the perfect finale to any Indian meal.

INGREDIENTS

1 kg/2 lb 4 oz sweet potatoes
850 ml/1½ pints milk
175 g/6 oz sugar
a few chopped almonds, to decorate

NUTRITIONAL INFORMATION	
Calories	234
Protein	5g
Carbohydrate	51g
Sugars	23g
Fat	3g
Saturates	1g

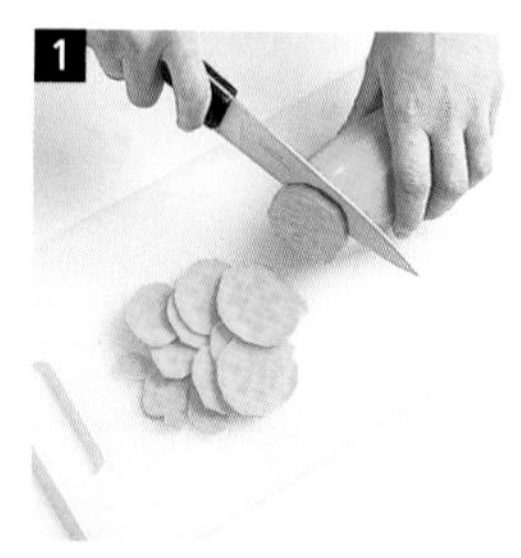

1 Using a sharp knife, peel the sweet potatoes. Rinse them under cold running water and cut them into slices.

2 Place the sweet potato slices in a large, heavy-based saucepan. Cover with 600 ml/1 pint of the milk and cook slowly until soft enough to be mashed.

3 Remove the saucepan from the heat and mash the sweet potatoes with a potato masher until smooth.

4 Add the sugar and the remaining milk to the mashed sweet potatoes, and carefully stir to blend together.

5 Return the saucepan to the heat and leave the mixture to simmer until it begins to thicken (it should reach the consistency of a cream of chicken soup).

6 Transfer the sweet potato dessert to a serving dish. Decorate with the chopped almonds and serve.

cook's tip

Sweet potatoes are longer than ordinary potatoes and have a pinkish or yellowish skin with yellow or white flesh. As their name suggests, they taste slightly sweet.

ground almonds cooked in ghee & milk

cook: 10 mins **prep: 5 mins** **serves: 2–4**

Traditionally served at breakfast in India, this almond-based dish is said to sharpen the mind! However, it can be served as a dessert.

NUTRITIONAL INFORMATION	
Calories	314
Protein	8g
Carbohydrate	23g
Sugars	18g
Fat	21g
Saturates	3g

INGREDIENTS

2 tbsp vegetable or pure ghee
25 g/1 oz plain flour
100 g/3½ oz ground almonds
300 ml/10 fl oz milk
50 g/1¾ oz sugar
fresh mint leaves, to decorate

1 Place the ghee in a small, heavy-based saucepan and melt over a low heat, stirring constantly so that it doesn't burn. Reduce the heat and add the flour, stirring vigorously to remove any lumps.

2 Add the almonds to the ghee and flour mixture, stirring constantly.

3 Gradually add the milk and sugar to the mixture in the saucepan and bring to the boil. Continue cooking for 3–5 minutes, or until the liquid is smooth and reaches the consistency of cream of chicken soup. Transfer to a large serving dish, decorate with mint leaves and serve hot.

cook's tip

Ghee comes in two forms and can be bought from Asian food shops. It is worth noting that pure ghee, made from melted butter, is not suitable for vegans, although a vegetable ghee is available.

indian fruit & custard

serves 6

prep: 15 mins, plus 1 hr 30 mins cooling/chilling

cook: 50 mins

This doesn't sound very Indian, but it is a popular dessert in north-west India, where it features tropical fruits and a fragrant custard.

INGREDIENTS

- 1 tbsp blanched almonds
- 1 litre/1¾ pints milk
- 400 ml/14 fl oz canned evaporated milk
- 1 tbsp rosewater
- 1 tsp ground cardamom
- a few drops of yellow food colouring (optional)
- fresh fruit, such as mango and paw paw slices and mixed berries
- 1 tbsp pistachio nuts, chopped, to decorate (optional)

NUTRITIONAL INFORMATION	
Calories	175
Protein	8g
Carbohydrate	17g
Sugars	17g
Fat	8g
Saturates	4g

1

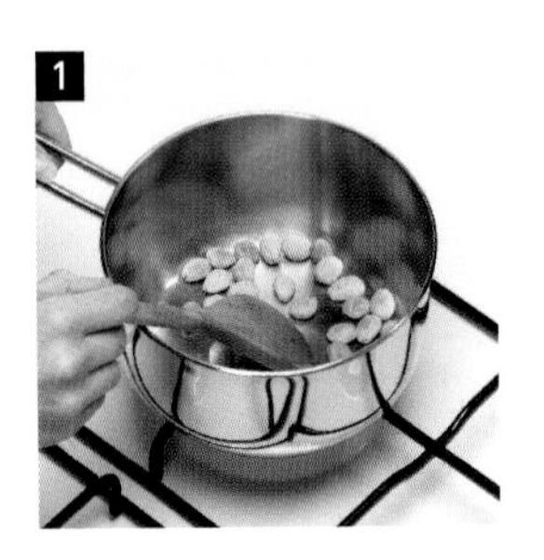

2

3

cook's tip

Reducing milk as a basis for desserts is a popular technique in India. Evaporated milk also features in a number of favourite desserts.

1 Dry-fry the almonds in a heavy-based saucepan over a low heat, stirring constantly, for 1–2 minutes, or until golden. Remove the saucepan from the heat and reserve.

2 Bring the milk to the boil in a separate saucepan, then reduce the heat and simmer for 30 minutes, or until reduced to about 500 ml/18 fl oz. Sieve into a clean saucepan, then place over a very low heat and stir in the evaporated milk, rosewater and cardamom. Add a few drops of food colouring to tint the custard an attractive golden yellow, if you like. Simmer gently, stirring frequently to prevent the custard catching on the base of the saucepan, for 15 minutes, or until thickened and smooth.

3 Pour the custard into a bowl and stir in the reserved almonds. Cover with clingfilm, leave to cool, then leave to chill in the refrigerator for at least 1 hour and up to 8 hours. Slice the fruit just before serving. Divide the custard between individual serving plates, arrange the fruit beside it and sprinkle with the pistachios (if using).

sago & coconut pudding

cook: 10–12 mins

prep: 25 mins, plus 30 mins cooling

serves 4

This milky dessert is an ideal choice after a spicy meal to settle the digestion. It uses fresh, rather than canned coconut milk.

NUTRITIONAL INFORMATION	
Calories	373
Protein	10g
Carbohydrate	51g
Sugars	38g
Fat	16g
Saturates	10g

INGREDIENTS

- ½ fresh coconut
- 225 ml/8 fl oz water
- 850 ml/1½ pints milk
- 85 g/3 oz caster sugar
- 25 g/1 oz raisins
- 55 g/2 oz sago
- seeds from 6–8 cardamom pods
- 25 g/1 oz flaked almonds, for sprinkling

1 To prepare the coconut milk, remove the flesh from the half-shell and grate it. Place in a food processor or blender, add the water and process until smooth. Sieve into a jug, pressing down on the coconut with the back of a wooden spoon. Discard the contents of the sieve and reserve the coconut milk.

2 Bring the ordinary milk to the boil in a large, heavy-based saucepan and continue to boil until it has reduced to 600 ml/1 pint. Reduce the heat, add the sugar and stir until dissolved. Stir in the raisins and sago. Simmer gently for 6–8 minutes, or until the sago is cooked.

3 Remove the saucepan from the heat and stir in the coconut milk and cardamom seeds, then pour into individual serving dishes. Sprinkle with the almonds and leave to cool before serving.

cook's tip

To crack a coconut, pierce 2 of the eyes with a skewer and drain off the liquid. Hit around the centre with a hammer, prise the halves apart, lever the flesh from the shell and peel with a peeler.

rice pudding

serves: 8–10 **prep: 10 mins** **cook: 30 mins**

Rice pudding is one of the most popular of all desserts in India. Serve with Pooris (see page 196), if you like.

INGREDIENTS

75 g/2¾ oz basmati rice
1.2 litres/2 pints milk
8 tbsp sugar
varq (silver leaf) or chopped pistachio nuts, to decorate

NUTRITIONAL INFORMATION	
Calories	152
Protein	5g
Carbohydrate	29g
Sugars	23g
Fat	3g
Saturates	1g

cook's tip

Varq is edible silver that is used to decorate elaborate dishes prepared for special occasions, such as weddings. You can buy varq from Asian food shops and store it in an airtight bag or box.

1. Rinse the rice under cold running water and place in a large, heavy-based saucepan. Add 1 pint/600 ml of the milk and bring to the boil over a very low heat. Cook until the milk has been completely absorbed by the rice, stirring occasionally.

2. Remove the saucepan from the heat. Mash the rice, making swift, round movements in the saucepan, for at least 5 minutes.

3. Gradually add the remaining milk and return the saucepan to the heat. Bring to the boil over a low heat, stirring occasionally.

4. Add the sugar and cook, stirring constantly, for 7–10 minutes, or until the mixture is quite thick in consistency.

5. Transfer the rice pudding to a heatproof serving bowl. Decorate with varq (silver leaf) or chopped pistachio nuts and serve.

almond sherbet

cook: 0 mins

prep: 45 mins, plus 3–8 hrs soaking

serves 2

Use whole almonds rather than ready-ground almonds for this dish as they give it a better texture.

NUTRITIONAL INFORMATION	
Calories	836
Protein	29g
Carbohydrate	36g
Sugars	33g
Fat	65g
Saturates	7g

INGREDIENTS

225 g/8 oz whole almonds

2 tbsp sugar

300 ml/10 fl oz milk

300 ml/10 fl oz water

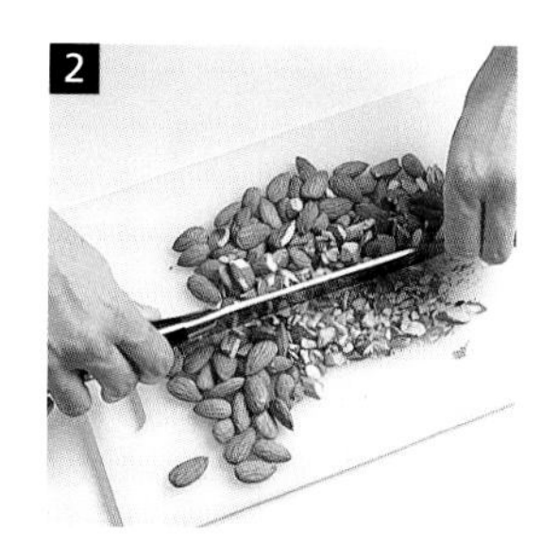

2

3

3

1 Soak the almonds in a large bowl of water for at least 3 hours or preferably overnight.

2 Using a sharp knife, chop the almonds into small pieces. Grind to a fine paste in a food processor or with a mortar and pestle.

3 Add the sugar to the almond paste and grind again to make a fine paste. Add the milk and water and mix well (in a blender if you have one).

4 Transfer the almond sherbet to a large serving dish. Leave to chill in the refrigerator for 30 minutes. Stir the almond sherbet just before serving.

cook's tip

An electric coffee grinder or spice mill will cut down the time taken to grind the almonds. If using a coffee grinder, remember to clean the grinder out thoroughly afterwards.

carrot dessert

serves 4–6 **prep: 10 mins** **cook: 1 hr**

This makes a very impressive dinner party dessert. It is best served warm, with a spoonful of fresh cream by the side, if you like.

INGREDIENTS

1.5 kg/3 lb 5 oz carrots
150 g/5½ oz ghee
600 ml/1 pint milk
175 ml/6 fl oz evaporated milk
10 cardamom pods, peeled and crushed
120–150 g/4¼–5½ oz sugar

TO DECORATE

25 g/1 oz pistachio nuts, chopped
2 leaves varq (silver leaf), optional

NUTRITIONAL INFORMATION	
Calories	509
Protein	8g
Carbohydrate	55g
Sugars	54g
Fat	30g
Saturates	19g

cook's tip

Use pure ghee for this dessert as it is rather special and tastes better made with pure ghee. However, if you are trying to limit your fat intake, use vegetable ghee instead.

1. Rinse, peel and grate the carrots.

2. Heat the ghee in a large, heavy-based frying pan. Add the grated carrots and stir-fry for 15–20 minutes, or until the moisture from the carrots has evaporated and the carrots have darkened in colour.

3. Add the milk, evaporated milk, crushed cardamoms and sugar to the carrot mixture in the frying pan and continue to cook for a further 30–35 minutes, or until it is a rich brownish-red colour.

4. Transfer the carrot mixture to a large, shallow serving dish. Decorate with the chopped pistachio nuts and varq (if using) and serve immediately.

almond & pistachio dessert

cook: 15–20 mins **prep: 10 mins, plus 1 hr setting** **serves 2**

Rich and mouthwatering, this dessert can be prepared in advance of the meal and chilled. It is best served cold.

NUTRITIONAL INFORMATION	
Calories	84
Protein	2g
Carbohydrate	20g
Sugars	20g
Fat	0g
Saturates	0g

INGREDIENTS

75 g/2¾ oz unsalted butter
200 g/7 oz ground almonds
200 g/7 oz sugar
150 ml/5 fl oz single cream
8 almonds, chopped
10 pistachio nuts, chopped

cook's tip

This almond dessert can be made a day in advance and stored in an airtight container in the refrigerator for several days.

1 Melt the butter in a heavy-based saucepan, preferably non-stick, stirring well. Add the ground almonds, sugar and cream, stirring well. Reduce the heat and stir constantly for 10–12 minutes, scraping the base of the saucepan.

2 Increase the heat until the mixture turns a little darker in colour.

3 Transfer the almond mixture to a large, shallow serving dish and smooth the top with the back of a spoon.

4 Decorate the top of the dessert with the chopped almonds and pistachio nuts. Leave to set for 1 hour, then cut into diamond shapes and serve cold.

mango ice cream

serves 6

prep: 10 mins, plus 3–8 hrs freezing

cook: 0 mins

Kulfi is the Indian equivalent of ice cream and is always made with fresh fruit or juice. This basic ice cream recipe is infinitely adaptable and incredibly easy to make.

INGREDIENTS

150 ml/5 fl oz double cream
2 tbsp caster sugar
425 ml/15 fl oz mango juice
½ tsp ground cinnamon
flaked almonds, to decorate

NUTRITIONAL INFORMATION	
Calories	257
Protein	1g
Carbohydrate	19g
Sugars	19g
Fat	20g
Saturates	13g

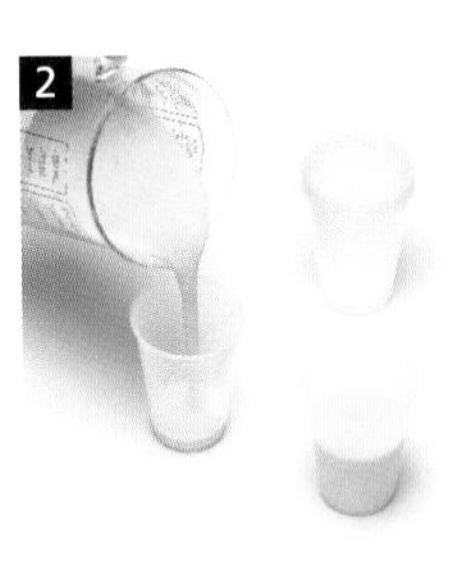

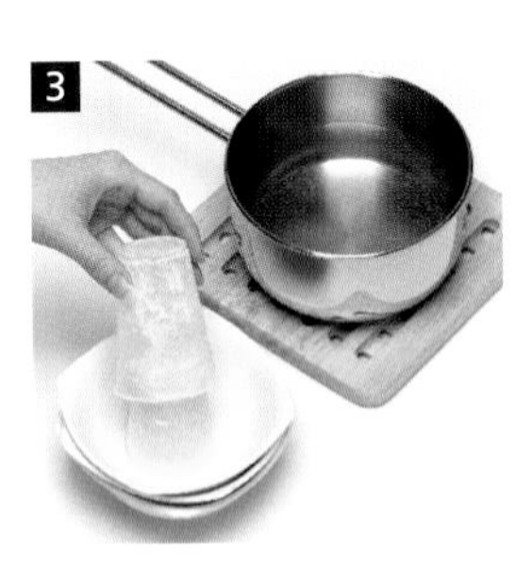

cook's tip

Don't beat the cream too vigorously – only whisk it enough to make a smooth mixture and to dissolve the sugar.

1. Pour the cream into a large bowl, add the sugar and whisk lightly until dissolved. Stir in the mango juice and cinnamon.
2. Pour the mixture into 6 freezerproof moulds, cover with foil and place in the freezer for 3 hours or preferably overnight, until set. During the first hour of freezing, gently shake the moulds 3 times.
3. To serve, dip the bases of the moulds in hot water, then invert on to individual serving plates. Decorate with flaked almonds and serve immediately.

fruit & nut ice cream

cook: 20 mins | **prep: 20 mins, plus 28–36 hrs chilling/freezing** | **serves 6**

This more elaborate, although still very simple, kulfi is sold throughout India by street sellers. It needs some advance preparation, but is well worth the effort.

NUTRITIONAL INFORMATION	
Calories	848
Protein	27g
Carbohydrate	94g
Sugars	92g
Fat	43g
Saturates	15g

INGREDIENTS

1.2 litres/2 pints canned evaporated milk
3 egg whites
350 g/12 oz icing sugar
1 tbsp rosewater
175 g/6 oz pistachio nuts, chopped, plus extra to decorate
85 g/3 oz flaked almonds
25 g/1 oz glacé cherries, roughly chopped, plus extra to decorate
85 g/3 oz sultanas
1 tsp ground cardamom

1 Begin preparing the day before you want to serve the ice cream. Place the cans of evaporated milk on their sides in a large, heavy-based saucepan. Pour in enough water to come about three-quarters of the way up their sides and bring to the boil. Reduce the heat, cover tightly and simmer for 20 minutes. Remove from the heat, leave to cool, then chill for 24 hours. Place a large bowl in the refrigerator to chill.

2 The next day, whisk the egg whites in a spotlessly clean, greasefree bowl until soft peaks form. Pour the evaporated milk into the chilled bowl and whisk until doubled in size. Fold in the egg whites, then the sugar. Gently fold in the pistachio nuts, almonds, cherries, sultanas and cardamom.

3 Cover the bowl with clingfilm and freeze for 1 hour. Remove the bowl from the freezer and beat the mixture with a fork. Spoon into a freezerproof container and freeze for 3 hours or preferably overnight, until set.

cook's tip

Don't forget to remove the labels from the cans before boiling the evaporated milk.

4 Scoop the ice cream into serving dishes, decorate with chopped pistachio nuts and glacé cherries and serve.

hot spiced tea

serves 4

prep: 5 mins, plus 4 mins standing

cook: 5 mins

It is hardly surprising that tea is drunk all over India. Although this is a hot drink, it is extremely refreshing in hot weather.

INGREDIENTS

500 ml/18 fl oz milk

500 ml/18 fl oz water

4 tsp Darjeeling tea leaves

55 g/2 oz fresh mint leaves

1 tsp ground ginger

1 tsp cardamom pods, lightly crushed

1 tsp fennel seeds

½ tsp freshly grated nutmeg

2 cinnamon sticks

sugar, to serve (optional)

NUTRITIONAL INFORMATION	
Calories	65
Protein	5g
Carbohydrate	6g
Sugars	6g
Fat	2g
Saturates	1g

1 Pour the milk and water into a heavy-based saucepan and bring to the boil.

2 Meanwhile, mix the tea leaves, mint leaves, ginger, cardamoms, fennel seeds, nutmeg and cinnamon sticks together in a teapot or heatproof jug.

3 As soon as it boils, pour the milk and water mixture into the teapot and stir well. Leave to brew for 4–5 minutes, then sieve into cups and serve, sweetened with sugar, if you like.

cook's tip

If you prefer to use teabags rather than loose leaves, then use 4. To keep the tea hotter for longer, warm the teapot or jug before using.

cold spiced tea

cook: 5 mins **prep: 5 mins, plus 50 mins standing, cooling/chilling** **serves 4**

Keep a jug of this cooling brew in the refrigerator to serve, Indian-style, as the sun goes down in the evening.

NUTRITIONAL INFORMATION	
Calories	20
Protein	0g
Carbohydrate	5g
Sugars	5g
Fat	0g
Saturates	0g

INGREDIENTS

1.2 litres/2 pints water

4 tsp Darjeeling tea leaves

4 tsp sugar

8 cardamom pods, lightly crushed

4 whole cloves

2 cinnamon sticks

fresh mint sprigs, to decorate

TO SERVE

crushed ice

lemon juice

1 Bring 300 ml/10 fl oz of the water to the boil in a heavy-based saucepan. Meanwhile, mix the tea leaves, sugar, cardamoms, cloves and cinnamon sticks together in a teapot or heatproof jug.

2 As soon as the water boils, pour it into the teapot and stir well. Leave to brew for 4–5 minutes, stir again, then sieve into a clean, heatproof jug. Stir in the remaining water, leave to cool, then cover with clingfilm and leave to chill in the refrigerator.

3 To serve, fill tall glasses with crushed iced and pour in the chilled tea. Top up with lemon juice and serve decorated with fresh mint.

cook's tip

Never make tea, either spiced or plain, by re-boiling water that has already been boiled. Always use fresh water. Make sure that the tea is completely cold before chilling in the refrigerator.

sweet lassi

serves 4 **prep: 5 mins** **cook: 0 mins** 

This cooling drink is sold everywhere in India and enjoyed by children and adults alike. Serve as part of an Indian meal as the yogurt is very good for counteracting the hotness of the chillies.

INGREDIENTS

500 ml/18 fl oz low-fat natural yogurt
225 ml/8 fl oz iced water
4 tbsp caster sugar
finely chopped pistachio nuts, to decorate
crushed ice, to serve

NUTRITIONAL INFORMATION	
Calories	164
Protein	6g
Carbohydrate	30g
Sugars	30g
Fat	3g
Saturates	1g

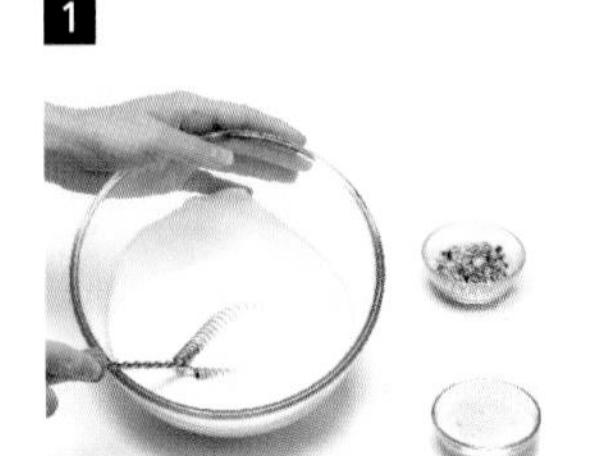

1 Pour the yogurt into a bowl and whisk with a balloon whisk or hand-held electric mixer for 1–2 minutes, or until frothy.

2 Add the water and sugar and whisk until the sugar has dissolved. Pour into a jug, cover with clingfilm and leave to chill in the refrigerator for 30 minutes.

3 To serve, fill tall glasses with crushed ice and pour in the lassi. Sprinkle with chopped pistachios to decorate and serve immediately.

cook's tip

For the best results, chill the glasses in the refrigerator for 15 minutes before serving. To prepare the ice, place ice cubes in a blender strong enough to crush them and whizz for a few seconds.

savoury lassi

cook: 0 mins

prep: 5 mins, plus 30 mins chilling

serves 4

The smooth texture of this delicious drink is the perfect counterbalance to highly spiced foods. It is just as popular throughout India as the sweet version (see opposite).

NUTRITIONAL INFORMATION	
Calories	63
Protein	5g
Carbohydrate	8g
Sugars	8g
Fat	1g
Saturates	1g

INGREDIENTS

425 ml/15 fl oz low-fat natural yogurt

300 ml/10 fl oz iced water

1 fresh green chilli, deseeded and very finely chopped

2.5-cm/1-inch piece fresh root ginger, very finely chopped

½ tsp ground cumin

salt and pepper

fresh coriander or mint leaves, to decorate

crushed ice, to serve

1 Pour the yogurt and water into a bowl and whisk with a balloon whisk or hand-held electric mixer for 2 minutes, or until thoroughly blended.

2 Stir in the chilli, ginger and cumin and season to taste with salt and pepper. Pour into a jug, cover with clingfilm and leave to chill in the refrigerator for 30 minutes.

3 To serve, fill tall glasses with crushed ice and pour in the lassi. Decorate with coriander or mint leaves and serve immediately.

cook's tip

The yogurt and water mixture should be the consistency of full-fat milk, so add more or less water, as required. The lassi is best served as soon as it is made.

sweet & sour lassi

serves 4 | **prep: 5 mins, plus 35 mins standing/chilling** | **cook: 0 mins**

In India, making lassi involves the laborious process of churning full-fat yogurt, then discarding the fat. Using low-fat yogurt is easier.

INGREDIENTS

- about 10 saffron threads, plus a few extra to decorate
- 1 tbsp boiling water
- 500 ml/18 fl oz low-fat natural yogurt
- 225 ml/8 fl oz iced water
- 2 tbsp caster sugar
- ½ tsp ground cardamom
- ½ tsp ground cumin
- crushed ice, to serve

NUTRITIONAL INFORMATION	
Calories	110
Protein	6g
Carbohydrate	20g
Sugars	19g
Fat	1g
Saturates	1g

1 Place the saffron in a small bowl and stir in the boiling water. Leave to stand for 5 minutes to infuse.

2 Pour the yogurt into a large bowl and whisk for 2 minutes, until frothy. Whisk in the iced water and sugar, then stir in the cardamom, cumin and saffron with its soaking water. Pour into a jug, cover with clingfilm and chill in the refrigerator for 30 minutes.

3 To serve, fill tall glasses with crushed ice, pour in the lassi and decorate with a few saffron threads.

cook's tip

Lightly crush the saffron threads between your finger and thumb before soaking in the water. Use a balloon whisk or hand-held electric mixer to whisk the yogurt and water together.

tropical fruit lassi

cook: 0 mins | prep: 5 mins | serves 4

This version of lassi is made with buttermilk rather than the usual mixture of natural yogurt and iced water.

NUTRITIONAL INFORMATION	
Calories	109
Protein	6g
Carbohydrate	19g
Sugars	19g
Fat	2g
Saturates	1g

INGREDIENTS

1 mango, peeled, stoned and roughly chopped

1 paw paw, peeled, halved and deseeded

350 ml/12 fl oz buttermilk

2 tsp clear honey

¼ tsp vanilla essence

4 tbsp full-fat natural yogurt, to serve

1 Place the mango in a blender or food processor. Slice the paw paw and reserve 4 slices for the decoration. Place the remaining flesh in the blender or food processor and add the buttermilk, honey and vanilla essence.

2 Process the mixture, scraping down the sides of the goblet if necessary, until smooth and frothy.

3 Pour the lassi into tall glasses and top each with a tablespoonful of yogurt. Decorate with the reserved slices of paw paw and serve immediately.

cook's tip

For the best results, make sure that the buttermilk and yogurt are well chilled before you begin making the lassi. Serve the drink as soon as it is made.

lime cooler

serves 4

prep: 5 mins, plus 3 hrs chilling

cook: 0 mins

Like many Indian drinks, this can be made in both sweet and savoury versions. Both are wonderfully refreshing and very easy.

INGREDIENTS

140 g/5 oz caster sugar
5 tbsp freshly squeezed lime juice
1 tsp finely chopped fresh mint
1 litre/1¾ pints water
crushed ice, to serve
fresh mint sprigs, to decorate

NUTRITIONAL INFORMATION	
Calories	140
Protein	0g
Carbohydrate	37g
Sugars	37g
Fat	0g
Saturates	0g

cook's tip

Each lime will yield 3–4 tablespoons of juice. You will get more juice if you roll the limes backwards and forwards on a work surface with the palm of your hand before squeezing them.

1 Place the sugar, lime juice and mint in a large bowl and stir in the water until the sugar has dissolved.

2 Cover the bowl with clingfilm and chill in the refrigerator for 3–4 hours.

3 Sieve the mixture into a jug, discarding the contents of the sieve. Fill tall glasses with crushed ice and pour in the lime cooler. Decorate with mint sprigs and serve immediately.

mango cooler

cook: 10 mins **prep: 10 mins, plus 30 mins cooling** **serves 4**

Made with slightly underripe mangoes, this delicious cold drink has a sharp edge to it that appeals to adult tastes.

NUTRITIONAL INFORMATION	
Calories	54
Protein	0g
Carbohydrate	14g
Sugars	9g
Fat	0g
Saturates	0g

INGREDIENTS

2 slightly underripe mangoes
1 litre/1¾ pints iced water
4 tsp sugar
salt
fresh mango slices, to decorate
crushed ice, to serve

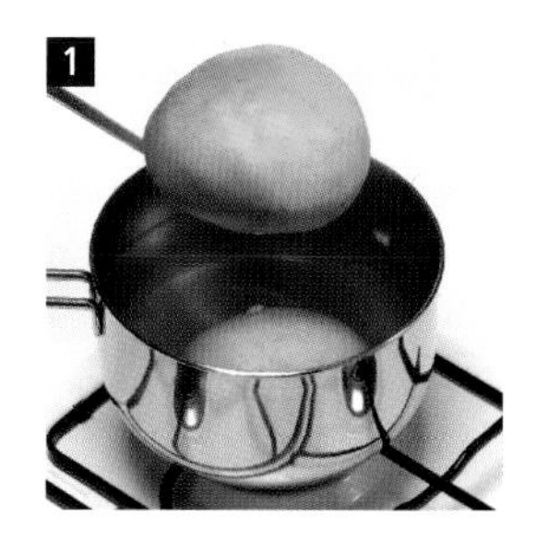

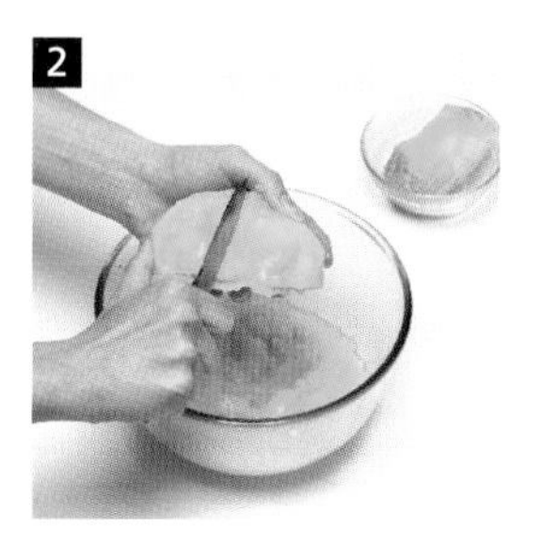

1 Place the mangoes in a heavy-based saucepan and add just enough water to cover. Bring to the boil, then reduce the heat and simmer for 10 minutes. Drain well and leave to cool.

2 Carefully peel off the mango skins, then, using a sharp knife, scrape the flesh away from the large central stones into a bowl.

3 Add the water and stir well to mix, then stir in the sugar and season with salt to taste. Stir well again, taste and add more sugar, if necessary. Fill tall glasses with crushed ice, pour in the mango cooler and decorate with mango slices. Serve immediately.

cook's tip

The colour of a mango's skin is not a good indication of its ripeness, as some varieties remain green. Test by cupping the fruit in your hand – ripe mangoes give slightly, while underripe mangoes don't.

index

index